Guilt Rules All

Irish Studies
Kathleen Costello-Sullivan, *Series Editor*

SELECT TITLES IN IRISH STUDIES

Fine Meshwork: Philip Roth, Edna O'Brien, and Jewish-Irish Literature
Dan O'Brien

Irish Questions and Jewish Questions: Crossovers in Culture
Aidan Beatty and Dan O'Brien, eds.

Laying Out the Bones: Death and Dying in the Modern Irish Novel
Bridget English

Political Acts: Women in Northern Irish Theatre, 1921–2012
Fiona Coleman Coffey

The Rebels and Other Short Fiction
Richard Power; James MacKillop, ed.

Respectability and Reform: Irish American Women's Activism, 1880–1920
Tara M. McCarthy

Science, Technology, and Irish Modernism
Kathryn Conrad, Cóilín Parsons, and Julie McCormick Weng, eds.

Trauma and Recovery in the Twenty-First-Century Irish Novel
Kathleen Costello-Sullivan

For a full list of titles in this series, visit
https://press.syr.edu/supressbook-series/irish-studies/.

GUILT RULES ALL

Irish Mystery, Detective, and Crime Fiction

Edited by

Elizabeth Mannion

and Brian Cliff

Syracuse University Press

Syracuse, New York 13244-5290

First Edition 2020
20 21 22 23 24 25   6 5 4 3 2 1

∞ The paper used in this publication meets the minimum requirements of the American National Standard for Information Sciences—Permanence of Paper for Printed Library Materials, ANSI Z39.48-1992.

For a listing of books published and distributed by Syracuse University Press, visit https://press.syr.edu.

ISBN: 978-0-8156-3673-1 (hardcover)
978-0-8156-3683-0 (paperback)
978-0-8156-5498-8 (e-book)

Library of Congress Cataloging-in-Publication Data

Names: Mannion, Elizabeth (Lecturer), editor. | Cliff, Brian, editor.

Title: Guilt rules all : Irish mystery, detective, and crime fiction / edited by Elizabeth Mannion and Brian Cliff

Description: First edition. | Syracuse, New York : Syracuse University Press, 2020. | Series: Irish studies | Includes bibliographical references and index. | Summary: “Irish crime fiction, long present on international Best Seller lists, has been knocking on the door of the academy for a decade. With a varied mix of Irish Studies scholars providing comprehensive analyses on essential Irish detective series, “Guilt Rules All” establishes once and for all that this genre has arrived”—Provided by publisher.

Identifiers: LCCN 2020003610 (print) | LCCN 2020003611 (ebook) | ISBN 9780815636731 (hardcover) | ISBN 9780815636830 (paperback) | ISBN 9780815654988 (ebook)

Subjects: LCSH: Detective and mystery stories, Irish (English)—History and criticism. | English fiction—Irish authors—History and criticism.

Classification: LCC PR8807.D48 G85 2020 (print) | LCC PR8807.D48 (ebook) | DDC 823/.087209415—dc23

LC record available at https://lccn.loc.gov/2020003610

LC ebook record available at https://lccn.loc.gov/2020003611

Manufactured in the United States of America

Contents

Acknowledgments

We are indebted to the contributors for their commitment to this book and their insights about Irish crime fiction. It has been an honor to work with them and with Syracuse University Press, particularly our editor, Deborah Manion, but also her colleagues in editorial and marketing.

Beth adds her thanks to the friends and colleagues with whom drafts were shared, whose feedback was instrumental in shaping this project. Thank you in particular to Mary McGlynn and the Irish Studies Seminar at Columbia University; and to Alan, Chip, and Sarah.

Brian also thanks the School of English, Trinity College Dublin for their support, and for the opportunity to teach Irish crime fiction seminars. He owes a particular debt to Aileen Douglas in that regard, and to Christopher Morash for collaborating on the first of those seminars. In all things, though, he is most grateful for the love and encouragement of his family, Marni, Maura, Elven, and Chuey.

Guilt Rules All

Introduction

ELIZABETH MANNION AND BRIAN CLIFF

Irish crime fiction has a long but fragmented history, as we have both discussed elsewhere, and as Ian Campbell Ross and Shane Mawe demonstrated in their contributions to *Down These Green Streets: Irish Crime Writing in the 21st Century* (2011), Declan Burke's invaluable anthology.[1] This history includes notable examples, but they are often isolated from each other and from the prevailing currents that grew to define perceptions of Irish literature. Writing as Nicholas Blake, for example, Cecil Day-Lewis had substantial success and ample crime-writing peers in British culture, but little recognition for his mystery novels within Irish literature. Similarly, Erskine Childers's *The Riddle of the Sands* (1903) effectively gave birth to the modern Anglophone espionage novel, but the book's influence was largely felt outside of Irish letters, within which the Childers name carried far more political than literary weight.

Despite these and other significant examples, Irish literary studies has been guilty of according a less than hospitable reception to popular fiction, for reasons material, ideological, and aesthetic, as Declan Burke and John Connolly have both argued.[2] In the face of that reception, antecedents can often remain to varying degrees isolated, overlooked, or assimilated to strands of Irish Studies like the Gothic and the fantastic. By tracing a

1. See Burke, *Down These Green Streets*; Mannion, *Contemporary Irish Detective Novel*; Cliff, *Irish Crime Fiction*.

2. See Burke, "Editor's Note," 9–11; Connolly, "No Blacks, No Dogs, No Crime Writers: Ireland and the Mystery Genre," 39–57.

diverse body of contemporary writing as it is emerging, however, scholars of Irish crime fiction have begun to establish a critical mass with which further accounts of the genre's role in Irish culture can be developed. These dynamics make this an interesting moment to publish this collection and present a rare chance to capture the developing patterns of a still-coalescing genre. Among the most apparent of these patterns has been the prominence of women authors, whose work is the focus of eight of the essays here. The genre's forebears in Ireland include mid-century novelists like Sheila Pim and Eilís Dillon as well as writers whose first novels appeared at the close of the twentieth century, like Julie Parsons and Gemma O'Connor, while novelists Alex Barclay, Jane Casey, Sinéad Crowley, Arlene Hunt, and Liz Nugent have clearly been among the genre's most recent highlights. However, despite that prominence, and unlike more canonical moments and clusters—the Irish Literary Theatre, the early Abbey, O'Faoláin's journal *The Bell*, the Belfast Group of poets, or Field Day—Irish crime fiction does not have a readily defined center (not even with due caveats about the sometimes constructed nature of such centers), nor do we advocate naming one. Instead, this collection emphasizes the mobility of Irish crime writing, with its journalistic links, its stubborn refusal to adopt an essential setting, and its generosity in fusing subgenres.

Guilt Rules All follows that mobility across a range of individual authors. This scope gives Irish crime fiction much of its energy, and—as a number of the essays here argue—means that it cannot be subsumed wholly within a single mode, nor wholly within familiar structures for critical discussion of Irish culture. The critical impulse toward a discrete narrative is complicated by maintaining a sense of these traits, but doing so is essential for understanding the genre's development. The essays in this collection illustrate these traits in part by connecting their subjects to Irish culture, literature, and history, but the emphasis here is not on familiar relationships to more canonical Irish Studies matters. That is deliberate: part of what is interesting and distinct about Irish crime fiction would be lost were we to bend these novels toward those familiar narratives of what constitutes Irish literature. Such narratives have at times equated Irish literature with texts that reflect directly on the nature of Irishness, an approach that can lead critics to shave too many corners off texts in the attempt to integrate them with the canon. *Guilt Rules All* seeks to keep those corners intact, recognizing that Ireland in crime fiction is a quite distinct category from Irish crime fiction, as novels by a number of authors here suggest, and as some of the work in Ian Campbell Ross and William Meier's 2014 interdisciplinary special issue of *Éire-Ireland* demonstrates.

In examining the genre's breadth, this collection necessarily includes series based in and around Dublin and Belfast (by writers including Arlene Hunt, Sinéad Crowley, Gene Kerrigan, Louise Phillips, Colin Bateman, and Adrian McKinty), as well as writing set outside of the prevailing urban settings (as with Eilís Ní Dhuibhne's Kerry-set novels, written in Irish and astutely discussed here by Caitlín Nic Íomhair). *Guilt Rules All* also examines novels set abroad, though—from Michael Russell's 1930s Danzig to Liz Nugent's Côte d'Azur—sometimes with few if any Irish characters, as in Steve Cavanagh's and Alex Barclay's novels set in contemporary America. This range demonstrates that while Irish crime fiction does many things—and representing shifting aspects of national identity is sometimes among them—its merits should not be confused with the extent to which it participates overtly in existing academic discussions about representing Ireland and Irishness.

Compounding Irish literature's specific issues around representation, identity, and the canon is the question of genre fiction's status in the academy and in wider literary discussions. Publishers, critics, booksellers, and the marketplace can all measure crime writers against each other and, at times, against Literature. Select genre writers like Wilkie Collins, Sheridan Le Fanu, Agatha Christie, Patricia Highsmith, and Raymond Chandler have all now become unambiguously canonical. Reaching that point took time, however, and was accompanied by considerable resistance to works dismissed as entertainments, as too accessible, as the province of less-educated readers, resistance that in Ireland was part of "an environment in which literary populism was regarded as suspect."[3] As any follower of crime writers on Twitter will have seen, such suspicions still shadow the reception of

3. Connolly, "No Blacks, No Dogs, No Crime Writers: Ireland and the Mystery Genre," 41.

contemporary genre novelists from Stephen King to Sara Paretsky. Despite such patterns, Irish crime fiction has built an increasingly articulated place in public culture. When the headline "'Untalented' Crime Writers Respond to Their No. 1 Critic" appeared in the *Irish Times*,[4] what was notable was less the familiar peremptory dismissal of crime fiction that occasioned the article, and more the quick rebuttal from writers, academics, and critics unapologetic about the genre. Both collectively and individually, the essays gathered here take this same approach to the genre's significance.

This unapologetic approach is one means by which Irish crime fiction participates in contemporary discussions about confronting privilege in Irish arts and letters. These discussions have been animated by threads such as #WakingTheFeminists and that movement's advocacy for gender representation in Irish theater. The accomplishments of Dublin's Tramp Press have been equally important, lobbying successfully for Irish publishers to be included in Booker Prize consideration, and reclaiming out-of-print and overlooked works, such as Dorothy Macardle's Gothic ghost stories *Dark Enchantment* (2019), *The Unforeseen* (2017), and *The Uninvited* (2015), and *A Brilliant Void: A Selection of Classic Irish Science Fiction* (2018), edited by Jack Fennell. Individual writers like Emma Dabiri and Melatu Uche Okorie have increased attention to writing by immigrants to Ireland, while Lisa McInerney, Frankie Gaffney, and Kit de Waal have advanced conversations on working-class representations in publishing houses and on the printed page. These conversations are being felt in the academy, too, as demonstrated by the work of Michael Pierse and others.[5] In terms of its genre, its authorship, its readership, and its content, Irish crime fiction both benefits from and contributes to these literary and cultural investments in inclusivity and reclamation.

The genre's porous nature is also seen in the diversity of settings, subgenres, and characterizations. In this collection, we have taken pains to avoid a prematurely homogenized sense of Irish crime fiction's themes, modes, and authors. Of course, we recognize that certain authors—Tana

4. Doyle, "'Untalented' Crime Writers."

5. Including Pierse, *History of Irish Working-Class Writing* and "Back to Class."

French, John Connolly, and John Banville among them—are widely known. French in particular has been ably discussed in numerous scholarly articles, however, including a special issue of *Clues: A Journal of Detection* (Spring 2014), edited by Rachel Schaffer, and valuable studies of French's fiction have been published by some of this volume's contributors: Brian Cliff, Rosemary Erickson Johnsen, and Maureen Reddy. However, *Guilt Rules All* seeks to reflect as much of the genre's diversity as could fit between these covers, not least by prioritizing authors whose work has, to date, received less scholarly attention. This will help both to develop the broadest possible base for considering the genre and to ensure that significant writers will not disappear from the discussion because their work less immediately fits understandings of Irish literature or crime fiction. Amidst this breadth, the essays here track certain themes—corruption and fractured families among them—across settings and time frames, allowing readers to follow the articulation of patterns that play a meaningful role in the genre. Crime fiction has often made use of outsider characters, whether as protagonists, victims, or villains, and many characters here are marked by their distance from a full integration into their community. In its adaptation of these and other established tropes to a small island, Irish crime fiction has become increasingly adept at building on international modes while using those modes to strengthen rather than sacrifice some sense of particularity.

The essays' individual subjects range widely, addressing less familiar models (the late Bartholomew Gill), active authors identified as trailblazers by their peers (Julie Parsons), current bestsellers (Adrian McKinty), and others on the cusp of developing a wide international readership (including Liz Nugent). Building on the important antecedents discussed in Part One, the subsequent sections proceed to address a series of markers in Irish crime fiction's development and in its engagement with the international genre. After Part Two examines historical crime fiction's uses of the past, Part Three is given over to readers and authors whose advocacy has helped establish the genre, and to some of the works they have found particularly notable. The widely varying adaptations of the hard-boiled detective novel considered in Part Four show how one of the best-known subgenres has, despite its American roots, been fertile ground for Irish crime writers' ingenuity, while Part Five—on domestic noir—demonstrates how Irish authors are contributing to the most contemporary forms of crime fiction.

With the mystery elements in Gothic fiction by writers such as Dublin-born Sheridan Le Fanu—whose short story "A Passage in the Secret History of an Irish Countess" (1838) would become the basis for *Uncle Silas: A Tale of Bartram Haugh* (1864)—or the detective series of North Roscommon's Matthias McDonnell Bodkin (1850–1933) and Cork's Nigel Fitzgerald (1906–81), Irish crime fiction has a generically and geographically varied but solid foundation. The authors examined in Part One, "Antecedents and Beginnings," represent periodic renewals of that foundation. As Shane Mawe explores in chapter 1, Crofts made a crucial contribution to the Golden Age of mystery fiction, a form that continues to define the popular image of mystery fiction. Bartholomew Gill, the pen name of Mark McGarrity, approaches the canon from a quite different direction, establishing through his long career one way in which a hybrid of European and American police procedural models can work in Irish settings. He also, as chapter 2 reveals, engaged with Ireland's emerging globalization in real time. Julie Parsons, whose Michael McLoughlin trilogy is the subject of Bridget English's essay on trauma in Irish crime writing, was one of the earliest writers in the contemporary wave of Irish crime fiction, and helped bring a new psychological depth to Irish forms of the genre, a path her work continues to chart. Caitlín Nic Íomhair breaks new ground here in chapter 4 with a searching examination of crime fiction *as Gaeilge*, addressing its key works, its thematic concerns, and some of the reasons it has received insufficient attention even within Irish-language studies.

The complexities of history in Irish fiction cannot be said to suffer from the same lack of attention. Crime and mystery novels set more than a few decades in the past, beyond what can be counted as contemporary, however, are a slightly rarer breed, and constitute a distinct subgenre. That subgenre is the focus of Part Two, with Eunan O'Halpin's account of Michael Russell's Stefan Gillespie series, set in Dublin and across the continent on the cusp of World War II, and Nancy Marck Cantwell's discussion of Conor Brady's Joe Swallow series, set in 1880s Dublin. While more distant historical fictions such as Cora Harrison's sixteenth-century Burren novels and

Peter Tremayne's Sister Fidelma series can find an empowering narrative in the past, modern historical settings like Brady's and Russell's—or those in work by their contemporaries, like Kevin McCarthy's Sean O'Keefe series (set in 1920s Dublin and West Cork) and Benjamin Black's Quirke series (anchored in 1950s Dublin)—often convey a more insistently skeptical view. Part of a long tradition of oppositional narratives in international crime fiction, this skepticism is apparent in Russell's and Brady's works, which depict heightened tipping points in Irish history (the Emergency in the former, and the Victorian Home Rule campaign in the latter).

Where the essays in Part Two do much with the particular settings of the novels they examine, Part Three's concerns are rather with readers. Crime fiction's prominence has its roots in the genre's popular reception, but it also owes much to the advocacy of devoted readers and novelists and to influential critics like Anthony Boucher, whose name still graces one of crime fiction's most prominent annual conventions. In recognition of this tradition, and in keeping with this collection's commitment to a wide angle on this diverse literature, we asked Declan Burke, Joe Long, and Gerard Brennan to select crime writers whose work inspires their tireless support of the genre. Burke and Brennan are established crime novelists in their own right who have also been promoting the merits of Irish crime writing for years, as has Long, who introduced the genre into the curriculum at New York University's Glucksman Ireland House as a student in their inaugural graduate program in Irish and Irish-American Studies. Brennan's and Burke's essays model the extent to which Irish crime novelists have often been important commentators on the genre. Burke in particular has been one of the centers of the Irish crime fiction community through his long-running blog, *Crime Always Pays*, and through his many *Irish Times* reviews. That newspaper's pages have been notably generous in their coverage of crime fiction, particularly through Burke's reviews and those of his fellow crime writer, Declan Hughes. The novelists Burke, Brennan, and Long chose to showcase here—Alex Barclay, Arlene Hunt, and Steve Cavanagh—feature protagonists who, even by the genre's dismal standards of work-life balance, are markedly unable to draw lines between their personal lives and their vocations. Every professional move of Barclay's Ren

Bryce, Hunt's QuicK partners, and Cavanagh's Eddie Flynn seems to open a wound of unfinished personal business, and a fresh sense of their own shortcomings, a pattern that has kept readers returning to these series.

Narrators' shortcomings, of course, are a familiar trope in crime fiction, not least in the hard-boiled detective narrative, Irish adaptations of which are the focus of Part Four. Maureen Reddy opens the section by establishing some of the key issues around Irish forms of this subgenre with her analysis of Declan Burke's Harry Rigby novels, which may appear to be among the most hard-boiled novels in Irish crime fiction but which at the same time, as she argues, break many of the genre's rules. Brandi Byrd's and Anjili Babbar's essays consider varying formal and historical pressures put on this subgenre through two Northern Irish series. Where writers including Keith Ridgway and Flann O'Brien have imported elements of crime fiction into metaphysical or postmodern fiction, Byrd suggests that Bateman instead imports the metaphysical into crime fiction, forming his own particularly effective fusion of humor and the amateur private eye. Babbar looks at McKinty's wryer Sean Duffy novels, tracing McKinty's use of intertextuality and gallows humor within his own adaptation of the police procedural. Finally, Richard Howard demonstrates how the crusading journalist Gene Kerrigan draws on some of the unique concerns of international hard-boiled models—particularly those involving corruption and the state, a preoccupation in the modern genre at least as far back as Dashiell Hammett's *Red Harvest* (1929)[6]—to frame his narratives set around Dublin during the Celtic Tiger years.

In the final section, the collection turns toward perhaps the most recently emerged crime subgenre, domestic noir. All crime subgenres develop from categories that stabilize to varying degrees over time. The stable segment then carries forward to absorb shifts in society and authorship, evolving into a new category that readers often recognize before it becomes fixed in generic classification. "Domestic noir" was similarly embraced even before the term was coined by the British novelist Julia Crouch in 2013, and reflects the broadening complexity of domestic narratives drawn,

6. For an astute examination of these matters, see Pepper, *Unwilling Executioner.*

in large part, by women crime novelists who have shifted the male literary gaze of female victimhood. From protagonist to plot, that misogynistic position faces death by a thousand narrative cuts in these novels. Each of the essays in this section—by Rosemary Erickson Johnsen, Vivian Valvano Lynch, Fiona Coleman Coffey, and Brian Cliff—addresses varied iterations of domestic noir, demonstrating how it can serve widely diverse narrative ends. Johnsen examines Louise Phillips's reconciliation of conflicting genre and market imperatives, and Lynch follows Claire McGowan's elaboration of a post-Troubles Northern Irish series around the private and the domestic. Emphasizing similarly intimate personal narrative matters, Coffey argues that Sinéad Crowley's Sergeant Claire Boyle series constitutes a specific maternal noir category within domestic noir, while the final chapter examines Liz Nugent's ability to navigate an uneasy relationship between empathy and evil through narrators whose acute malignancy is profoundly entangled with their familial dysfunctions and traumas. These novelists' works are representative of both the international subgenre's still-growing scope and its centrality in contemporary Irish crime writing. These are not, however, pure genre exercises: they all contribute to an Irish domestic noir, but they do so in part through their innovative use of other subgenres, particularly psychological thrillers and police procedurals. In this, the examples of domestic noir here reflect the best and the breadth of Irish crime fiction, its dynamic and fluid development, its malleability in the hands of writers as inventive as those discussed throughout this book.

Bibliography

Burke, Declan, ed. *Down These Green Streets: Irish Crime Writing in the 21st Century*. Dublin: Liberties Press, 2011.

———. "Editor's Note." In Burke, *Down These Green Streets*, 9–11.

Childers, Erskine. *The Riddle of the Sands*. London: Smith, Elder, & Co., 1903. Reprint, London: Penguin, 1999.

Cliff, Brian. *Irish Crime Fiction*. London: Palgrave Macmillan, 2018.

Connolly, John. "No Blacks, No Dogs, No Crime Writers: Ireland and the Mystery Genre." In Burke, *Down These Green Streets*, 39–57.

Dabiri, Emma. *Don't Touch My Hair*. London: Penguin, 2019.

de Waal, Kit. "Make Room for Working Class Writers." *Guardian* (Manchester), 10 February 2018.

Doyle, Martin. "'Untalented' Crime Writers Respond to Their No. 1 Critic." *Irish Times*, 20 March 2017, http://www.irishtimes.com/culture/books/untalented-crime-writers-respond-to-their-no-1-critic-1.3017198. Accessed 5 April 2017.

Fennell, Jack, ed. *A Brilliant Void: A Selection of Classic Irish Science Fiction*. Dublin: Tramp Press, 2018.

Gaffney, Frankie. *Dublin Seven*. Dublin: Liberties Press, 2015.

Harding, Michael. *Staring at Lakes*. Dublin: Hachette Books Ireland, 2013.

Macardle, Dorothy. *Dark Enchantment*. 1953. Reprint, Dublin: Tramp Press, 2019.

———. *The Unforeseen*. 1945. Reprint, Dublin: Tramp Press, 2017.

———. *The Uninvited*. 1941. Reprint, Dublin: Tramp Press, 2015.

Mannion, Elizabeth, ed. *The Contemporary Irish Detective Novel*. London: Palgrave Macmillan, 2016.

McInerney, Lisa. "Don't Tell Me That Working-Class People Can't Be Articulate." *Guardian* (Manchester), 5 May 2017.

Okorie, Melatu Uche. *This Hostel Life*. Dublin: Skein Press, 2018.

Pepper, Andrew. *Unwilling Executioner: Crime Fiction and the State*. Oxford: Oxford Univ. Press, 2016.

Pierse, Michael, ed. "Back to Class: Ireland's Working-Class Literature." *The Honest Ulsterman* (June 2018). https://humag.co/features/back-to-class. Accessed 22 October 2018.

———. *A History of Irish Working-Class Writing*. Cambridge: Cambridge Univ. Press, 2017.

Schaffer, Rachel, ed. "Special Issue on Tana French." *Clues: A Journal of Detection* 32, no. 1 (2014). Accessed 19 March 2018.

PART ONE

Antecedents and Beginnings

1

Freeman Wills Crofts and the Inverted Mystery

SHANE MAWE

Dublin-born Freeman Wills Crofts played a major role in the development of detective fiction during its Golden Age, a period defined mainly by British authors in the years between the two world wars. With his successful debut, *The Cask* (1920), Crofts was front and center of this group, many of whom are still celebrated today. He was a prolific author whose sales figures rivaled the bestsellers of the period, yet he remains largely omitted from discussions of Irish crime fiction. A contemporary of Agatha Christie and Dorothy L. Sayers, Crofts's books remain in print,[1] but his reputation has failed to match that of these luminaries. The low-profile nature of his fictional detectives and pacing of his plots are certainly contributing factors to this and to limiting his work's screen adaptations. Unlike Christie's cast of characters in particular, Crofts's fictional Inspector French failed to successfully morph from print to celluloid. The lack of drama in Crofts's personal life correlated directly with a low news-media profile. Marital affairs, divorces, or sensational disappearing acts were not to feature during his writing career, but Crofts matched his colleagues when it came to plot structure, and this—specifically the inverted mystery—is what made his detective novels popular during the Golden Age and explains why he remains a key figure in crime fiction today.

1. Recent reissues include *The Pit-Prop Syndicate* (Harper Collins, 2018), and Crippen and Landru plan to issue a volume of Crofts's essays, plays, and short stories in 2020.

Crofts and his fellow members of the Detection Club (including Sayers, Christie, and G. K. Chesterton) have become synonymous with this era in the same way Raymond Chandler, Dashiell Hammett, and James M. Cain are taken to represent the hard-boiled American genre. Although frequently referred to as a "humdrum" writer from the school of police procedurals,[2] Crofts had the ability to adapt this style to incorporate the inverted mystery, a back-to-front work that cross-fertilizes a study of criminal behavior with a detective story.[3] At the time this was a relatively new approach to crime fiction.

Crofts was born in Dublin in 1879 to an army surgeon, also named Freeman Wills Crofts, and his wife Cecilia Frances Wise. His father died on duty in Honduras before young Crofts was born. After a short time in Dublin, Crofts and his mother moved to Belfast when she remarried in 1883. Educated at the Methodist and Campbell colleges in the city, Crofts seemed destined for a career in engineering, having secured an apprenticeship in 1896 with his uncle, Berkeley D. Wise, chief engineer on the Belfast & Northern Counties Railway. By 1910 he had risen to the role of chief engineer of the Northern Counties Committee Railway. Not unlike Hammett's entrance into fiction, an illness suffered by Crofts in 1919,[4] followed by a period of convalescence, gave him the time to devote to writing a novel. He completed the manuscript after his recovery, and submitted the final draft to Collins, who published *The Cask* in 1920. *The Cask* marks the beginning of a writing career that spanned thirty-seven years, up to *Anything to Declare?*, published in 1957, the year of his death. A prolific author, Crofts averaged a book for every year, with Inspector French featuring in thirty titles.

With the recent Golden Age of Scandinavian noir or indeed the Golden Age of Irish crime fiction, it might be harder to identify a time when the crime and mystery genres were *not* covered in gilt. That gilt can imply

2. See Evans, *Masters of the "Humdrum" Mystery*, for an overview of this subgenre.

3. Edwards, *Story of Classic Crime*, 199.

4. Curtis Evans suggests that the work was written three years earlier and Crofts revisited the work in 1919.

the dawn of the genre, but Victorian and Edwardian exponents such as Arthur Conan Doyle, Sheridan Le Fanu, Wilkie Collins, Edgar Allan Poe, and Émile Gaboriau—all of whom retain their popularity—predated the Golden Age of detective fiction.

Contrary to its sometimes staid reputation, the Golden Age was an era of experimentation in forms of detection writing and in audience engagement with the genre. Audience participation was popularized by the competition story, of which Edgar Wallace was an early exponent, with mixed results. In Wallace's locked-room mystery, *The Four Just Men* (1905), British Foreign Secretary Sir Philip Ramon is killed at a predicted time (8 o'clock) after his life was threatened by the vigilante group "The Four Just Men." Ramon's death occurred while he was in a secure environment surrounded by a police guard. Wallace left the case unsolved, and "the publishers invite[d] the reader to solve this mystery and offer prizes to the value of £500 (first prize £250) to the readers who will furnish on the form provided the explanation of Sir Philip Ramon's death."[5] Unfortunately, Wallace underestimated the ingenuity of his audience, many of whom submitted the correct answer, thus bankrupting the author when income generated from sales failed to match the expenditure of payouts.

Audience engagement also took the form of contributory novels (or round-robins), which begin in the Golden Age and remain popular nearly a century later, particularly within the location-specific subgenre.[6] As a member of the Detection Club, Crofts contributed to the round-robin novel *The Floating Admiral* (1931). Referred to in its introduction by Dorothy L. Sayers as "the detection game as played out on paper by certain members of the Detection Club among themselves,"[7] the work includes twelve chapters

5. Wallace, *Four Just Men*, Cover.

6. Florida has been a most popular setting in this category, beginning with *Naked Came the Manatee* (New York: G. P. Putnam's Sons, 1996), which included contributions from Elmore Leonard, Paul Levine, and Carl Hiaasen. Irish settings have also been used, including Dublin in *Yeats Is Dead!* (London: Vintage, 2002) and *Finbar's Hotel* (London: Picador, 1997).

7. Detection Club, *Floating Admiral*, 2.

written by twelve different club members including Chesterton, Christie, and Sayers. Contributors had to write a chapter to follow the previous one without any collaboration on the final outcome of the story. Each author then submitted their solutions at the end of the text. The members were to collaborate again in 1936 with *Six Against the Yard* and the Gollancz publication *Double Death* (1939), which, unlike the earlier collaboration, also included contributions from nonmembers such as Anthony Armstrong. *Double Death* would further cement the Detection Club's prominence in the public mind.

The origins of the Detection Club can be traced to the late 1920s. Complete with its own constitution, rules, and initiation ceremony, the Club invited crime writers of two or more titles (with some exceptions) to join as members and help develop the genre. How seriously the authors took their attachment to the Club is open to scrutiny. As part of the initiation ceremony, for example, members had to swear what seems a slightly tongue-in-cheek oath composed by Sayers: "Do you promise that your detectives shall well and truly detect the crimes presented to them using those wits which it may please you to bestow upon them and not placing reliance on nor making use of Divine Revelation, Feminine Intuition, Mumbo Jumbo, Jiggery-Pokery, Coincidence, or Act of God?"[8] The fact that members had to swear an oath, let alone its wording, suggests the Club is best described as a loose gathering of authors with an irreverent or humorous slant. It is hard to argue however with the talent among the members. Along with Sayers, early club members included Chesterton, G. D. H. Cole, M. Cole, Christie, Anthony Berkeley, and Crofts's fellow Irish member, Mrs. Victor Rickard.[9]

Sayers's oath was in response to Detection Club member Ronald A. Knox's introduction to *The Best Detective Stories of the Year 1928* (1929), which included a set of ten rules—his Decalogue—that codified what became known as the Fair Play conventions of the genre:

8. Brabazon, *Dorothy L. Sayers*, 144.

9. Like Crofts, Rickard was born in Dublin, though she also had a Cork connection (as did Crofts's father). A prolific author of fiction and history, Rickard is perhaps best known for her detective novel *Not Sufficient Evidence* (1926), which is oddly absent from the National Library of Ireland.

1. The criminal must be mentioned in the early part of the story, but must not be anyone whose thoughts the reader has been allowed to follow.

2. All supernatural or preternatural agencies are ruled out as a matter of course.

3. Not more than one secret room or passage is allowable.

4. No hitherto undiscovered poisons may be used, nor any appliance which will need a long scientific explanation at the end.

5. No Chinaman must figure in the story.

6. No accident must ever help the detective, nor must he ever have an unaccountable intuition which proves to be right.

7. The detective himself must not commit the crime.

8. The detective is bound to declare any clues upon which he may happen to light.

9. The stupid friend of the detective, the Watson, must not conceal from the reader any thoughts which pass through his mind; his intelligence must be slightly, but very slightly, below that of the average reader.

10. Twin brothers, and doubles generally, must not appear unless we have been duly prepared for them.[10]

Knox's fifth rule stands out for its directness. Christopher Frayling suggests this was in response to the success Sax Rohmer enjoyed with his Fu-Manchu stories,[11] which were also often guilty of shattering the second rule on a consistent basis. Although Crofts tried to obey Knox's amusing rules of detective fiction, and his inverted stories can be viewed to some extent as examples of Fair Play, their very structure fails to adhere to Knox's first rule. Crofts—who, like Knox, had a strong religious faith—created protagonists who were a good deal less scrupulous about the original Ten Commandments revealed to Moses on Mount Sinai. In *Antidote to Venom* (1938) alone there is evidence of murder (obviously), extramarital affairs, gambling, and deceit.

Well before the Detection Club or *Antidote to Venom*, Crofts's writing career was firmly established by the enormous success of *The Cask*,

10. Knox, *Best Detective Stories*, xi–xiv.

11. Frayling, *Yellow Peril*, 276.

which sold well over one hundred thousand copies worldwide. *The Cask* introduces Inspector Burnley of Scotland Yard who is alerted to strange happenings on the docks in London.[12] Arriving from France on board the steamship *Bullfinch*, a heavy cask splits as it is being unloaded on the dockside to reveal its bounty: a hoard of gold sovereigns. Digging further, the workers, while filling their pockets, uncover a woman's hand. On arrival at the scene, Burnley learns of the cask's disappearance and so begins the tale that proved so popular in the 1920s.

Three more novels appeared in the next three years: *The Ponson Case* (1921), *The Pit-Prop Syndicate* (1922), and *The Groote Park Murder* (1923). Crofts was on a roll. Further success came in 1924 with *Inspector French's Greatest Case*, which marked the first appearance of Crofts's most celebrated character, Inspector Joseph French of Scotland Yard. Howard Haycraft describes this bestseller as "a volume worthy in almost every way to find its place on the shelf beside *The Cask*."[13] The case in question revolves around a theft and murder at a London diamond merchant. Scotland Yard are alerted and the first appearance of Inspector French in print ensues. Much of what was to become familiar in later French titles can be found here, not least a persistent detective working the leads and descriptive passages of locations (France, Holland, Spain, Portugal, and Switzerland), including carefully detailed shipping and rail timetables. Crofts's passion for travel, which featured in many of his titles, is very much evident here.

The Inspector who was to become associated with Crofts's career is "a stout man in tweeds, rather under middle height, with a clean shaven, good-humoured face and dark blue eyes, which, though keen, twinkled as if at some perennially fresh private joke. His air was easy-going and leisurely, and he looked the type of man who could enjoy a good dinner."[14] Though his Inspector may have seemed "perennially fresh," further health issues prevented Crofts himself from continuing in his dual role as writer and railway engineer. He sacrificed the latter and moved to the village of Blackheath

12. Burnley is a precursor to Inspector French, the detective figure for whom Crofts is most well known.

13. Haycraft, *Murder for Pleasure*, 123.

14. Crofts, *Inspector French's Greatest Case*, 14.

near Guildford, Surrey in 1929, where he concentrated on his writing, later moving in 1953 to Worthing in southeast England to avail of its temperate climate as his health further deteriorated. Upon his death in 1957, Crofts bequeathed the copyright of his works to the Royal Society of Arts, which had elected him a Fellow in 1939, in order to help struggling authors.

From early in this long career, Crofts was among the very first advocates of the inverted mystery, "in which the identity of the murderer or criminal is given away at the beginning."[15] Much like competition stories, this format was designed to include and engage the reading audience, who enjoy full knowledge of the circumstances of the crime and can concentrate on the unraveling of the case, which moves from "whodunit" to "howcatchem." Knowledge is power, and with inverted mysteries, authors offer their readers the feeling of participation. The inverted mystery is probably most associated today with the television show *Columbo* (1971–2003), whose creators—William Link and Richard Levinson—used this device to announce the arrival of their pioneering and long-serving police lieutenant. Inspector French and Lieutenant Columbo share much in common. Both characters, while humble, are dogged in their pursuit of murderers. In his inverted works, Crofts builds the storyline and establishes the plot long before French appears on the scene.[16] The initial result was *The 12.30 from Croydon* (1934).[17] Publishers Hodder & Stoughton issued three more of Crofts's inverted mysteries—*Mystery on Southampton Water* (1934),[18] *Antidote to Venom*, and *The Affair at Little Wokeham* (1943)[19]—as well as *Murderers Make Mistakes* (1947), a collection of inverted stories.[20]

15. Murphy, *Encyclopaedia of Murder and Mystery*, 264. Richard Austin Freeman, a contemporary of Crofts, pioneered the inverted fiction format with *The Red Thumb Mark* (1907). This was his first work to feature Dr. Thorndyke, and is generally regarded as the first example of an inverted mystery story.

16. Examples include: Crofts, *12.30 from Croydon*, 180; Crofts, *Mystery on Southampton Water*, 99; and Crofts, *Cheyne Mystery*, 154.

17. Published in the United States as *Wilful and Premeditated* (New York: Dodd, Mead).

18. Published in the United States as *Crime on the Solnet* (New York: Dodd, Mead).

19. Published in the United States as *Double Tragedy* (New York: Dodd, Mead).

20. Crofts refers to his inverted short stories in the author's note as "double stories."

In between the publication of the novels and short stories, Todd Publishing Company (London) reissued Crofts's inverted tale *The Hunt Ball Murder* (1944) as an illustrated pamphlet. As he does in many of the titles, Inspector French appears late in this text. It is not until page 13 (of only 16) that French (now Chief Inspector) enters the story to solve the murder of Justin Holt and arrest Howard Skeffington for the act. There are two further matters of interest in this story: a rare attempt by Crofts at humor in describing French and Sergeant Carter's efforts at reconstructing the murder; and his use of clue finders where he addresses the reader directly, asking, "Where had Skeffington given himself away?"[21] He had made greater use of this device, steeped in the tradition of Fair Play,[22] in *The Hog's Back Mystery* (1933),[23] where at the end of the text French directs the reader back to the actual pages where he made progress in the case.

Crofts's works featuring Inspector French not only satisfied a public demand for crime fiction, they were also well received by critics in the United Kingdom and Ireland. Favorable reviews for his early works were published in the *New Republican*, *Outlook*, and *New Statesman*. On the publication of *Sir John Magill's Last Journey* (1930), the *Irish Book Lover* referred to Crofts's reputation as "the greatest writer of detective fiction."[24] Although he was deemed worthy of comment in the United States, his Stateside reputation and popularity failed to match that in the United Kingdom and Ireland. Features on Crofts and his work often cite Raymond Chandler as an admirer.[25] The evidence is largely based upon one line in Chandler's classic essay "The Simple Art of Murder" (1950), which refers

21. Crofts, *Hunt Ball Murder*, 13.

22. Fair Play in the Golden Age of detective fiction refers to authors playing fair with the readers by revealing all the clues and vital information so that they are afforded an opportunity to solve the mystery.

23. Published in the United States as *The Strange Case of Dr. Earle* (New York: Dodd, Mead).

24. *Irish Book Lover*, 132. With a similar enthusiasm, *Crime at Guildford* (US title, *The Crime at Nornes*) is listed in "What Dublin Is Reading," *Irish Times*, 25 May 1935.

25. See, for example, Fowler, "Invisible Ink"; Evans, *Masters of the "Humdrum" Mystery*, 159; and Woolven, "Crofts, Freeman Wills."

to Crofts as "the soundest builder of them [Golden Age authors] all, when he doesn't get too fancy."[26] While the description suggests Crofts's plots are elaborate in structure and somewhat intricate, it does not quite portray Chandler as a paid-up member of the Crofts fan club, and leaves the reader wondering just how much Chandler really admired Crofts. It could even be argued that as backhanded compliments go, this one, like Chandler's fictional detective Marlowe, takes some beating.[27]

Chandler's background would suggest he was well versed on the canon of Golden Age writing. Born in Chicago, he received his education at Dulwich public school and later contributed book reviews, essays, and even verse to London literary periodicals. The fact that he was thoroughly familiar with the genre makes his often-quoted line on Crofts all the more lukewarm. Further evidence of his opinion on Crofts can be seen in a letter written in 1948 to James Keddie in which he suggests that "no normal reader could solve a Crofts mystery because no normal reader has that exact a memory for insignificant details."[28] Later correspondence with Keddie in 1950 shows no sign of Chandler reappraising the author's ability, referring to Crofts's writing as dull.[29]

Criticism of Crofts's style is valid. His later works were not always well received and the quality of his output is uneven.[30] As a writer, he leaves himself open to accusations of overindulgence in describing irrelevant

26. Chandler, *Simple Art of Murder*, 325.

27. To put it further in context, Chandler's essay takes numerous swipes at Golden Age authors. After slating Agatha Christie's *Murder on the Orient Express*, suggesting "only a halfwit could guess it," and suggesting that "the English may not always be the best writers in the world, but they are incomparably the best dull writers," he cedes that "there may be one [story] somewhere that would really stand up to close scrutiny. It would be fun to read it, even if I did have to go back to page 47 and refresh my memory about exactly what time the second gardener potted the prize-winning tea-rose begonia" (Chandler, *Simple Art of Murder*, 325–26).

28. Chandler, *Selected Letters*, 109.

29. Chandler, *Selected Letters*, 226.

30. "Unfortunately . . . for in recent years some impatient readers claim to have noticed evidence of weariness in the methodical Inspector's adventures" (Haycraft, *Murder for Pleasure*, 123–24).

detail. Consider this passage from *Mystery on Southampton Water*: "Did the Chief-Inspector know anything of the manufacture of cement? French's ideas were of the haziest. Very well, roughly what happened was that chalk and earths of various kinds were mixed and ground with water into a slurry."[31] It is crying out for the blue pencil of a heavy-handed editor. There are many more examples of this overly descriptive style in his writing. Yet Crofts's talent is also in the detail and his plots rely heavily on descriptions of what appear to be watertight alibis. Although much enjoyment is gained from observing how Inspector French arrives at the solution, the journey there could have been spared the extraneous detail and described in more direct prose—typically the reader ambles, rarely sprinting, with French minutely examining the evidence frequently involving travel plans and timetables. Such granular examination contributed to the "humdrum" label.

The Inspector's method is of "untiring thoroughness directed by flashes of inspiration which is the secret of his unfailing success."[32] Crofts's writing skills lack the ability for solid character development. Apart from perhaps our instinctive empathy with the side of law and order in Golden Age fiction, modern readers will rarely feel any emotional connection to Crofts's victims or villains. All too often it feels that his characters exist solely as devices to develop a particular alibi-related event. Moreover, his fictional work is generally devoid of humor, although his reference to fellow crime writer R. Austin Freeman in *The 12.30 from Croydon* and a reference to *The Cask* in his later novel *The Sea Mystery* (1928) would have made his loyal readership smile. Crofts is not alone in such limitations; Golden Age police procedurals can have a one-dimensional style. Perhaps this is part of their attraction. Readers are presented with a crime and can concentrate on observing the resolution of the case free of any distraction.

The maxim "write what you know" can be applied to much of Crofts's output. Inspector French titles feature locations familiar to Crofts, including

31. Crofts, *Mystery on Southampton Water*, 136.

32. Crofts, *Inspector French and the Cheyne Mystery*, "About This Book" verso of cover.

Cork in *Fatal Venture* (1939),[33] Northern Ireland in *Sir John Magill's Last Journey*, and Surrey in *The Hog's Back Mystery* and *The Affair at Little Wokeham*. As a railway engineer, Crofts deploys his interest in various methods of transportation to good effect. Yet, his familiarity with the workings of Scotland Yard was limited, as he confesses in *Meet Inspector French* (1935): "I knew nothing about the Yard or C.I.D. What was to be done? The answer was simple. I built upon the great rock which sustains so many of my profession: if I knew nothing of my subject, well, few of my readers would know any more."[34]

Despite this casual attitude toward precise procedural detail, Crofts's titles champion the role of law and order in society. His attempts to bring a sense of authenticity to depictions of the police force can be viewed as a rebuke to the fiction of E. W. Hornung's Raffles and his fellow gentleman-thief Arsène Lupin. Crofts draws rather on antecedents like Charles Dickens's Inspector Bucket, who—middle-aged and friendly in appearance, but tenacious and perceptive—solves the murder that forms the climax of *Bleak House* (1853).

Meet Inspector French, for example, sees Crofts explain his decision to portray French as an uncomplicated character. This self-deprecating piece gives an insight into the origins of French's personality and Crofts's initial ambitions for the Inspector. French was always to be front and center as the main protagonist. From Shakespeare's Dogberry in *Much Ado about Nothing* to Arthur Conan Doyle's depiction of Inspector Lestrade, literature is littered with examples of bumbling or boastful policemen. Crofts, however, was among the first in the established genre to develop a member of the police force as the central character.[35] Equipped with the necessary crime-solving skill set, matched with humble characteristics, French gained the admiration of his associates and that of generations of readers.

33. US title published as *Tragedy in the Hollow* (New York: Dodd, Mead).

34. Full text available at http://www.classiccrimefiction.com/fwcrofts-inspectorfrench.htm.

35. Josephine Tey also tasted success with her Inspector Alan Grant series beginning with *The Man in the Queue* (1929) and ending with the posthumously published *The Singing Sands* (1952).

In his foreword to the eightieth anniversary edition of *The Floating Admiral* (2011), Simon Brett argues that "Berkeley is one of the contributors . . . whose name is still reasonably well known . . . the same can be said of Monsignor Ronald A. Knox, Freeman Wills Croft [*sic*] and Clemence Dane."[36] The misspelling of his name suggests that Crofts's profile is less than prominent. Circulation figures for Crofts's titles in the Library of Trinity College Dublin similarly suggest the author lacks popularity among the college community with just twenty-eight checkouts since the 1980s from the eighty-four volumes held in the library. Interestingly, however, the London Library's copy of *Mystery on Southampton Water* has alone seen over one hundred loans over the same period, a figure that suggests at least pockets of popularity.

Despite his limitations as an author, Crofts was a ground-breaking precursor to what is now recognized as the distinct subgenre of the police procedural. His religious upbringing and lifelong devotion to the Church,[37] while influencing his work—nowhere more so than in *Antidote to Venom*—failed to deter him from fictionalizing the most despicable of crimes. He deserves to be remembered more as an innovator than a great writer. Nevertheless, he had the ability to adapt his writing skills to various formats (monographs, short stories, radio plays) and styles (whodunits, inverted mysteries, multiple-narrator works, juvenile crime fiction, and round-robin works). Crofts's influence is evident in the majority of police procedurals that followed, including Georges Simenon's Maigret, crucially exemplifying how crime novels can allow the reader to follow the investigation step by step. For this his reputation deserves greater recognition.

Bibliography

Brabazon, James. *Dorothy L. Sayers: A Biography*. London: Gollancz, 1981.

Chandler, Raymond. *The Selected Letters of Raymond Chandler*. Edited by Frank MacShane. London: Macmillan, 1983.

———. *The Simple Art of Murder*. London: Hamish Hamilton, 1950.

36. Detection Club, *Floating Admiral*, vi.

37. Crofts was a strong advocate for the Christian evangelical organization The Oxford Group.

Crofts, Freeman Wills. *The 12.30 from Croydon*. London: Hodder & Stoughton, 1934.

———. *Antidote to Venom*. London: Hodder & Stoughton, 1938.

———. *The Hunt Ball Murder*. London: Todd Publishing Company, 1944.

———. *Inspector French and the Cheyne Mystery*. London: Penguin, 1953.

———. *Inspector French's Greatest Case*. London: W. Collins Sons, [1925].

———. *Mystery on Southampton Water*. London: Hodder & Stoughton, 1934.

Detection Club. *The Floating Admiral*. London: HarperCollins, 2011.

Edwards, Martin. *The Golden Age of Murder: The Mystery of the Writers Who Invented the Modern Detective Story*. London: HarperCollins, 2015.

———. *The Story of Classic Crime in 100 Books*. London: British Library Publishing, 2018.

Evans, Curtis J. *Masters of the "Humdrum" Mystery: Cecil John Charles Street, Freeman Wills Crofts, Alfred Walter Stewart and the British Detective Novel, 1920–1961*. Jefferson, NC: McFarland, 2012.

Fowler, Christopher. "*Invisible Ink*: No 184—Freeman Wills Crofts." *Independent* (London), 3 August 2013. https://www.independent.co.uk/arts-entertainment/books/features/invisible-ink-no-184-freeman-wills-crofts-8744830.html. Accessed 12 April 2017.

Frayling, Christopher. *The Yellow Peril: Dr. Fu Manchu & the Rise of Chinaphobia*. London: Thames & Hudson, 2014.

Haycraft, Howard. *Murder for Pleasure: The Life and Times of the Detective Story*. New York: Carroll & Graf, 1984.

Irish Book Lover, The. Vol. 18 (1930).

Knox, Ronald Arbuthnott. "Introduction." In *The Best Detective Stories of the Year 1928*, edited by Ronald Arbuthnott. London: Faber & Faber, 1929.

Murphy, Bruce. *The Encyclopaedia of Murder and Mystery*. London: Palgrave, 2001.

Wallace, Edgar. *The Four Just Men*. London: Tallis Press, 1905.

"What Dublin Is Reading." *Irish Times*, 25 May 1935. https://www.irishtimes.com/newspaper/archive/1935/0525/Pg007.html#Ar00704. Accessed 9 April 2017.

Woolven, Robin. "Crofts, Freeman Wills (1879–1957), Railway Engineer and Writer of Detective Stories." *Oxford Dictionary of National Biography*, 23 September 2004. https://www.oxforddnb.com/view/10.1093/ref:odnb/9780198614128.001.0001/odnb-9780198614128-e-38560. Accessed 14 May 2018.

2

Before the Tiger Roared

Bartholomew Gill's Ireland

ELIZABETH MANNION

Decades before Irish crime fiction emerged on international bestseller lists, American journalist Mark McGarrity staked a claim as the first author of a contemporary Irish detective series. Under the pen name Bartholomew Gill, he published the Peter McGarr series from the late 1970s until his death in 2002.[1] McGarr is chief superintendent of the Serious Crimes Unit (SCU) of An Garda Síochána (nicknamed the "Dublin Murder Squad"),[2] a position to which he was recruited from Paris. He is European-trained, but Inchicore born-and-raised, and his working-class Dublin roots are on display whenever he has to weigh the needs of the community with the wants of the privileged. McGarr prides himself on viewing "the world as it is."[3] But this pragmatism, like the ease with which he bridges the social strata, is often challenged. McGarr is urbane with spine, equally content at posh restaurants and in the docklands of his boyhood. Considering the massive socioeconomic changes that Ireland underwent in the twenty-five years the series covers—from joining the Common Market and the establishment of the European Union to the early Celtic Tiger—this malleability is put to good use. McGarr is simultaneously a face of New Ireland and a

1. He also published several novels under his given name, from *Little Augie's Lament* (1973) to *White Rush/Green Fire* (1991).

2. Others, most notably Tana French, would adopt this nickname too.

3. Gill, *Irish Politician*, chap. 5.

surrogate for working-class figures who fear economic and political disenfranchisement in an increasingly globalized country. In its snapshot of these societal changes, the series exemplifies early transnational Irish crime fiction and offers a template for the police procedurals that emerge in the following decades.

When the series begins, McGarr has been away from Ireland for fourteen years, serving on the French police force and Interpol. His emigration was not by choice but was, as for many of his generation, due to limited career prospects. While ascending the career ladder in Europe, he regularly applied for senior posts back in Dublin. But "he had to wait until somebody died for a position to be offered to him."[4] When McGarr does join the SCU, it mirrors the country's turn from the "economic nationalism . . . that found its ideological basis in post-Independence isolationism."[5] Where McGarr's long-serving predecessor at the SCU was "notorious" for having "ruthlessly pursued and . . . murdered renegade IRA gunmen," McGarr was selected precisely because he was free of such political entanglements.[6] This contrast anchors the series on the edge of socioeconomic change, anticipating an accompanying shift in criminality, including an increased drug trade that gains prominence throughout the series. In recruiting McGarr, the SCU gains a lawman who knows the past but possesses the skills the force will need to face the ever-changing present. The Irish public grasps this too because he is a public figure: during his years in Paris, he broke a series of big cases that were followed closely in the press, and became himself a subject of public curiosity. So when he finally returns to Ireland, he is not merely new Superintendent McGarr, he is *the* Peter McGarr: local Dub who climbed the ranks of an elite European police force and made a name for himself. The public consider him one of their own, as much as the administration does.

Mirroring this negotiation of power and authority within the novels, the series' authorship (American), setting (increasingly globalized Ireland),

4. Gill, *Irish Politician*, chap. 2.

5. McCarthy, *Modernisation, Crisis and Culture in Ireland*, 12.

6. Gill, *Cold, Wild River*, 28. The only indication of his political leanings is a portrait of Wolfe Tone (1763–98) that adorns his office wall. He occasionally contemplates his youthful lack of involvement in Republican causes, but keeps these thoughts to himself.

and literary antecedents (European and American) problematize its place in the history of transnational Irish detective fiction. The complicated publishing history—renaming titles, switching publishing houses, periodically going out of print—has further complicated the series' exposure. As part of his homage to Georges Simenon's Maigret, for example, Gill included his detective's name in book titles while under contract with Scribner's.[7] At the close of that relationship, however, the titles of reissued editions were revised to be more genre- rather than character-specific, with an explicit emphasis on their Irishness.[8] *McGarr and the Politician's Wife* (1977) became *The Death of an Irish Politician*, *McGarr and the Sienese Conspiracy* (1977) became *The Death of an Irish Consul*, *McGarr on the Cliffs of Moher* (1978) became *The Death of an Irish Lass*, and *McGarr at the Dublin Horse Show* (1979) became *The Death of an Irish Tradition*. The next three were published by Viking and returned to making the detective the selling point: *McGarr and the P.M. of Belgrave Square* (1983), *McGarr and the Method of Descartes* (1984), and *McGarr and the Legacy of a Woman Scorned* (1986). Gill then joined William Morrow, which published the rest of the series, following the revised titles established by Scribner's: *The Death of a Joyce Scholar* (1989), *The Death of Love* (1992), *Death on a Cold, Wild River* (1993), *The Death of an Ardent Bibliophile* (1995), *The Death of an Irish Sea Wolf* (1996), *The Death of an Irish Tinker* (1997),[9] *The Death of an Irish Lover* (2000), *The Death of an*

7. This, along with McGarr's penchant for hats, smoking, alcohol, and good food, plus his reliance on a "faithful four" core group of colleagues, is part of his homage to Simenon, who often put his Inspector Maigret in the titles of that series.

8. Charles Scribner pitched the paperback rights to Pocket Books as "destined to become an Irish Inspector Dalgliesh (P. D. James)," suggesting the possibility that title changes were under consideration before Gill left Scribner's. Letter from Charles Scribner to Florence Torrino, 1 May 1979. Series 3: Author Files; 1968–89; Archives of Charles Scribner's Sons, Manuscripts Division, Department of Rare Books and Special Collections, Princeton University Library.

9. The 1997 UK edition by Severn House is instead titled *The Death of a Busker King*; it appears this title was subsequently adopted in future North American paperback editions. It is noteworthy that the original title was used at all, since its publication (1990) was well

Irish Sinner (2001), and the posthumously issued *Death in Dublin* (2003).[10] There are no cliffhangers and few recurring criminal nemeses. Instead, the series' arc consists largely of tracking both McGarr and Ireland as Irish society changes, particularly around the regulatory aspects of the Common Market/European Union (EU).[11]

Ireland joined the Common Market (the predecessor to the EU) in 1973. This put Ireland on a path toward globalization that would see an unprecedented financial return, including infrastructural advancements that benefited rural and urban communities alike, particularly decades of major road and power projects. But membership brought regulations along with a return on investment, and these were based largely on economic partnerships as a path to postwar peace and stability.[12] Trade laws and economic parity were also the foundation for the civil rights cornerstones of EU legislation, including gender equality. The 1957 Treaty of Rome included Article 119, "establishing the principle of equal pay for women and men."[13] Economic principles meant to assure ease of trade thus led to gender equity laws that helped facilitate progress for women's rights in Ireland. At the start of the McGarr series (1977), contraceptives and divorce were both illegal in Ireland; the Family Home Protection Act, ending the practice of limitations on married women's legal property rights, had only recently been signed; and the Employment Equality Act of 1977 had only just passed. In contrast, by the publication of the final novel in 2003, Mary McAleese was already the second woman elected president of Ireland.

---

after the Traveler Community in Ireland had begun lobbying for civil rights. Pavee Point, the Dublin-based NGO in support of Traveler and Roma communities, had already been in existence for five years.

10. Paperback and UK rights went to presses other than Scribner's, Viking, and William Morrow, but first editions were with those three American publishing houses.

11. In March 1957, The Treaty of Rome established the European Economic Community (EEC) aka the Common Market: signatories were Belgium, France, Italy, Luxembourg, the Netherlands, and West Germany. Ireland joined in 1973.

12. See, for example, "1960–1969, A Period of Economic Growth."

13. Burri and Prechal, "EU Gender Equality Law Update 2010."

These seismic shifts are tracked in the McGarr series, with gender matters incorporated—either as subtext or overtly—in all cases, but particularly those that highlight issues around EU integration.

McGarr's wife, Noreen, is established from the start as intelligent, confident, and successful. Her training in art restoration has given her a sharp eye for detail that McGarr calls on fairly regularly. McGarr "discussed every aspect of his job with her, and she was scrupulously discreet about the details. 'Two for the price of one,' a former minister for justice had always joked when introducing them."[14] Yet McGarr's respect for her does not initially extend to all women, and he is frequently misogynistic in the early novels. When the series opens, as he interrogates a wealthy socialite and celebrated beauty suspected of murder, she begins to cry. Just glimpsing a tear in the corner of her eye sets him off: "McGarr hated to admit it, but that the very sound of his voice had made such an extraordinary woman cry rather excited him. She had the sort of beauty he would like to crush. . . . Briefly he wondered if his allowing his wife to [witness] his obvious enjoyment in grilling this woman in a brutal fashion, was some odd psychological foible of his."[15] Well, yes, it is, and Noreen calls out his "barbarous" behavior.[16] His "foible" reappears, but this middle-aged man slowly sheds his misogynistic skin as the series moves along, with a significant shift occurring in the seventh volume, *McGarr and the Legacy of a Woman Scorned*. The title's sexist idiom is ironic for a novel that serves as a tipping point away from the normalizing of sexist commentary, but it is timely and contextually apt. *Legacy* was written during a key period for women's rights in Ireland, and released soon after the Tenth Amendment of the Constitution Bill (1986) was defeated. That bill sought to remove the prohibition on divorce, and its defeat energized the fight for equality.

Legacy concerns neighboring farm families—each under matriarchal control—who have been fostering a long-held grudge that is revealed to be the result of a power play for land ownership. The intermittent sexual

14. Gill, *Irish Politician*, chap. 1.
15. Gill, *Irish Politician*, chap. 1.
16. Gill, *Irish Politician*, chap. 1.

fantasies of McGarr, so prevalent in early titles, give way to those of Noreen, who is unofficially working undercover on the case. Her role includes getting close to one family's son, whom she compares to McGarr. He is "younger . . . more fit, and then he and she had horses and the country and banter in common. When, she asked herself, had she and her husband last had a playful conversation together, to say nothing of a flirt?"[17] These musings remind Noreen of her mother warning her against marrying a man twenty years her senior: "The difference," her mother had argued, "isn't distinct now, but it will be as years go by. I've seen it."[18] Noreen smiles at the memory, suddenly aware that her mother was trying to draw attention to the impact his age would have on their sex life as years moved on. Noreen flirts her way through her unofficial role and even comes to understand the circumstances surrounding the extramarital affairs of her friends, but, like her husband, she does not venture into infidelity. This case gives Noreen an additional level of agency, allowing the series to compensate in part for some of McGarr's own "foibles." This evolution is acknowledged in a metaliterary bit of dialogue when a man of McGarr's generation states that he has "sworn off sexist gaffes."[19] For the remainder of the series, McGarr avoids them too. By the eleventh installment, he is calling out "blatantly sexist"[20] points of view, and is appalled to discover, upon attending the wake of a legendary sportswoman (and former lover), that her body has been dressed and made up to be more "feminine and ladylike" than she ever chose to appear in life.[21] He deems it "the ultimate indignity" to be inflicted on a woman he knew relished living in defiance of gendered expectations.

Gill gives McGarr's increasingly progressive articulation of gender equality a prominence to match that of the series' debates over EU trade policies in a globalizing Ireland, debates that bind the series together. Even a task as innocuous as McGarr tending to his kitchen stove is accompanied by the narrator's observation that it was run on "EU-acceptable composite

17. Gill, *Legacy of a Woman*, 42.
18. Gill, *Legacy of a Woman*, 43.
19. Gill, *Legacy of a Woman*, 112.
20. Gill, *Cold, Wild River*, 29.
21. Gill, *Cold, Wild River*, 36.

fuel (which produced little smoke)."[22] The books set farthest west—*Sea Wolf*, set on Clare Island, and *Cold, Wild River*, set in the Donegal village of Ardara—make the most of this, with plots that document the impact of Brussels-mandated policies on local communities.

River's Nellie is a professional fly-fishing instructor and writer whose business attracts wealthy tourists, who keep the pubs and hotels flush.[23] But she has her dissenters, those who condemn fly fishing for salmon as "a pastime of the idle rich . . . who are seeking to deprive traditional Irish fishermen of their livelihoods."[24] A local drift netter, Hal Shevlin, is an early suspect in Nellie's murder because of his vocal opposition to regulations that he feels restrict his livelihood on local waters, while benefiting tourism-drivers like Nellie or foreign trawlers: "Dublin is prohibiting Irish fishermen from taking their share, while permitting the Spanish and Portuguese to 'hammer' every feckin' species they can search out with all the newfangled electronics *their* governments give them . . . all subsidized."[25]

Shevlin's disdain for what he sees as a fixed playing field is paralleled by Paul O'Malley in *Sea Wolf*: "It's the EC or EU—they now call themselves—playing Puck . . . the bloody Common Market t'ugs from Brussels telling us how to live."[26] O'Malley considers McGarr (and anybody else based in Dublin) to be ignorant of the negative consequences that EU membership has brought to rural communities. But McGarr's internal monologue shows the series' sympathies:

> Having designated much of the West of Ireland "severely disadvantaged," Brussels had decided that it could keep people on the land by encouraging "traditional farming practices," one of which was raising sheep. But the subsidy did not reward farmers for animals brought to market, which

22. Gill, *Death of an Ardent Bibliophile*, 23.

23. Gill is drawing here on a world he knew well. He was an avid angler and wrote about the sport in his column for the *Newark Star-Ledger*. His many allusions to Samuel Beckett are likewise the result of a personal interest, reflected in his MLitt thesis at Trinity College Dublin on "Language and Narrative Voice in the Novels of Samuel Beckett" (1971).

24. Gill, *Cold, Wild River*, 20.

25. Gill, *Cold, Wild River*, 99.

26. Gill, *Sea Wolf*, 84.

would depress sheep prices. Instead, it paid them according to the number of sheep on the land—aged, infirm, or ill; it did not matter—which had led to overgrazing and the destruction of native plant habitats.[27]

The end result is a community forced to turn to tourism for economic survival. Adding insult to injury, a seasonal influx of tourists hinders the murder investigation.

As it navigates this social terrain, the series draws on tropes now standard in a contemporary Irish detective novel, albeit with less irony and edge than they have since gained. Emigration, the economy, the Troubles, and the politics of social standing are all on display. Like Declan Hughes's Ed Loy, McGarr is a Dubliner who is in his home city after decades abroad, providing a running commentary on the changes it has undergone since his younger days. But where Loy tends to view his new Dublin with a hard-boiled cynicism, McGarr often projects a tempered wistfulness that accentuates romantic notions of his homeland, notions not uncommon in American literary and cinematic portrayals of Ireland. This is established in the first book, when McGarr surveys Inis Mór as he approaches the island on a case, viewing it as "the Ireland of the picture books he had read as a child."[28] This distanced perspective is a method by which both the Loy and McGarr series comment on, among other things, the consequences of economic changes, whether Hughes's Celtic Tiger or Gill's European Union. Newer Dublin-set Irish crime fiction tends to center on a rise of criminality at the height of the Celtic Tiger, often with only passing commentary on the building blocks that led to Ireland's emergence on the global economic stage.[29] Gill fills that gap, and reading him today affords a glimpse at globalization's emergence in Irish crime fiction as it developed.

Gill's writing also shares a fondness for the literary allusion and epigraph shared by many leading Irish detective authors, including Jane Casey, Hughes, John Connolly, and Ken Bruen. But where these newer authors

27. Gill, *Sea Wolf*, 84.

28. Gill, *Irish Politician*, chap. 3.

29. One notable exception is Declan Hughes's *The Wrong Kind of Blood*, which examines generations of corruption.

are inclined to mix the canonical with the popular, Gill sticks with the former. Chapters open with a range of writers from Thoreau to Yeats, but allusions favor the Irish canon and frequently become plot devices. Jonathan Swift is central to *Ardent Bibliophile*, and appears in each volume that deals with working-class Dublin. The Dean is also summoned when absurdity reaches a peak, as when a Squad team member is serving undercover at a posh Kerry resort and finds himself "surrounded by a hotel of Brobdingnagians."[30] *Bibliophile* cuts the widest Swiftian swath, with a victim (Brian Herrick, the Keeper of Marsh's Library) whose obsession with Swift knows no bounds, and a plot framed around Swift's most scatological writings. Herrick is poisoned during the filming of his home porn films, or weekly "frolics" as he called them, performances replete with Stellas, Vanessas, and as many participants as Herrick can cast in his Swift parodies, all set against a replica of Marsh's Library that Herrick constructed in the side parlor of his Shrewsbury Road home. Herrick is one of the more memorable Dublin characters to appear in the series, but it is a crowded field, and one often connected to canonical Irish writers.

The doubles, doubling, and mistaken identities favored by Irish Gothic writers like Joseph Sheridan Le Fanu, for example, appear in *Irish Politician* and as late as *Death in Dublin*. The poetry and political speeches of Yeats are used on a regular basis, and Sean O'Casey is called on to shorthand the venting of unhappy wives, a situation McGarr encounters regularly when interviewing domestic cases. References to Samuel Beckett often combine the biographical with the literary, most notably in *McGarr and the P.M. of Belgrave Square*, where a missing Sisley masterpiece, *L'Inondation à Port-Marly*, is part of a crime scene. The crime has roots in Occupied Paris, the city Beckett escaped when his Resistance cell was exposed. When Noreen is examining another painting in the series under the annoying supervision of a member of the Murder Squad's Technical Unit, she cheekily "hand[s] him the hammer. 'You to play,'"[31] she says, providing the first of the novel's many *Endgame* references. Beckett is also referenced in *Sea Wolf* (which,

30. Gill, *Death of Love*, 62.

31. Gill, *Belgrave Square*, 128.

like *Belgrave Square*, alludes to Ireland's relationship with Germany during World War II, in this case the provision of sanctuary for a former Nazi sympathizer)[32] and in *The Death of a Joyce Scholar* (where a Trinity College graduate student kills his professor, in part, "for lov[ing] Joyce instead of Beckett").[33] But pride of place is reserved for Joyce's *Ulysses*, which, as either a literary or historical touchstone, appears in all sixteen novels.

Sometimes the Joycean references are slight, as with the Eccles Street crime scene of *Horse Show*, the minor character in *Belgrave Square* who is "the son but not the son," or the murder victim in *Cliffs* who "was a Joyce aficionado."[34] But *Joyce Scholar* embraces Joyce's oeuvre entirely. The murder of Trinity College professor Kevin Coyle occurs on Bloomsday at the conclusion of a tour retracing Bloom's path through the city. The investigation reveals professional jealousies (the academy, particularly as housed at Trinity, being a frequent target of derision throughout the series) and disdain for the commercial enterprises of Joycean tourism. Coyle's new book, "a critical reappraisal of modern Irish literature in English that focuses mainly on Joyce and Beckett,"[35] is about to launch, and it promises to advance the reputation of this young professor from Dublin's Liberties ahead of those of his colleagues, all of whom have more traditional pedigrees. Class warfare in the series is not limited to the material economic commentaries; it also operates internally, with a working-class figure like Coyle dismissed by his rarified Trinity students and colleagues. *Joyce Scholar* may, as has been argued, "verge on a parody"[36] of academic discourse, but its foregrounded class divisions also constitute one of the series' most direct hits on a social divide that it seldom hesitates to circumnavigate. The series is written in a manner that bears the bruises of a pastiche. In a follow-up to

32. Ireland's position in World War II is also the focus of other Irish crime novels, including Stuart Neville's *Ratlines* (2013), Joe Joyce's *Echoland* (2013), and Michael Russell's *City of Lies* (2017).

33. Mangialavori, "Ghost of James Joyce in Contemporary Detective Fiction," 170. This essay also offers an interesting mapping of the Gill novel against *Ulysses*.

34. Gill, *Belgrave Square*, 46; Gill, *Cliffs of Moher*, 190.

35. Gill, *Joyce Scholar*, 31.

36. Murphy, "The Strange Case of Detective Fiction," 38.

his pitch letter to Scribner's (the first publisher of the series), Gill expressed a desire to emulate the "style and ease of manner"[37] of Simenon's Maigret series. The European influence is evident, but it is overshadowed by echoes of the American Dashiell Hammett. The age differences, socioeconomic backgrounds, and banter between McGarr and Noreen call to mind Nick and Nora Charles of *The Thin Man* films, based on Hammett's work of the same name, and McGarr can hold his drink and throw a punch in the manner of Hammett's Sam Spade. As this might suggest, there is a limit to McGarr's romantic notions of Ireland. But Gill writes landscapes and secondary characters from a distinctly (and unfortunately dated) Irish American point of view. There is sometimes a limited complexity in Gill's secondary characters and the Ireland they inhabit. Feisty colleens, IRA men on the run in New York, Irish Americans looking to return to the land of their ancestors, the pugilist, the wily old farmer, and the Yeats-quoting publican all dot Gill's landscape, as do idealized notions of Irish living and copious amounts of simplified history. But Gill plays both sides of the fence, depicting Americans in Ireland as naïve and vicious (not least in their ill-informed enthusiasm for Irish republicanism) and among the series' most brutal murderers.[38] His predisposition to highlight American influence as tarnishing an Irish idyll, and Irish characters succeeding in America at the expense of their safety or dignity, relies on stereotypes that infantilize Ireland and condemn America.

The novels are peppered with characters whose time in America has been an opportunity to make it big but also contributed to their downfall or served as an incubator for their criminality. This is explored most extensively in *Cliffs of Moher*, which opens with the victim, May Quick, "propped against the other side of the wall, dressed in a stylish full-length leather coat . . . through her violet-tinted glasses her eyes seemed to be

37. Letter from McGarrity to Brian Dumaine, 24 April 1976, Series 3: Author Files; 1968–89; Archives of Charles Scribner's Sons, Manuscripts Division, Department of Rare Books and Special Collections, Princeton University Library.

38. The murderers in *Cold, Wild River* are both Americans: one a disgruntled academic who reinvents himself as the "Cowboy Fly Fisherman" and the other his wife, a gun-happy Midwesterner.

focused on a point distant in the Atlantic. She had four punctures where somebody had jabbed a pitchfork through her upper chest."[39] Colored by such heavy symbolism, her journalistic celebrity in urban America results in her murder in rural Ireland.

One of three friends who emigrated from County Clare to New York, May, who made a name for herself as a freelance journalist, is known for hard-hitting exposés on political heavyweights, and her career is soaring until she is assigned to write about "how the IRA is financing the operations in the North and where all the American donations go."[40] New York tabloids, worried a negative portrayal of the IRA will alienate their Irish American readership, drop the story, but she pursues it on her own. She is under watch by the Provisional IRA in New York, and again when she travels back to Clare to research the article locally. McGarr's investigation of her murder takes him to New York, where he is soon surrounded by misty-eyed cops singing "Danny Boy" along with the jukebox. Although McGarr expresses mild sympathy for people clinging to a cultural identity of which they have limited direct understanding, the experience alters his opinion of Americans considerably. When they were tourists on his home turf, marveling at their surroundings, he was mildly amused. After uncovering the extent to which they facilitated the murder of May, though, he proclaims there are "none more savage" than Irish Americans.[41]

May was the only woman among the three ambitious, talented Irish friends who found success in New York, and the only one McGarr refers to as "inordinately ambitious,"[42] even though all three strove for success. The novelist will get on, although by writing books he feels make him something of a sell-out rather than the literary lion he hoped to be; the doctor turns out to have used his chemistry training to make bombs for the IRA, but ideology—explicitly fostered during his years in Manhattan—rather than ambition kills him. The only one whose professional ambitions lead

39. Gill, *Cliffs of Moher*, 2.
40. Gill, *Cliffs of Moher*, 73.
41. Gill, *Cliffs of Moher*, 156.
42. Gill, *Cliffs of Moher*, 115.

directly to demise is May, the lone woman and hardly the first female character in crime fiction to pay for being ambitious.

Cliffs of Moher is the most overt example, but the series as a whole problematizes consideration of transnationalism in Irish crime fiction as it pertains to Irish American influences and settings. It is now well-established that American crime writing has influenced Irish writers. The legacies of Chandler and Hammett are clear in the work of Hughes and others, while the female private detectives crafted by Sara Paretsky and Sue Grafton can be seen in the police procedurals of Jane Casey and Stuart Neville. The influence of earlier American crime writers is just as clear in Gill's work, but he set out to pay homage to European crime fiction, particularly that of Simenon, and then proceeded to infuse his series with a cross-Atlantic perspective. As Brian Cliff notes, the genre "has used diverse characters, settings, and plots to move in some outward-looking directions,"[43] but one is hard-pressed to think of another Irish crime series that looks out and in simultaneously. Certainly, no crime writers to date have used the Irish setting to look outward toward Irish America at such length and with such an unflinching eye.

Bibliography

"1960–1969, A Period of Economic Growth." European Union. Europa. http://europa.eu/european-union/about-eu/history_en. Accessed 22 June 2017.

Archives of Charles Scribner's Sons (C0101). Manuscripts Division, Department of Rare Books and Special Collections, Princeton University Library. Accessed 19 April 2017.

Burri, Susanne, and Sacha Prechal. "EU Gender Equality Law Update 2010." Updated by Susanne Burri. European Network of Legal Experts in the Field of Gender Equality. http://ec.europa.eu/justice/genderequality/files/dgjustice_eu genderequalitylaw_update_2010_final24february2011_en.pdf. December 2010. Accessed 20 June 2017.

Cliff, Brian. *Irish Crime Fiction*. London: Palgrave Macmillan, 2018.

Gill, Bartholomew. *The Death of an Ardent Bibliophile*. New York: William Morrow, 1995.

43. Cliff, *Irish Crime Fiction*, 146.

———. *Death on a Cold, Wild River.* 1993. Reprint, New York: Avon, 1994.

———. *Death in Dublin.* New York: Avon, 2003.

———. *The Death of an Irish Politician.* 1977. Reprint, New York: HarperCollins, 2009. Kindle edition.

———. *The Death of an Irish Sea Wolf.* New York: William Morrow, 1996.

———. *The Death of a Joyce Scholar.* New York: William Morrow, 1989.

———. *The Death of Love.* New York: William Morrow, 1992.

———. *McGarr on the Cliffs of Moher.* New York: Charles Scribner's Sons, 1978.

———. *McGarr and the Legacy of a Woman Scorned.* New York: Viking, 1986.

———. *McGarr and the P.M. of Belgrave Square.* New York: Viking, 1983.

McCarthy, Conor. *Modernisation, Crisis and Culture in Ireland, 1969–1992.* Dublin: Four Courts Press, 2000.

Mangialavori, Maria Domenica. "The Ghost of James Joyce in Contemporary Detective Fiction: The Case of Amanda Cross and Bartholomew Gill." In *Joyce in Progress: Proceedings of the 2008 James Joyce Graduate Conference in Rome*, edited by Franca Ruggieri et al., 162–74. Newcastle upon Tyne: Cambridge Scholars, 2009.

Murphy, P. J. "The Strange Case of Detective Fiction." In *Beckett in Popular Culture: Essays on a Postmodern Icon*, edited by P. J. Murphy and Nick Pawlink, 33–52. Jefferson, NC: McFarland, 2016.

"Makes Us Human"

Julie Parsons's Michael McLoughlin Trilogy

BRIDGET ENGLISH

The psychological thrillers that make up Julie Parsons's Michael McLoughlin trilogy—*Mary, Mary* (1998), *I Saw You* (2007), and *The Therapy House* (2017)—are preoccupied with human suffering, both physical and psychological. They are plot-driven mysteries, but, more crucially, they seek to understand the impact of crime on individual victims and, in doing so, expose the larger social and economic systems that produce violent acts. The questions that underlie each of these novels are ultimately: What makes us human? What happens when our humanity has been stripped away? How do crime victims regain agency? While these questions have no easy answers, Detective Michael McLoughlin's pursuit of justice reveals the impact personal suffering has on the larger community, highlighting the ways that neoliberalism operates as an external force and as a naturalized ideology that has far-reaching implications.

Despite being foundational to the genre of Irish crime writing, the McLoughlin Trilogy, and particularly the first novel, *Mary, Mary*, is often overlooked by critics. Parsons's fellow crime writers, however, continue to hold her work in high regard. Declan Hughes contends that "Parsons was Irish Crime Fiction before there was Irish Crime Fiction."[1] Born in New Zealand to Irish parents, Parsons moved to Ireland at the age of twelve,

1. Hughes, "*The Therapy House* Review."

following the disappearance of her father during a medical mission to the remote Tokelau Islands. While his boat was eventually recovered, her father and the twenty-five others aboard were never found. Parsons has referenced her father's disappearance as the main impetus for her stories: "I will never know how and why my father disappeared in the middle of the Pacific Ocean, but I can now see that I can do in my fictional and creative life what I cannot do in my 'real' life. I can solve the mystery."[2] This incentive to "work through" grief by writing lends itself to the interpretative framework of trauma theory, which examines texts for gaps that mirror cracks in memory and point to difficulties in the expression of human suffering. But the victim-turned-perpetrator paradox in Parsons's novels troubles this kind of therapeutic approach. Nearly every character has been or becomes a victim of violence, even Detective McLoughlin himself. These shared traumas must be resolved by challenging the neoliberal ideologies that dominate contemporary Irish society.

McLoughlin, the reluctant hero of the series, is the opposite of a tough, hard-boiled detective. He is compelled to solve these crimes out of compassion for the victims and obligation to their families. In this concentration on the tortured humanity of these characters and the pasts that continue to haunt them, the McLoughlin Trilogy addresses social and political concerns such as suicide, child sexual abuse, and the Troubles, but its breezy seaside settings also indicate a desire to break with noir's gritty realities and to reorient Irish crime fiction in a wider global context.[3] Depictions of Margaret Mitchell's movements between Ireland and New Zealand in *Mary, Mary*, as well as McLoughlin's own journeys beyond Irish borders in *The Therapy House*, demonstrate a concern not only with Irish national identity but also with universal notions of victimhood. Beyond their engagement with Ireland's history of trauma, Parsons's novels focus on her

2. Hunt, "Interview with Julie Parsons."

3. Writers such as John Connolly, Alex Barclay, and Ken Bruen have demonstrated a similar concern with Ireland's place in a global world by setting their novels abroad. For an account that links the emergence of crime fiction to the consolidation of the modern state in a transnational context, see Pepper, *Unwilling Executioner*. For more on crime fiction and world literature, see Nilsson, Damrosch, and D'haen, *Crime Fiction as World Literature*.

characters' grief and suffering, raising questions about victimization, individual suffering, and communal trauma in an increasingly globalized and secularized society.

The Trilogy was published in a trajectory that loosely traces the progression of the Celtic Tiger from its height in 1998 (*Mary, Mary*) to the international financial crash of 2008 (*I Saw You*) and the more recent recession and recovery leading up to 2017 (*The Therapy House*). This fits them neatly into a larger narrative of Irish crime fiction, which asserts that the emergence of the genre during the Celtic Tiger period reflects its unique ability to register social and cultural change in Ireland.[4] Fintan O'Toole argues that crime fiction is the closest thing contemporary Ireland has to literary realism, indicating the genre's ability to depict the realities of Irish life and social conditions.[5] While crime fiction may address these wider shifts in Irish culture, it does not simply reflect one dominant ideology or act as a barometer of social change. It incorporates many coexisting and conflicting ideologies. Parsons makes particular use of the psychological thriller subgenre, through which her series not only registers the psychological upheavals of this tumultuous period but also, more importantly, shapes human agency by refusing binary notions of victimhood.

According to trauma theory, the repetition of traumatic experiences through narrative works to recover lost memories, allowing the trauma victim to gain control of these experiences by mentally reliving them. This process of recovery ultimately exposes past truths and allows them to be integrated into the present. In her discussion of Irish crime fiction and trauma theory, Shirley Peterson describes how Tana French's Dublin Murder Squad series "'speak[s] through' the experience in tropes associated with trauma."[6] Parsons's novels follow this paradigm of the police procedural as "speaking through" trauma in the sense that the process of

4. For an overview of Irish crime fiction, see Ross, "Introduction," 14–35; Kincaid, "Down These Mean Streets," 39–55; and Mannion, *Contemporary Irish Detective Novel*, 1–15.

5. O'Toole, "From Chandler and the 'Playboy' to the Contemporary Crime Wave," 358–61.

6. Peterson, "Voicing the Unspeakable," 110.

solving the crime reveals difficult truths buried in the characters' pasts. For instance, the series documents McLoughlin's struggle to come to terms with his father's death during an IRA robbery, when McLoughlin senior, the on-duty garda, was shot. But the Trilogy also shows resistance to these ideas of working through trauma. Characters often remain haunted by their losses and are unable to achieve closure. This includes both McLoughlin, who becomes increasingly preoccupied with the deaths of his father and Mary, and also Margaret, who remains mired in the harsh realities of bodily wounds and scars that will not heal.

In a further nod to Parsons's interest in psychological states and trauma, the title of the most recent book in the series is *The Therapy House*, referring to the house that McLoughlin purchases in his retirement, a place where therapists and analysts practiced. This setting is metaphoric in more ways than one as McLoughlin is forced to confront his own traumas when he encounters James Reynolds, the man who killed his father. *The Therapy House* also focuses on McLoughlin's burgeoning relationship with Elizabeth Fannin, the one remaining psychiatrist who still treats patients in the building, who offers him the chance to move on from his failed marriage and unrequited love for Margaret. Elizabeth is a freethinking woman who was deeply influenced by the doctor who started the Therapy House as a kind of commune for World War II veterans with PTSD. A conversation between McLoughlin and Elizabeth midway through the novel highlights the novel's concerns with suffering. After Elizabeth remarks that McLoughlin's best qualities are "Sensitivity, empathy, [and] understanding," he scoffs at her, remarking that he would hardly be coming to speak to her if he had those traits. McLoughlin then reveals that he went for counseling once when he was with the guards, and "was looking for something to kill the pain," but found "whiskey more effective."[7] This exposes McLoughlin's character and gets to the heart of the series' concern with psychotherapy's effectiveness in dealing with trauma. McLoughlin, despite his empathetic nature, remains caught up with macho ideals of drinking away psychological wounds instead of verbalizing them. But all is not as hopeless as it may

7. Parsons, *Therapy House*, 176.

seem: Hughes notes that the ending of the novel, which sees McLoughlin beginning a relationship with Elizabeth, offers some hope that he might overcome these pressures, implying that psychotherapy might provide a way forward.[8]

Female therapists feature throughout the trilogy and serve as dialogic counterpoints to masculine cultures of violence and repression. Though these women are successful in helping people work through traumas, violent actions ultimately win out over psychotherapy: Margaret Mitchell, a noted psychiatrist whose specialty is women's mental health, fails to cope with her own grief, ultimately enacting revenge on her daughter's killer; Dr. Gwen Simpson's patient commits suicide from her office window mere moments after speaking to the doctor; and Elizabeth Fannin's treatments of Samuel Dudgeon do not prevent him from mutilating a judge's corpse in retaliation for past abuses. The trilogy suggests that while therapy may help individual victims, it fails to interrogate the social injustices that allowed their victimization to occur.

In Parsons's fiction, physical and psychological wounds are mutually significant. This is also true of the larger matrix of victim and perpetrator in crime fiction, where the body of the deceased victim is of central importance. Lee Horsley observes that the physicality of corpses (especially their dissection), traumatic wounds, and psychologically damaged minds are concerns particular to late twentieth-century crime fiction. According to Horsley, it is during this period—from the late 1990s onward—that "wound culture" gains currency and crime fiction moves away from the sanitized bodies of classic detective fiction to the ideas of wounding and psychological trauma that come to characterize the late-twentieth-century "cult of abjection."[9] In this context the gruesomely fragmented bodies of crime victims act to break down boundaries, blurring distinctions between the inner and outer so that all bleed together. Parsons's many mutilated corpses—including Mary's brutally raped and disfigured body in *Mary Mary* and Judge Hegarty's bound, shot, and bludgeoned body in

8. Hughes, "*The Therapy House* Review."

9. Horsley, *Twentieth-Century Crime Fiction*, 117.

The Therapy House—act as narrative starting points or as ruptures that expose the dark underside of ordinary life. McLoughlin pins photographs of Mary's body on noticeboards around the incident room: "The colours, scarlet, black, white, purple, stood out vividly against the drab monotony of the grey walls, ceiling and floor. A reminder, he thought, of what we're dealing with here."[10] Despite the brutality of the crime that McLoughlin has just described, the "reminder" that he posts is curiously abstracted into colors, which contrast with the grey room, implying a division between the surfaces of ordinary life and the graphic nature of the crime. Similarly, in *The Therapy House*, McLoughlin's discovery of Judge Hegarty's body is described in visceral detail: "There wasn't much left of his face. Blood, bone and brain tissue on the carpet."[11] Here human life is reduced to basic matter—blood, bone, brain tissue—and serves as a reminder of mortality. Mary's body likewise reveals the fragility of human life, and reminds its viewers of the extreme evil of which humans are capable. In both instances, the fluids that spill from these maimed bodies cross the boundaries that separate victim and perpetrator and draw the living characters, such as McLoughlin, into the realm of the dead.

In contrast, the second novel, *I Saw You*, centers on the drowning of a young woman whose body bears no indication of foul play. The violence in *I Saw You* is largely self-inflicted and psychological: victims die by their own hand as a result of bullying or other past traumas. The number of deaths by suicide is so high that readers unfamiliar with the dramatic rise in Irish suicide rates over recent decades may find it unimaginable.[12] Thus in its concerns with both the physicality of victims' bodies and their damaged minds, *I Saw You* brings to the fore contemporary sociological issues

10. Parsons, *Mary, Mary*, 97.

11. Parsons, *Therapy House*, 33.

12. From an average suicide rate of two to three per 100,000 people in the 1970s, the rate rose to fourteen by the late 1990s. See O'Sullivan, *Ireland and the Global Question*, 37. According to the Central Statistics Office of Ireland, suicide rates decreased slightly throughout the 2000s and went down to 10.9 deaths per 100,000 in 2010. However, the most recent records indicate that suicide is on the rise again as the rates were up to 12.1 in 2011 (Central Statistics Office, "Suicide Statistics 2011").

such as suicide. In doing so, it traces the complex interplay between past psychological traumas and present action in order to complicate notions of victimhood and agency in an increasingly neoliberal society.

Neoliberalism's conception of victimhood is challenged by Rebecca Stringer, who argues that such rhetoric sets up a false opposition between victimhood and agency and posits victimhood as backward, resulting in a "victim-blaming conception of victimization as subjective and psychological rather than social and political."[13] Through the psychological thriller, Parsons critiques this conception by depicting characters who are shaped by their sociohistorical environments and whose agency is achieved through further violent acts, such as Margaret's imprisoning of her daughter's killer or Helena's drowning of her ex-husband's daughter. The result is a subtle critique of contemporary Irish politics as more closely aligned with American neoliberalism than with European social welfarism, as perhaps best exemplified by the Irish banking crisis.

Mary, Mary opens with the disappearance of Mary Mitchell, a twenty-year-old woman who recently moved to Dublin from New Zealand with her mother, Margaret, a well-known psychiatrist. The novel begins with the phone call Margaret makes asking the barely interested Detective McLoughlin for assistance in finding her daughter, before shifting to a scene that depicts Mary and her killer, Jimmy. As Jimmy shears away Mary's long, dark hair, he asks if Mary would do anything for him. When she asks if she has a choice, he replies: "Oh, we all have a choice. That's what separates us from the beasts of the field. Makes us human." But when Mary questions his definition of the word by repeating "human," Jimmy concludes that she is not human after all, and therefore has no choice.[14] He systematically eliminates physical evidence of her humanity through torture: lacerating her genitals and breasts, and burning her with cigarettes. It is implied that Jimmy's actions are a result of his own abusive childhood, thus Mary's damaged body comes to represent the evil that people are

13. Stringer, *Knowing Victims*, 9.

14. Parsons, *Mary, Mary*, 13–14.

capable of when their own humanity is subsumed by trauma that renders them devoid of empathy.

The trilogy repeatedly measures notions of empathy, asserting that this condition is essential to what makes people human. In this figuration, victims possess agency that can bridge the gap between past failures and future possibilities. In the case of Margaret Mitchell, however, this agency is thwarted by a neoliberal society that confines victimhood to the realm of the psychological. Mary's murder disturbs what Margaret calls "the crust of accepted memory," forcing a reevaluation of the past that reverberates through her social circles into greater Dublin society and beyond.[15] McLoughlin too views the crime as a catalyst, as if "a shot bursts from the barrel of a gun and a flock of crows wheel into the sky. A butterfly flaps its wings and on the other side of the world a tidal wave roars in from the sea. A girl is murdered, and throughout the city the stain of the crime disturbs, awakens, shuffles the deck of past anger and suspicion."[16] This imagery distills Parsons's critique of neoliberalism's effects on Ireland, while simultaneously implying that the changes to Ireland carry global implications.

For Margaret, Mary's murder forces consideration of the gulf between rational empiricism (associated with modernity and medicine) and premodern, religious, and mythic structures that offer consolation in the face of loss. This conflict is particularly apparent in Margaret's failed efforts to understand her own grief through medical knowledge of the body. Considering the patients whose lives she helped to end through medically assisted suicide, Margaret thinks that she understands "what happens when the heart stops pumping oxygen through the body, pushing its sweetness into every blood vessel. But I don't understand the loss of being, the negation of existence. It must be why so many people believe in an afterlife. To make sense of the essentially meaningless. I know in an abstract way, but I can't accept it."[17] Margaret's thoughts here are indicative of a larger cultural cri-

15. Parsons, *Mary, Mary*, 87.

16. Parsons, *Mary, Mary*, 41.

17. Parsons, *Mary, Mary*, 59.

sis in meaning as religious ways of making sense of loss have been replaced by the hard science of medicine, which offers logical explanations but limited consolation. This crisis in meaning also indicates a possible reason why late twentieth-century crime novels so frequently feature autopsies: they represent efforts to understand human life by studying what remains of it.

Perhaps the most significant aspect of loss in the novel is the way that Margaret's grief transforms her:

> I look like the same woman that I was three weeks ago, she thought. But this isn't Margaret. This is a changeling. The fairies have stolen away the real Margaret and replaced her with this thing with the same colour hair and eyes, the same mouth and teeth, the same hands and feet. This thing is reduced to nothingness by the attentions of a madman. . . . This thing will never allow the real Margaret back into its skin. Not unless the real Margaret does something about it.[18]

Margaret's vision of herself as a changeling conflicts with her modern faith in psychiatry, and harkens back to folkloric beliefs in changelings, who were left in place of children or other people who were taken by the fairies. These beings resembled the stolen person, but were sickly and evil. Efforts to bring a person back from this state included subjection to the elements, particularly fire, which resulted in accidental deaths that were covered up to protect the people who believed in these superstitions.[19] In an intriguing reversal of the child-as-changeling trope, it is Margaret (not Mary) who imagines herself as a changeling, implying that her grief has deprived her of human agency and made her victim to forces beyond her control. Believing that a prison sentence will not be punishment enough, Margaret tracks Jimmy down, lures him to an abandoned Wicklow cottage, and imprisons him in a shed without access to food or water. Justifying her crime by remembering the way Jimmy turned Mary into "an object, a shapeless, inhuman creature," Margaret does the same to him.[20] Tearing up the

18. Parsons, *Mary, Mary*, 156.

19. For a real-life example, see Bourke, *Burning of Bridget Cleary.*

20. Parsons, *Mary, Mary*, 427.

crime scene photos in front of Jimmy before she abandons him, Margaret replaces one dehumanized body with another, shifting her role from victim to perpetrator, in an attempt to compensate for her daughter's lost future.

The idea of gaining agency through vigilantism raises many ethical questions, which are sharpened by Margaret's particular narrative: as a renowned psychiatrist she knows how to treat the grief of others, but as a grieving mother she cannot treat herself and so that professional understanding offers her little comfort or guidance. Through this characterization, Parsons troubles neoliberal notions of victimhood and agency. Discussing such notions, Stringer observes that the "ideal neoliberal citizen is often explicitly figured as one who avoids 'victim mentality,' one who assumes personal responsibility for guarding against risk of victimization, instead of focusing on their right not to be victimized." This redefinition of victimhood "drains all legitimacy from the idea that suffering can be social, political and collective, rather than merely subjective, psychological and individual."[21] In line with such neoliberal views of individual suffering, Margaret experiences her pain as hers alone, an isolation that drives her to seek personal revenge. The ethical violations involved in that revenge, however, have repercussions that extend far beyond her individual agency, and they suggest a critique of neoliberal conceptions of victimhood and agency.

I Saw You begins with the discovery of Jimmy's skeleton, and Margaret's return to Ireland from New Zealand, where she has spent the five years since Mary's death. The novel's main plot, though, centers on the body of yet another dead young woman, Marina Spencer, whose corpse is found near her family's summer home in the Wicklow mountains. The Gardaí have declared the death a suicide—large quantities of drugs were found in her blood—but her mother suspects foul play and contacts the now-retired McLoughlin for help solving the crime. Meanwhile, Margaret coincidentally befriends Marina's half-sister, Vanessa, eventually acting as a source of support for the girls' mother, Sally, who is struggling in the wake of her daughter's death. Building on the questions raised by Mary's

21. Stringer, *Knowing Victims*, 2–3.

death, *I Saw You* further interrogates neoliberal notions of victimhood that construe human suffering as purely psychological and individual. The agency Margaret sought by punishing Jimmy has only further exacerbated her pain, but her grief has some communal currency and she finds power in the emotional suffering she shares with Sally. The dead also pervade McLoughlin's thoughts, motivating him to pursue closure. His identification with victims represents the human core of the novel, one that is resistant to the dehumanizing forces of neoliberalism: through his empathy with the shared suffering of these two mothers and obligations to their dead daughters, Parsons foregrounds the collective aspects of victimhood that bond people together.

The focus on humanizing victims in *I Saw You* is also apparent through the depictions of the devastating psychological effects that bullying has on individuals and, in turn, on their communities. The further McLoughlin pursues Marina's case, the more the novel's body count increases. Midway through the narrative, he takes inventory: "Ben Roxby, death from a fall. Marina Spencer, death by drowning. Rosie Webb, née Atkinson, sister of Poppy, death by drug overdose. McLoughlin sat down at his computer and tapped out their names on the keyboard. He highlighted and enlarged the type. Suicide or accident? Or was there some other reason?"[22] By recording the names of these suicide victims, McLoughlin ensures their inclusion in the narrative, and draws attention to a larger social problem. Though Marina's death turns out to be murder rather than suicide, this investigation reveals the problem of suicide in contemporary Ireland. In this way, Parsons uses the form of the psychological thriller to draw together the victims of violent crimes, pointing to larger social ills rather than exclusively to individual pathologies.

Parsons's focus on suicide—one of Ireland's biggest and least understood social problems—situates individual victims in a broader cultural context. Kieran Keohane and Derek Chambers note that public discourses surrounding suicide in Ireland problematically focus on medical or psychological causes such as depression or substance abuse, which are useful in

22. Parsons, *I Saw You*, 187.

individual cases but fail to yield an understanding of why suicide rates in Ireland increased exponentially in recent decades. According to Keohane and Chambers, suicides are best understood as the result of "the historical experience of cultural collisions: collisions between the vestiges of traditional community and accelerated modern society, the rural and the urban, the local and the global; and collisions that impact traumatically on the life histories of individuals."[23] These collisions are found throughout the trilogy, indicating that characters' tragedies are not only the product of an individual's damaged mind or a singular traumatic event but also the result of social and cultural forces that have come together in unpredictable ways. This is not meant to suggest that Parsons is taking a determinist approach, as the characters in these novels ultimately take responsibility for their actions. The point here is rather that crimes are not committed in isolation. They are the product of various social, cultural, and psychological circumstances with impacts that reach far beyond the individual to a communal and even global relevance that is a hallmark of contemporary Irish crime fiction.

The repercussions of Mary Mitchell's death resound throughout the trilogy, as when *I Saw You* ends with Margaret's decision to confess to Jimmy's death. True to its title, the novel is full of surveillance and watching. Yet despite this kind of policing, the punishment of crimes and the meting out of justice take place largely outside the bounds of jails in a cycle of suicide and vigilante violence.

The final and most accomplished novel in the trilogy, *The Therapy House*, pushes the conflict between individual ethics and institutions even farther. Both of the men who inflict violence were themselves victims of crimes that went unpunished and now inflict the same suffering on others; indeed, all of the novel's characters become victims of traumatic pasts that provide an impetus for present action. The portrayal of the complex web of violence spun by sectarian divisions, sexual abuse, and petty grievances does not simply rehash a tired narrative of renewal and recovery achieved by a psychological working-through of past traumas. Instead, it conveys a

23. Keohane and Chambers, "Understanding Irish Suicides," 36–37.

sense that this violence will continue if the institutions that foster victimization do not change.

Through the suffering her characters experience and inflict, Parsons depicts the social pressures and human failings behind both victims and perpetrators, destabilizing neoliberal notions of justice, distributing blame across wider social institutions, and ultimately suggesting that these notions must be redefined if violence is to cease. The bludgeoned bodies of late twentieth- and early twenty-first-century crime fiction force readers to face the visceral realities of human life, as if dissecting the human body will offer insight into human nature. Consequently, critics have begun turning to Irish crime fiction for answers to the capitalist crisis of the Celtic Tiger and the subsequent crash. While the trilogy cannot be simply read as a response to that crisis, it does interrogate the ways that neoliberal victim-blaming has separated the psychological interior world of the individual from social and political realities.

Joe Cleary identifies neoliberal globalization as one of the most difficult challenges facing contemporary Irish literature, arguing that Irish literature needs to "give narrative visibility to the persistent contradictions of contemporary capitalism."[24] While Parsons's trilogy is not experimental in form nor is it particularly radical in its politics, its portrayal of victims whose bodies have been dehumanized gives visibility to many of the capitalist contradictions that Cleary highlights, tracing their tangible repercussions on wider Irish society. Parsons's depictions of an affluent, cosmopolitan Dublin poised on the edge of the sea seem generic enough to describe any European city. At the same time, the trilogy's focus on the traumas of sexual abuse, suicide, and the Troubles, along with other culturally specific references, make it distinctly Irish in setting. As a result, Parsons emphasizes the problematic aspects of the global novel, which must make its concerns at once local and widely marketable, even as it seeks to challenge capitalist values. Taking Irish crime fiction from the alleyways of Dublin to the lush seascapes of Dun Laoghaire, and shifting the action from the arteries of the city to its peripheries, the series broadens the scope of the genre to include

24. Cleary, "Horseman, Pass By!," 146.

Dublin's coastline, indicating a desire to look beyond Irish shores to a wider context. Focusing on universal themes of human suffering, these novels do not simply chronicle the social and economic changes that Ireland has undergone over the course of the past two decades. They subvert the neo-liberal ideas of victimization that have begun to dominate its culture and, in so doing, challenge the ideologies that underpin globalization.

Bibliography

Bourke, Angela. *The Burning of Bridget Cleary: A True Story.* New York: Penguin, 1999.

Burke, Declan, ed. *Down These Green Streets: Irish Crime Writing in the 21st Century.* Dublin: Liberties Press, 2011.

Central Statistics Office of Ireland (CSO). "Suicide Statistics 2011." http://www.cso.ie/en/releasesandpublications/er/ss/suicidestatistics2011/. Accessed 24 October 2017.

Cleary, Joe. "'Horseman, Pass By!': The Neoliberal World System and the Crisis in Irish Literature." *Boundary* 2 45, no. 1 (2018): 135–79.

Horsley, Lee. *Twentieth-Century Crime Fiction.* Oxford: Oxford Univ. Press, 2005.

Hughes, Declan. "*The Therapy House* Review: A Devastating Testament on Behalf of the Victims." *Irish Times*, 3 June 2017.

Hunt, Catherine. "Interview with Julie Parsons." *Shots: Crime and Thriller EZINE.* 2006. http://www.shotsmag.co.uk/archive/interviews2006/j_parsons/j_parsons.html. Accessed 1 August 2018.

Keohane, Kieran, and Derek Chambers. "Understanding Irish Suicides." In *Ireland Unbound: A Turn of the Century Chronicle*, edited by Mary P. Corcoran and Michel Peillon, 36–50. Dublin: Institute of Public Administration, 2002.

Kincaid, Andrew. "Down These Mean Streets: The City and Critique in Contemporary Irish Noir." *Éire-Ireland* 45, nos. 1–2 (Spring–Summer 2010): 39–55.

Mannion, Elizabeth, ed. *The Contemporary Irish Detective Novel.* London: Palgrave Macmillan, 2016.

Nilsson, Louise, David Damrosch, and Theo D'haen, eds. *Crime Fiction as World Literature.* London: Bloomsbury, 2017.

O'Sullivan, Michael. *Ireland and the Global Question.* Syracuse: Syracuse Univ. Press, 2006.

O'Toole, Fintan. "From Chandler and the 'Playboy' to the Contemporary Crime Wave." Afterword. In Burke, *Down These Green Streets*, 358–61.

Parsons, Julie. *I Saw You*. London: Pan Macmillan, 2007.

———. *Mary, Mary*. London: Pan Macmillan, 1998.

———. *The Therapy House*. Dublin: New Island Books, 2017.

Pepper, Andrew. *Unwilling Executioner: Crime Fiction and the State*. Oxford: Oxford Univ. Press, 2016.

Peterson, Shirley. "Voicing the Unspeakable: Tana French's Dublin Murder Squad." In Mannion, *The Contemporary Irish Detective Novel*, 107–20.

Ross, Ian Campbell. "Introduction." In Burke, *Down These Green Streets*, 14–35.

Stringer, Rebecca. *Knowing Victims: Feminism, Agency and Victim Politics in Neoliberal Times*. East Sussex: Routledge, 2014.

"A Land of Shame, a Land of Murder and a Land of Strange, Sacrificial Women"

Representations of Wealth, Gender, and Race in Modern Irish-Language Crime Fiction

CAITLÍN NIC ÍOMHAIR

The ghosts of history do not rest easy in Irish-language crime fiction.[1] Famine, sectarianism, and rebellion still feature in the texts surveyed in this chapter, as do more contemporary but still typical concerns of Irish Studies, including immigration and ethnic minorities, reproductive and LGBT rights, and the excesses of the Celtic Tiger. Many of the novels surveyed in this chapter express serious misgivings about preservation and integration in a neoliberal Ireland, and it is tempting to read the demography of their victims as illustrative of these concerns. Throughout the Celtic Tiger and its demise, Irish society has witnessed a seemingly endless cycle of scandal and inquiry involving the abuse of women: from laundries to mother and baby homes to forced symphysiotomy and knowingly botched cervical cancer screenings, not to mention the gruesome consequences of the constitutional ban on abortion that was repealed in late 2018. The Celtic Tiger also brought the first significant immigration to Ireland in centuries, with attendant concerns about exploitation, trafficking, and integration.

1. The quotation in the chapter title is from O'Brien, "Scandalous Woman," 940.

It is perhaps unsurprising, then, that the victims of these texts are overwhelmingly female and often ethnic minorities. Yet if Irish-language and English-language crime writing are broadly thematically similar in their focus on Tiger-era Ireland, their authors are writing in different milieux, for different audiences with different expectations. Before surveying the most significant contemporary crime writing in Irish, then, it is worth briefly examining how genre fiction has fared in a literature that was only resurrected, with great effort, around a century ago.[2]

As noted elsewhere, poetry in particular was elevated by the Celtic Revival as the "truest" medium to express the Irish soul,[3] and poetry remains arguably the strongest form of Irish-language writing today. However, the architects of language revival had more pressing concerns than the English-language Celtic Revivalists, urgently seeking to preserve what was left of the language, which was in severe decline. One of the greatest prose writers of the last century put it bluntly when he questioned the emergence of the first major poets in modern Irish, arguing that it was far easier to write "harmless little eight-line lyrics" than a full story.[4] This sense of "the more the better" was certainly embraced by the language's first major crime writer, Cathal Ó Sándair, among whose epic 160-book output were some of the preciously few genuinely populist works in Irish. As Ó Sándair was a mid-century writer who wrote mostly for children, and especially since he has already received critical attention elsewhere,[5] he won't be examined here. But it would be unjust not to mention, in passing, his pioneering work in the genre.

Though Ó Sándair was not the only populist writer of the time—Críostóir Ó Floinn deserves honorable mention—none lived up to the

2. The story of the decline and revival of Irish is too complex to discuss here, but it should be noted that the tradition of literacy in the Irish language had all but collapsed by the time Conradh na Gaeilge (The Gaelic League) was founded in 1893 (O'Leary, *Prose Literature*, 1).

3. Cliff, *Irish Crime Fiction*, 2.

4. Ó Cadhain, *Páipéir Bhána*, 37. Throughout this article, rough English translations are provided by the present author.

5. See, e.g., Adams, *Forbairt Litríocht Ghaeilge na nÓg*.

apex of Ó Sándair's Réics Carló series. Indeed, critics later lamented "an t-úrscéal nár tháinig,"[6] the failure of the novel to break ground in Irish. What prose there was shifted toward more "literary" work by authors like Liam Ó Flaithearta, Máirtín Ó Cadhain, "Robert Schumann," and Séamas Mac Annaidh.

With the exception of Ruaidhrí Ó Báille's perennially popular early crime novel *Dúnmharú ar an Dart* (1989) (*Murder on the Dart*)[7]—now on its thirty-eighth imprint—crime fiction only really began to gain traction in Irish around the turn of the millennium. Two historical novels by Seán Ó Dúrois aside, the texts surveyed below can be considered very much of the Celtic Tiger era and its aftermath. Wealth and multiculturalism are probably the two most consistently remarked-on features of the era, and both can be said to be regarded with ambivalence. There is, in general, much less emphasis in Irish on genre staples like state corruption, and the Garda Síochána—the Irish police force—does not play a particularly important role in the majority of novels, which can be said to be located somewhere between the poles of seedy underbelly and "cosy village mystery."[8] In general it is the public, rather than the Gardaí, who are at the forefront of solving the crimes, perhaps another iteration of lingering Irish ambivalence towards security forces. Ó Dúrois's work aside, the Troubles remain conspicuously absent in these books, possibly because far fewer people speak Irish in the northern state, where protective measures for the language remain bitterly contested.

The earliest text to be explored here is *Dúnmharú sa Daingean* (*Murder in Dingle*), published in 2000 by the bilingual writer Éilís Ní Dhuibhne. The novel follows the chic, urban, but somewhat bratty Saoirse on a journey south to the Gaeltacht when her love life and career as a PR agent in an art gallery in Dublin go awry. Saoirse is, we are encouraged to believe,

6. Ó hÁinle, "An tÚrscéal nár Tháinig."

7. A number of texts that could be considered crime fiction are excluded from this survey. Among those are translations into Irish, elementary fiction for adult learners, novels that are aimed at secondary-school students, and Biddy Jenkinson's two collections of intertextual comedy detective short stories.

8. Cliff, *Irish Crime Fiction*, 68.

the quintessential Dublin girl—materialistic, conformist, proudly embracing modern Ireland:

> Bean óg as príomhchathair na hÉireann ba ea í. Gan tír gan chreideamh agus bródúil as.[9]
>
> She was a young woman from Ireland's capital city. Without nation nor religion, and proud of it.

It is fitting that Saoirse sees her move south in consumerist terms, describing it as a "health package."[10] There are several examples of her condescension toward country people in the early pages of the novel, prompting the following quip during her first interaction with the locals on arrival in Dingle:

> Ó fuaireamar an leictreachas níl deireadh leis na háiseanna nua-aimseartha atá againn![11]
>
> Since we got electricity there's no end to the modern conveniences we have!

Saoirse soon learns that Dingle combines the progressive culture of a city with the famed friendliness of the countryside. She discusses organic farming over a lunch of lobster thermidor and Sancerre with her new friends, who toast her arrival "to our beautiful, friendly, Gaelic area free from GM and artificial fertilizer."[12] However, not all of the typically "urban" features of Dingle are as wholesome: drug smuggling is a significant problem, we are told, though Saoirse is far from perturbed by a gang-related murder that she finds "boring and common."[13] She concludes that there are more similarities between Dublin and Dingle "than Bord Fáilte let on,"[14] yet Dingle, where acceptance is much easier to come by, is clearly the preferred of the two.

9. Ní Dhuibhne, *Dúnmharú sa Daingean*, 58.
10. Ní Dhuibhne, *Dúnmharú sa Daingean*, 61.
11. Ní Dhuibhne, *Dúnmharú sa Daingean*, 57.
12. Ní Dhuibhne, *Dúnmharú sa Daingean*, 77.
13. Ní Dhuibhne, *Dúnmharú sa Daingean*, 75.
14. Ní Dhuibhne, *Dúnmharú sa Daingean*, 114.

Although there is a deep skepticism about "the new Ireland of the .com shares"[15] throughout the book, *Dúnmharú sa Daingean* is for the most part a light-hearted, almost kitsch example of genre fiction. However, it does presciently describe the experience of many, then and now, who are pushed out of parts of Ireland that have more employment opportunities by a chronic lack of affordable housing:

> Níl a fhios agam cad tá ag tarlú don tír seo. £250,000 ar thigh nach bhféadfá dhá chat a thabhairt suas ann, gan trácht ar chlann! Cíos £500 ar sheomra amháin agus cistin. Níl aon dealramh leis.[16]
>
> I don't know what's happening to this country. £250,000 for a house that you couldn't raise two cats in, nevermind a family! £500 rent for one room and a kitchen. It's ridiculous.

Two of the novel's characters, Garda Máirtín Ó Flaithearta and his artist girlfriend Saoirse Ní Ghallchóir, reappear in Ní Dhuibhne's second crime novel *Dún an Airgid* (2008) (*Silver Fort* or *Money Fort*), with which *Dúnmharú sa Daingean* shares numerous plot points. Both books seem to condemn modern Ireland as materialistic and shallow, and Liam Burn, the villain in *Dún an Airgid*, can be considered a victim of the Celtic Tiger as well as a psychopath.

Once again, the victims are all female, but they also have some tenuous connection to what Burn perceives as an injustice. We find out at the end of the novel that his first victim, Laoise, around whose disappearance the book is centered, had bought his house after the bank foreclosed on him for failing to keep up mortgage payments. His revenge on this woman who comes to epitomize Tiger-era excess is to starve her slowly to death in his caravan on the margins of the utopian development of Dún an Airgid. Though Burn's marginalization is not by choice—we are told he was loaned the caravan by an antipoverty charity—he clearly rejects the values of Dún an Airgid, and his other two victims are connected, however tenuously, to

15. Ní Dhuibhne, *Dúnmharú sa Daingean*, 21.
16. Ní Dhuibhne, *Dúnmharú sa Daingean*, 44.

"the engines and the builders and the new life, constantly destroying the old one."[17]

A brilliant scholar whose gifts contemporary society did not value, Liam Burn exacts his revenge by reenacting the goriest of mytho-historical battles in this new utopia, which is literally built on the ruins of Old Ireland:

> De réir Liam Burn, láthair mhór seandálaíochta amháin a bhí sa cheantar ar fad. Agus anois, níorbh ann dó. Bhí Dún an Airgid tógtha ar na hiarsmaí ar fad. Bhí stair na háite tréigthe ar mhaithe leis an dul chun cinn, ar mhaithe leis an saibhreas.[18]

> According to Liam Burn, the entire area was an important archeological site. And now, it was gone. Dún an Airgid was built on its remains. The history of the area had been abandoned for progress, for wealth.

Part of Liam's protest against this new, ahistorical Ireland is to leave a calling card on each victim, which put together spells his name in Ogham—a crude early alphabet—thus compelling his pursuers to learn about Gaelic history if they wish to decode his messages.

Though the book clearly has some sympathy with Liam's disgust at a shallow, money-obsessed modern Ireland, it is countered intelligently by one of his would-be victims, who points out the plurality and transnationality of early Irish history itself:

> Sraith eile den stair sin is ea sinne, dar liom. Bhíodh daoine anseo sa Nua-Chlochaois. Bhí na Ceiltigh anseo. Bhí na Lochlannaigh anseo. Bhí na Normannaigh anseo. Bhí na Spáinnigh agus na hIodálaigh agus Sir Walter Raleigh féin anseo. Agus d'fhág siad go léir iarsmaí éigin in[a] ndiaidh.[19]

> We're another link in the chain of history, if you ask me . . . there were people here during the New Stone Age. The Celts were here. The Vikings were here. The Normans were here. The Spanish, the Italians and Sir

17. Ní Dhuibhne, *Dún an Airgid*, 224.
18. Ní Dhuibhne, *Dún an Airgid*, 251.
19. Ní Dhuibhne, *Dún an Airgid*, 251.

> Walter Raleigh himself was here. And they all left some traces in their wake.

Like *Dúnmharú sa Daingean* before it, *Dún an Airgid* shows a deep ambivalence toward the Celtic Tiger, at times virtually ridiculing the pretensions of Ireland's nouveau riche. Liam's concerns may be legitimate, but no reasonable alternative is offered. The tension between the two views above is never resolved in the book, but the winners are clear as the story closes with the popping of champagne corks across the wealthy development of Dún an Airgid.

The accomplished noir novel *Sceon na Mara* (*Terror At Sea*) by Liam Ó Muirthile is also concerned with the inequalities and excesses of the Tiger era. Published in 2010, it is one of the few to integrate the severe recession that followed the boom in Ireland, almost seeming to welcome it as salutary to the country:

> [Bhí] an cúlú tosaithe cheana féin. Bhainfeadh sé an teaspach gan bhrí den saol. An uair is measa a bhí an fuadar santach, bhraith sé ina stróinséir ina thír féin, mar a bheadh anfa ag gabháil thairis á fhágaint ar an trá fholamh.[20]

> The recession had already begun. It would take some of the empty arrogance away. When the greedy hustle was at its worst, he felt like a stranger in his own country, as though a storm was blowing through him and leaving him defenseless.

The novel takes place in Killiney, a prosperous seaside village outside Dublin whose "maoin gháifeach"[21] ("extravagant wealth") epitomizes the excess of the Tiger years. Likened both to the Coast of Amalfi and the Gold Coast, we are told Killiney houses some of the wealthiest people in Ireland. In the early pages of the novel, a decadent, cocaine-addled Ireland is contrasted unfavorably with the old, rural way of life: "cnámhdhroma na tíre le ceart, amach as an gcré agus as an gcloch, nuair is iad na

20. Ó Muirthile, *Sceon na Mara*, 42.

21. Ó Muirthile, *Sceon na Mara*, 8.

scaothairí is mó a bhí in uachtar anois,"[22] "the backbone of the country by rights, borne of earth and stone, while the extravagant elite were having their moment."

More than any other novel, *Sceon na Mara* shows a large and varied immigrant community largely working in the service industry. That this remains a novelty is clear, and throughout the story Ó Muirthile explores the differing receptions the workers receive from the Irish:

> Muintir na Polainne, agus roinnt Síneach i mbun cuntar éisc is mó a bhí ag obair san ollmhargadh, agus bhí sé béasach leo. Bhí dornán Indiach nó dream cneasdorcha éigin dá leithéid ag pacáil earraí ar na seilfeanna. Bhí fáilte aige féin roimh eachtrannaigh, níorbh ionann agus cuid den chosmhuintir a labhraíodh leo go maslach, faoi mar a bheadh an goblach á bhaint as a mbéal acu.[23]

> For the most part it was Polish people who were working at the supermarket, with some Chinese people at the fish counter, and he was polite to them. There were a few Indians or a similarly dark-skinned folk packing shelves. Personally, he welcomed foreigners, unlike some of the working class who spoke down to them, as though they were taking the food out of their mouths.

The novel centers around a serial killer, George McCullough, who targets primarily Filipina women. When the Filipino community closes in on itself in response to the murders, he then reluctantly targets a Polish woman. More psychopath than criminal, and avowedly pro-immigration, there seems no explanation for McCullough exclusively choosing foreign women to rape and murder before tying them up "like Christmas gifts" and dumping them in the sea.[24]

The novel is peppered with racist sentiments from various classes of Irish society, including the Garda Síochána whose upper echelons are reluctant to investigate the case. Yet though race is undoubtedly a feature of the

22. Ó Muirthile, *Sceon na Mara*, 13.
23. Ó Muirthile, *Sceon na Mara*, 41–42.
24. Ó Muirthile, *Sceon na Mara*, 68.

book, *Sceon na Mara* is not about racism: passing racist comments and the condescension of the Irish toward migrant workers both seem more designed to add authenticity than to interrogate race relations in wealthy neoliberal Ireland.

Though evincing a certain nostalgia for pre-Tiger Ireland, the complexity of that past is not disguised. One character seems to lament the passing of English occupation, while another's alienation is, at least partially, attributed to his ancestors' involvement in strike-breaking and their role as landlords during the boycott era. Nevertheless, *Sceon na Mara*'s focus is firmly contemporary, taking place in a new Ireland whose "extravagant wealth announced that the days of guilt were over."[25]

The sexualized exploitation of migrant women is once again central to the plot in *Fianaise* (2012) (*Evidence*) by Mícheál Ó Ruairc, an off-the-wall novella about a gay sadomasochist, family dysfunction, and Garda corruption. Seán O'Connor—the only author not based in Ireland—deals with similarly extravagant, taboo-laden plots involving group sex, abortion, child sex abuse, and filicide in his three-part series centered around the Garda detective Seán Ruiséal.

Sexualized violence and taboo are not, however, ubiquitous in Irish-language crime fiction. Among the earliest and best examples of the genre, Seán Ó Dúrois's two-part series *Crann Smola* (2001) (*Blighted*) and *Rí na gCearrbhach* (2003) (*King of the Gamblers*) are set in the post-Famine era, exploring rising sectarian tension in Belfast and the profound scars left by hunger, language shift, and mass emigration. Ó Dúrois's novels are ambitious and subtle, with a depth of characterization unusual in comparison with the other texts surveyed here. As historical novels, it is unsurprising that they have little in common with the other texts. Unfortunately, space prohibits the thorough reading warranted by these outliers.

The last author to be considered in this survey is Anna Heussaff, a multi-Oireachtas award-winning author for both children and adults.[26]

25. Ó Muirthile, *Sceon na Mara*, 8.

26. Oireachtas na Gaeilge is the annual Irish-language literary and cultural competition, similar to the Welsh Eisteddfod.

Heussaff's three detective novels can be loosely considered as a trilogy as they center around the same family, while two of the three feature the same Garda, Réamonn Seoighe. The heroine throughout is undoubtedly Aoife Nic Dhiarmada, a retired journalist who maintains her tenacious nose for a story when she moves with her husband, Pat Latif, and their children, Sal and Rónán, to the Beara Peninsula in the southwest of Ireland to open a guesthouse.

The first book in the series, *Bás Tobann* (*Sudden Death*) (2004), sees the family initially struggling to adjust to life in the country. Like many of the authors already discussed, Heussaff is interested in immigration and integration, and race features throughout the series writ both small and large. One of the less dramatic examples of this is that Aoife's husband, Pat, is Malawian (albeit with some Irish ancestry), and their children are mixed-race. This is shown as gratifyingly unremarkable most of the time, and very little in general is made of Pat's race throughout the series. *Bás Tobann* does, however, explore the potential difficulties faced by an urban, mixed-race family moving to a remote part of the country.

Though human movement is shown as totally normal, and Pat in particular has experienced life in many countries, the novel does not shy away from the potential for people like Pat to be treated as novelties or a "one man multicultural show."[27] Indeed, there are some instances of cultural insensitivity in this early novel, as one of the least sympathetic characters frequently comments on Pat's race in a supposedly friendly, jocular way:

> Here we have Paddy the African man, ordering a pint of Guinness.
>
> A black man returned from the missions, and called by one of our own fine names.[28]

Sometimes this sort of othering is seemingly well-intentioned, as when the local pub landlady sympathizes with Pat about having to withstand Irish weather:

27. Heussaff, *Bás Tobann*, 15. I am indebted to Aonghus Ó hAlmhain for access to his copy of this out-of-print text.

28. Heussaff, *Bás Tobann*, 25.

> Mo ghraidhín tú . . . ach ní foláir nó go n-airíonn tú féin an fuacht go nimhneach in Éirinn? Is dócha go bhfuil sé deacair duit, a bheith ag tarraingt éadaí troma ort, mar a bhímidne?[29]

> You poor thing . . . you must feel the cold terribly in Ireland? I'm sure you find it difficult, having to layer on the heavy clothes like we do?

Pat responds politely to these questions while Aoife bites her tongue, tempted to remind the landlady that Pat was not raised wearing a grass skirt and had spent more of his life in cold countries than hot. Aoife seems to realize, however, that this will not change the landlady's view of Pat as wholly foreign, and she also accepts that the condescension was unintended.

Another source of conflict between the new arrivals and the locals is that Aoife and Pat have decided to raise their children secularly, which becomes a source of considerable tension when their son, Rónán, enrolls in the local school during Communion year. In Ireland, Catholic children are prepared for their First Holy Communion during school hours, and Aoife in particular objects to her son being present for those classes, fearing that he will be indoctrinated along with the others:

> Cuirfear in iúl dó gurb iad na Críostaithe amháin a bhíonn go deas lena chéile, agus nach dtuigeann ar leithéidí cad is olc ná maith ann, nuair nach bhfuil duais na síoraíochta romhainn.[30]

> He'll be told that only Christians are good to one another, and that our type don't understand good and evil, since we don't have an eternal reward waiting for us.

The book maintains a skeptical tone when talking about religion throughout—"financial greed and holy sacrament, they obviously go very well together"[31]—while acknowledging that à la carte spirituality is no panacea either. A particularly marginalized character, Sinéad, suffers from acute anxiety disorder and tries to soothe herself by any means necessary:

29. Heussaff, *Bás Tobann*, 65.
30. Heussaff, *Bás Tobann*, 20.
31. Heussaff, *Bás Tobann*, 135.

> Bhí triail bainte aici as réimse teiripe le blianta anuas, de réir cosúlachta, idir theiripe intinne, colainne is anama. Comhairleoireacht is suathaireacht, *yoga* is *reiki*. Drugaí nádúrtha is mínádúrtha ar aon, damhsa *sufi* is damhsa seite féin . . . bhí tairbhe le cuid acu, a dúirt sí, agus a mhalairt le cuid eile. An chuid ba mheasa acu, bhí siad ag teacht i dtír ar dhaoine a bhí briste, cráite mar a bhíodh sí féin ar feadh i bhfad. . . . Slám airgid fágtha aici le mangairí an tsonais.[32]

> She had tried a variety of therapies over the years, it seems, covering body mind and spirit. Counseling and massage, yoga and reiki . . . some of them were helpful, she said, and some were not. The worst among them took advantage of broken, tormented people like she had been for a long time. . . . She had left wads of cash with these slingers of solace.

Sinéad is also the sole example of a "good" character with mental health problems. The stigma associated with these problems is cleverly expressed throughout the book, as others refer to them to undermine her credibility to suit their own agenda, beginning when she was seduced and abandoned as a teenager by the seemingly upstanding headmaster of Rónán's school.[33]

Land ownership and access rights prove to be yet another source of contention, as Aoife learns that she had unwittingly outbid two local people for the guesthouse, who had plans to turn it into a retirement home.[34] Indeed it appears that many were interested in the plot, with a local woman mentioning that it had been identified as a potential place to build either a Direct Provision hostel for asylum seekers or holiday homes, which have become synonymous with deprived rural areas. Consequently, Aoife and Pat are faced with sets of resentful neighbors who try to block their access to land they need for their business. Although these sorts of disputes seem cynical and petty—greed for land being a trope associated with the inhabitants of rural Ireland—the author stresses that inhabitants of remote areas like Beara have been struggling to subsist on smallholdings for decades and longer:

32. Heussaff, *Bás Tobann*, 178.
33. Heussaff, *Bás Tobann*, 28, 179.
34. Heussaff, *Bás Tobann*, 73.

> Bhí dísheabhú le léamh ar an tírdhreach, tailte á dtréigean ón nGorta Mór i leith. Úinéireacht na talún bainte amach le fada, ach pobal dúchasach ag cailliúint dóchais dá ainneoin. Istigh i nGleann Inse Choinn, ní raibh ach corrtheach le feiceáil cois locha nó ar imeall na gcnoc. Saol an ghleanna ag athrú de shíor, gan mórán daoine fágtha ag streachailt chun slí beatha a scríobadh ó ghabháltais bheaga. Lucht saoire i gcuid de na tithe, iadsan ar thóir an uaignis seachas a bheith ag teitheadh uaidh.[35]
>
> Dispossession could be read on the landscape, lands being deserted from the Great Famine onwards. Landownership had long been achieved, but the native population was losing hope nonetheless. In Gleann Inse Choinn, there were only a few houses to be seen, by the lough or on the brow of the hills. Life in the valley was ever-changing, with few people left to struggle to scrape a living from small holdings. Holiday makers were in some of the houses, those who came searching for loneliness instead of fleeing it.

This passage speaks to genuine social problems in increasingly deserted parts of rural Ireland, where many villages face imminent extinction if some means of employment is not found urgently. The irony that urban Ireland associates underpopulation with tranquility is succinctly expressed elsewhere in the book:

> Tá's agam go mbíonn bhur leithéidí ag trácht de shíor ar áilleacht na gcnoc is a leithéid, ach maidir le muintir na tuaithe, 'séard is mó a fheicimidne lasmuigh ná saothar is anró.[36]
>
> I know that your lot are always going on about the beauty of the hills and so on, but as far as country folk are concerned, what we see when we look outside is work and hardship.

A final noteworthy feature, begun in *Bás Tobann* and continued throughout the series, is Heussaff's language strategy. All three novels take place in a world where Irish is spoken by all, with varying registers and dialects accorded to different classes and regions. In the newest novel, *Scáil an*

35. Heussaff, *Bás Tobann*, 148–49.

36. Heussaff, *Bás Tobann*, 65.

Phríosúin (2015) (*The Shadow of the Prison*), even the immigrant characters imported for sexual exploitation speak Irish. Yet throughout the series, Aoife's daughter Sal constantly codeswitches between Irish and English, seemingly an attempt at linguistic authenticity, which is somewhat distracting when all other sections of society have embraced Irish as the lingua franca.

The second novel in the series, *Buille Marfach* (*Deadly Blow*), published in 2010, takes place for the most part on the same peninsula though its focus is more global, covering drug smuggling, war crimes, and the arms race. It is clear throughout the novel that the boom has reached the Beara Peninsula, where Mercedes and BMWs are not unusual sights, and Aoife's guesthouse boasts both eco-consciousness and luxury. It is equally clear that this is no rising tide that lifts all boats: one of several subplots finds a boatload of immigrant workers stranded on a ship in the peninsula, deserted by their Russian employers who have filed for bankruptcy. The workers remain at the periphery throughout the story, depending on locals for daily provisions, while the novel's main villain blandly defends the obvious injustice of the situation in one of his very few instances of direct speech:

> Dá mbeimis ag brath ar mhoráltacht i gcúrsaí trádála . . . bheimis go léir chomh bocht le foireann na loinge. . . . Nach dtuigeann tú . . . go bhfuilimidne ag brath ar allas na milliún duine i gcéin chun saol compordach a bheith againn in Éirinn. Agus is mise atá buíoch go bhfuil.[37]
>
> If we depended on morality in matters of trade . . . we'd all be as poor as the ship's staff. Don't you understand . . . that we depend on the sweat of millions of people far away in order to have a comfortable life in Ireland. And I'm very glad that we do.

These are the words of Oscar Mac Ailpín, simultaneously the murder victim and main villain of *Buille Marfach*. As a victim he is highly atypical of the texts surveyed here: he is not only a powerful, wealthy Irish male but also a hardened criminal and serial rapist. We find out through the course

37. Heussaff, *Buille Marfach*, 62.

of the novel that Mac Ailpín was an international arms broker with a specialty in torture tools. It is perhaps not surprising, then, to find him defending the inequalities of neoliberal Ireland, but his speech does speak to the uncomfortable novelty of a historically poor country embracing the roles of host and client of poorer places. Though many of these stories show a genuine sympathy for the vulnerable migrant population, this tension is rarely directly addressed as above. It is striking, too, that the system of Direct Provision, grimly reminiscent of the Magdalene laundries, is mentioned only once in all the books surveyed here, given the prevalence of migrant characters throughout.

The final book to be briefly discussed is the latest installment in Heussaff's trilogy, *Scáil an Phríosúin*. This is the most ambitious of the three novels, as it tries to tie together a contemporary crime borne of contemporary ills with a historical murder mystery. At first, the only connections apparent between the two are that both victims—yet again, female—are found dead in the same prison. Published on the eve of the 1916 centenary, much of the novel takes place in the appropriately loaded setting of the iconic Kilmainham Gaol, where the leaders of the Easter Rising were imprisoned and executed in its aftermath. The use of the jail to establish a panoscopic view of Dublin's underbelly from the eras of famine and land war to the present day is the most accomplished feature of the novel, genuinely managing to root both mysteries in "their" Dublin. This book, of all those examined here, also features the one true iteration of the bent cop trope, and for once the gender of the victims seems deliberate and purposeful rather than a convenience.

It is perhaps appropriate that *Scáil an Phríosúin* is the most recent crime novel discussed here, as it is the most generically typical, replete with bent cops, drugs, corrupt elites, class tension, red herrings, and dramatic scenes of peril. It also shares many features with its predecessors, especially regarding the juxtaposition of several different Irelands. Perhaps most telling is that both of the story's main plots, set over a century apart, center around victims of poverty and colonialism, but the role of victim and perpetrator has shifted entirely so that the Irish are no longer, in general, the victim.

The year 2018, with Ireland firmly back in boom mode, may prove to be a banner year for Irish-language crime fiction, with at least three new titles expected by year's end. The novels surveyed above represent the development and growing confidence, over two decades, of a genre that had previously, tellingly, been the domain of adult learners and schoolchildren. That some of the most highly regarded "literary" authors writing in Irish today have embraced the genre is perhaps also a sign of a growing respect for the value of *scíthléitheoireacht*—reading for pleasure rather than edification.

However lighthearted some of these books are, they speak both implicitly and explicitly to serious problems in Irish society. Even leaving aside the worrying demographic profile of the murder victims in a large majority of the stories, these novels show a keenness to reflect and to some extent challenge Ireland's enthusiastic embracing of capitalism and commercialism at the expense of environment and heritage. They anticipate and represent the growing divide between rich and poor and city and country. They show a sympathy for those left behind by the boom, and seem particularly concerned that the Irish will perpetuate the exploitation of immigrants once visited upon themselves. Though they clearly have much in common with their English-language counterparts, it could be argued that the Irish texts have their own priorities, which can be summed up in two words: preservation and integration. That they should be looking both backward and forward is typical for Irish-language writing, always aware of its own history and precarity. That there is a strong solidarity with the vulnerable should come as no surprise from a minority community with extensive experience of emigration, which has been fighting for its own survival in the face of cultural change and economic expediency for over a century.

Bibliography

Adams, Róisín. *Forbairt Litríocht Ghaeilge na nÓg, 1926–1967*. Unpublished PhD thesis. Dublin: Trinity College Dublin, 2014.

Cliff, Brian. *Irish Crime Fiction*. London: Palgrave Macmillan, 2018.

Heussaff, Anna. *Bás Tobann*. Baile Átha Cliath: Cois Life, 2005.

———. *Buille Marfach*. Indreabhán: Cló Iar-Chonnacht, 2012.

———. *Scáil an Phríosúin*. Indreabhán: Cló Iar-Chonnacht, 2015.

Ní Dhuibhne, Éilís. *Dún an Airgid*. Baile Átha Cliath: Cois Life, 2008.

———. *Dúnmharú sa Daingean*. Baile Átha Cliath: Cois Life, 2000.

Ó Báille, Ruaidhrí. *Dúnmharú ar an Dart*. Indreabhán: Cló Iar-Chonnacht, 1989.

O'Brien, Edna. "A Scandalous Woman." In *Seven Novels and Other Short Stories*. London: Collins, 1978, 917–40.

Ó Cadhain, Máirtín. *Páipéir Bhána agus Páipéir Bhreaca*. Indreabhán: Cló Iar-Chonnacht, 1969, 2003.

O'Connor, Seán. *Seán Ruiséal agus na Corpáin ar Shiúlán na hAille*. Baile Átha Cliath: Coiscéim, 2013.

———. *Seán Ruiséal agus an Guth Istoíche*. Baile Átha Cliath: Coiscéim, 2008.

———. *Seán Ruiséal agus Iníon an Oileáin*. Baile Átha Cliath: Coiscéim, 2007.

Ó Dúrois, Seán. *Crann Smola*. Baile Átha Cliath: Coiscéim, 2001.

———. *Rí na gCearrbhach*. Baile Átha Cliath: Coiscéim, 2003.

Ó hÁinle, Cathal. "An tÚrscéal nár Tháinig." *Promhadh Pinn*. Má Nuad: An Sagart, 1978.

O'Leary, Philip. *The Prose Literature of the Gaelic Revival*. University Park, PA: Pennsylvania State Univ. Press, 1994.

Ó Muirthile, Liam. *Sceon na Mara*. Baile Átha Cliath: Cois Life, 2010.

Ó Ruairc, Mícheál. *Fianaise*. Baile Átha Cliath: LeabhairCOMHAR, 2012.

PART TWO

Historical Crime Fiction

5

Hospitality and Surveillance

Imperial Crime in Conor Brady's Victorian Dublin

NANCY MARCK CANTWELL

Exploring the criminal environments of Victorian Dublin in four novels featuring Detective Inspector Joe Swallow, Conor Brady argues that "modern Ireland was shaped in the 1880s."[1] From Dublin Castle to the Liberties, Rathmines to Phoenix Park, Detective Swallow unravels the political ramifications of seemingly personal crimes, as Irish national identity responds to historical events ranging from the Land Wars to the struggle for Home Rule. The pressure toward independence grows even as the country prepares for Queen Victoria's 1887 Golden Jubilee in *A June of Ordinary Murders* (2012), and political tensions escalate in *The Eloquence of the Dead* (2013), where Swallow's murder investigation discovers the sinister power undermining land reform. In *A Hunt in Winter* (2017), Swallow must navigate public criticism of the Dublin Metropolitan Police (DMP) as the British government moves to discredit Charles Stewart Parnell, a threat further elaborated in Brady's most recent novel, *In the Dark River* (2018). In these two last works, the detective's growing moral disillusionment rises as he uncovers a corrupt colonial bureaucracy. All four novels register the increasing pervasiveness of English imperial rule as it extends its grip on Dublin's law enforcement agencies to exert control over the Irish home and family, an encroachment on privacy and self-determination that motivates growing political resistance in Ireland.

1. Wallace, "Conor Brady."

Although Brady's detective generally thinks more about solving crimes than about colonial politics, the series charts his increasing nationalist sentiment, repeatedly emphasizing the apparent contradiction in his position as a Dublin "G-man" who is both native Irish and a civil servant ultimately answerable to English colonial authorities.[2] In each novel, Swallow endures criticism from fellow Irishmen who accuse him of collaborating with the imperial enemy, as one jeers at "the great Sergeant Swallow, doing England's work in Dublin Castle. . . . There's a long tradition attaching to your kind, Sergeant Swallow, of selling their country for 30 pieces of silver."[3] The strain of Swallow's conflicting loyalties manifests chiefly in Brady's representation of the intersection of private and public spheres, complicated by the flexing of English imperial muscle. Brady's novels ask: Whose home is this Ireland? Whose laws are to be upheld, and whose peace defended? The operation of two systems of authority run by two historical figures—John Mallon's Dublin Metropolitan Police and the English colonial administration overseen by Joseph West Ridgeway as Under-Secretary for Ireland (1887–92)—radicalizes even the essentially conservative Swallow by unmasking the English state's invasion of that most private space, the Irish home.

I want to situate the political dimension of Brady's series in the context of home and hospitality in order to make a claim for the radical political possibilities implicit in both domestic and detective fiction. Like other contemporary Irish crime writers, Brady engages with current postcolonial efforts to document and analyze Ireland's historical and cultural inequalities; his nineteenth-century setting offers a unique position from which to comment on what Charlotte Beyer describes as the "contestation of the past by reimagining its power structures."[4] While the power structures

2. Brady refers to Swallow and his colleagues as "G-men," noting that "the plain-clothes G Division based at Exchange Court was supposedly the elite of the Dublin Metropolitan Police" (*June*, 4).

3. Brady, *June*, 106.

4. Beyer, "Third Ireland," 61. Critics addressing postcolonial issues in Irish crime fiction include Declan Burke, John Scaggs, David Clark, Eoin Flannery, Valerie Coughlan, John Cawelti, and Andrew Kincaid.

are imperial and English in the Swallow novels, Brady takes pains to position the political struggle for Ireland in the colonized Irish home.

Discussing the private sphere in *Of Hospitality*, Jacques Derrida defines "absolute hospitality" as the unconditional opening of one's home to a foreigner, an unrestricted offering that appears impossible because such openness is typically contravened by other laws that border or limit a guest's access to all the host might potentially offer.[5] Unconditional hospitality sets the stage for foreign invasion and appropriation of the host's home, inviting a colonization of sorts. As Derrida explains, "Anyone who encroaches on my 'at home,' on my ipseity, on my power of hospitality, on my sovereignty as host, I start to regard as an undesirable foreigner, and virtually as an enemy. The other becomes a hostile subject, and I risk becoming their hostage."[6] This unbounded invasion upends power relations between the native host and the foreign guest, inverting their roles; the host becomes the hostage, or constrained guest, of the foreigner, who takes control of the home and establishes what were formerly foreign rules as laws, now instituted and enforced by an enemy authority. This dynamic accurately describes the "hostile subject" position occupied by English colonial administrators in Brady's series.

While Brady's English officials are colonial administrators, not "guests" in the usual sense of the term, they act in concert with the Anglo-Irish landowners who took control of Irish property, establishing political and authoritarian lines of defense and effectively taking Ireland hostage, in Derrida's terms. In Brady's series, English laws supersede and countermand Irish ones, escalating resentment and nationalist sentiment expressed by both Dublin's criminals and its law officers through the series as "the guest becomes the host's host."[7]

Appropriating Ireland, imperial law enforcement becomes politically charged by paranoia and characterized by an unremitting vigilance anticipating organized rebellion by groups including the Fenians, the Hibernian

5. Derrida and Dufourmantelle, *Of Hospitality*, 75.

6. Derrida and Dufourmantelle, *Of Hospitality*, 55.

7. Derrida and Dufourmantelle, *Of Hospitality*, 123.

Brotherhood, and the Invincibles. The title of Brady's first novel, *A June of Ordinary Murders*, refers to the DMP's distinction between "ordinary murders," which are not politically motivated, and "special crimes" that threaten the Empire and its representatives. Reflecting the historical urgency of these "special crimes," Brady's Swallow first rises to prominence through his role in solving the infamous 1882 Phoenix Park murders, attacks on the top two British colonial administrators by members of the Invincibles.[8] Brady's DMP and the G-men who form its detective force remain alert to any threats to imperial representatives, particularly with the state visit of the Prince of Wales approaching in *A June of Ordinary Murders*.

This heightened security, in which colonial forces scrutinize the colonized for signs of rebellion, links police surveillance with social class in the search for a born criminal embedded in the Irish resistance. An inverted model of hospitality in which the host becomes the guest's hostage means that the guest must continually defend against the host's efforts to regain home and ipseity, or selfhood. While surveillance is a usual part of detective investigations, it typically serves publicly sanctioned institutions and the law. For instance, while detectives may shadow suspects in an effort to gather evidence and solve a crime, journalists in Brady's series also shadow police and critique their efforts in the press. As former editor of the *Irish Times* and former commissioner of the Garda Síochána Ombudsman Committee, Brady appreciates the public interest that guides both efforts, describing police and journalists equally as "seekers after truth" who "claim to protect and defend the weak."[9] However, this common understanding of Ireland's laws is under siege in Brady's series, as English political prerogatives supersede and countermand Irish law. In the Swallow novels, English agents are assigned to work alongside the Irish police, but

8. In the early evening of 6 May 1882, newly appointed Chief Secretary for Ireland, Lord Frederick Cavendish, and the Under-Secretary for Ireland, Thomas Henry Burke, were attacked and stabbed to death while walking in Dublin's Phoenix Park. Cavendish had just arrived in Dublin. Earlier that day, Irish Home Rule leader Charles Stewart Parnell had been released from Kilmainham Jail, where he had been held following violent public speeches condemning the 1881 Land Act.

9. Brady, "Journalist and the Policeman," 193.

suspicion prompts them to operate their own investigations, which often undermine Irish procedures. While the Irish G-men aim to prevent and contain criminal activity, the English forces constantly survey Irish subjects for any signs of insurrection.[10] Swallow uncovers one such effort when he is assigned to protect the prominent Alderman Thomas Fitzpatrick in *A June of Ordinary Murders*, only to discover that he himself is under surveillance by English intelligence operatives. Although Swallow protects Fitzpatrick and Under-Secretary Smith Berry during a potentially fatal attack by members of the Hibernian Brothers, he nonetheless suspects that Fitzpatrick is connected to two unidentified bodies discovered in Phoenix Park, and so conducts his own surveillance of Fitzpatrick. The lead English operative, Major Nigel Kelly, apprehends and forcibly detains Swallow as he watches Fitzpatrick's Merrion Square house, disabusing the detective of any illusion that both police forces work collaboratively. Kelly makes the distinction clear: "Like you, I represent the civil authorities, but at a different level. Should I suggest . . . a higher level of authority? . . . My work isn't done in the public eye. My duties are of a, well, more clandestine nature.'"[11] As it turns out, Kelly's assignment is to obstruct Swallow and Mallon's investigation. As a well-to-do Irish official committed to conciliation, the alderman is a valuable commodity whose reputation must remain untarnished. When Swallow uncovers evidence linking Fitzpatrick to a third corpse, he realizes that Fitzpatrick is "being shielded by powerful people—probably including yourself—because you need him to perform in some sort of political pantomime next week" when the Prince of Wales visits Dublin.[12] The alder-

10. Irish police forces include the Dublin Metropolitan Police (DMP), composed of alphabetized divisions that reflect city districts, and the Royal Irish Constabulary (RIC), which covers the rural areas outside city limits. While most divisions have responsibility for an area of the city, G Division is a plainclothes elite force. English police units include the Special Irish Branch of New Scotland Yard as well as "teams of secret police agents . . . formed in Scotland Yard and Dublin Castle" to discredit Parnell and destabilize subversive organizations (Brady, *June*, 53). Major Kelly belongs to the new secret squads, which report directly to the English Under-Secretary for Security, not to Chief Superintendent Mallon.

11. Brady, *June*, 244–45.

12. Brady, *June*, 246.

man's public performance of Irish allegiance to Great Britain would ratify England's claim to Ireland, easing Queen Victoria's fear of increasingly dangerous protests that could threaten the prince's safety.

The various nationalist groups represented in the novels maintain associations with the Dublin criminal underworld, but they simultaneously introduce the private sphere of the Irish family. Sparrow's sister Harriet is romantically and politically involved with James O'Donnell of the Hibernian Brothers, a radical organization dedicated to the overthrow of English rule. Intervening to prevent an attempted shooting of Fitzpatrick at the Royal Hibernian Academy, Swallow uncovers a plot to assassinate the Prince of Wales during his visit to Dublin. The two assailants are members of a criminal network run by the historical figure known as Cecelia or Ces "Pisspot" Downes. Downes rose from lowly beginnings as a Dublin housemaid to preside over the most powerful gang in Dublin, a personage of such recognized importance that she is the subject of ongoing surveillance by Mallon's G-men, and Swallow feels compelled to attend her funeral in *A June of Ordinary Murders*.

Defying Major Kelly's orders, Swallow directs a controversial full search of Fitzpatrick's Merrion Square manse, a breach of Irish domestic privacy he justifies because the third corpse is a woman who was formerly a servant in Fitzpatrick's home, and the two Phoenix Park victims were also seen entering that address. Swallow's surveillance unveils Fitzpatrick's "secret family": two adult children the alderman fathered by Ces Downes, and an infant secretly buried on the grounds of the Merrion Square home. At this point Derrida's remarks on the crypt and encryption further the idea of concealed identity, as Linden Peach notes that the "topoi," the grounds in which a crypt is situated, are "intended to hide at least as much as hold the crypt," emphasizing "the close relationship between what is hidden and, as far as contemporary Irish fiction is concerned, the individual or national consciousness in which it is concealed."[13] Fitzpatrick's secret backyard crypt, in which he has entombed the infant corpse, stands for the host's repressed ipseity. He must conceal his true family, "encrypting" the

13. Peach, *Contemporary*, 44.

birth to maintain his public position, yet his emotional attachment to family prevents him from denying the birth in private, and since he feels compelled to claim the infant by assigning a grave within his grounds, the crypt both conceals and identifies home and family identity. On a deeper level, Fitzpatrick does not wish to deny his secret family; while Ces has raised their daughter, he has provided for his son's education and assists his rising career as a journalist. He also keeps the evidence of the infant corpse close to home, subjecting it to eventual discovery, exhumation, and reidentification as evidence in a criminal act that also invokes the family—the Phoenix Park victims are Fitzpatrick's daughter and his grandson, their murderer Fitzpatrick's son.

Although Fitzpatrick's grief is compounded when he realizes his son has brutally murdered his daughter, he nonetheless attempts to conceal the fact, partially to shield his one remaining offspring from execution, and partly to protect his own reputation. This calls on the national consciousness: Fitzpatrick stands for a narrative of successful assimilation that endorses imperial conquest, but his own family's violation of cultural taboos makes his endorsement worthless. From Brady's postcolonial vantage point, the imperial "family" presided over by Victoria takes priority over and dictates the terms of the local, intimate family drama, in contrast to John Cawelti's remark that in crime narratives of the nineteenth century, "the social order is not responsible for the crime because it was the act of a particular individual with his own private motives."[14] In the Swallow novels, it is impossible to separate personal motives from their broader imperial significances. Once Swallow uncovers Fitzpatrick's connection with Downes and identifies the murderer, Fitzpatrick's value as an imperial mouthpiece declines, and assimilation appears compromised, again nudging Swallow toward a nationalist political stance. Instead of offering a nineteenth-century detective who is "a detached eccentric with no worldly stake in the action," Brady allows Swallow space for a more modern awareness of the irresolvable tensions that complicate both individual and national identities.[15]

14. Cawelti, *Adventure*, 95–96.

15. Cawelti, *Adventure*, 95.

Surveillance, exposing secret narratives, heralds "the emergence of socially marginalized groups: once what was formerly acknowledged only in secret surfaces in the public domain, it becomes a significant 'other' within the dominant discourse."[16] The criminal, now revealed and unveiled in his blood relation to the public/political figure of the alderman, must be explained as a manifestation of Irishness, particularly of its lower depths, rather than simply a man acting on his pro-British politics. How has this class boundary become porous, and what impact might this porosity have on the Empire's grip on the host as hostage? Fitzpatrick turns to a scientific explanation, to ineffable atavism as the cause of criminality, explaining his son's criminality as inherited:

> Cecilia was utterly wayward. I suppose that was part of the attraction for me. She didn't accept authority. She didn't accept her position as a servant. She didn't respect the laws of property or anything else. She was a born troublemaker and unfortunately a born criminal, as I'm sure a policeman knows better than anyone.[17]

The "born criminal" narrative resurfaces in the murderer's justification of the crime as self-defense: "My sister was like her mother—my mother. She inherited her low ways and her low standards. . . . when she realised it was me she flew into a rage and started to abuse me. . . . She said I had got all the privileges and that she had got nothing. Then suddenly she took a knife from somewhere and went for me."[18] Both explanations shift responsibility from male to female perpetrators while referencing innate Irish violence. Fitzpatrick and his son thus incriminate female "throwbacks" whose viciousness they see as distinctly Irish. While the Fitzpatrick men claim a more civilized identity through their British affiliations, they descry these passionate women who embody Ireland's historical grievances as well as class differences. David Clark adds that in using "the markers of Otherness as signs of potential or actual deviance," nineteenth-century crime

16. Peach, *Contemporary*, 9.

17. Brady, *June*, 350.

18. Brady, *June*, 362–63.

narratives employed atavism as a means of "effectively criminalising both the western working classes and the victims of colonialism."[19] The born criminal argument unsuccessfully deflects the host/guest tension by suggesting that inheritance rather than politics motivated the crime, but the resurgence of atavistic violence characterizes the crime as a gothic manifestation of what Vera Kreilkamp has described as "the subversive power of an archaic and uncivilized Ireland."[20] In each case, the born criminal justifies continued colonial dominance, increasing the anxiety attending surveillance by reinvigorating English stereotypes of Irish violence. Brady calls particular attention to the class dynamic, as Major Kelly's effort to secure Fitzpatrick and his residence from penetration by the Dublin G Division extends English class privilege. Fitzpatrick is above the law insofar as the English officials are concerned, but Swallow's own surveillance enables him to pinpoint the exact time to conduct the thorough search of the house and the interview of the alderman needed to obtain his evidence.

Both *A June of Ordinary Murders* and *A Hunt in Winter* center on a brother's murder of his sister, merging political and personal motives. In *The Eloquence of the Dead*, the victim's sister is the prime suspect, again calling attention to the family as the locus of criminal violence, and in all three novels secret families are exposed. As recurring themes, sororicide and the secret family point to the effacement of the boundary between private and public spheres; surveillance exposes the Irish family to the English operative's power to scrutinize, invade, and punish. As Michel Foucault has famously noted, "It is this fact of being constantly seen, of being able always to be seen, that maintains the disciplined individual in his subjection."[21] In *The Eloquence of the Dead*, surveillance uncovers two secret Irish families, both attempting concealment for political reasons. But while the Clinton family hides to evade prosecution for fraud and murder, the secret illegitimate family of Charles Stewart Parnell and Katherine O'Shea also becomes

19. Clark, "Mean Streets," 256.
20. Kreilkamp, *Anglo-Irish*, 97.
21. Foucault, *Discipline*, 187.

part of the larger investigation in the latter two novels.[22] Mr. Clinton is part of an organized effort to defraud the Crown of government money paid out through the Land Purchase Act of 1885. Once Swallow traces Clinton's organization back to the Treasury Office, it becomes clear that the land transfer program is in jeopardy. As Assistant Under-Secretary Smith Berry observes, "If it were to become generally known that it had been corrupted, right up to the level of the Treasury Office, we might well have threats by Mr. Parnell or leaders of the tenants' organisations to have nothing to do with it."[23] The need to discredit Parnell propels English operatives to press G Division for their records of surveillance of Parnell's Dublin home, records that would invariably expose his relationship with Mrs. O'Shea. Assigned to routine surveillance of Parnell, Swallow is "uncomfortable with the espionage. As an Irishman, he recognised Parnell as the greatest leader of his country since Daniel O'Connell."[24] With Mallon's tacit if unofficial approval in *A Hunt in Winter*, Swallow conceals the surveillance records, again defying Major Kelly, but inadvertently prompting an invasion of his own home and family.

Swallow's domestic life develops alongside his political views through the series, but his mixed allegiances begin to tilt toward Ireland with his increasingly personal experience of imperial invasion and corruption. Maureen Reddy observes that while the contemporary Irish crime novel often reflects conventions of the American hard-boiled detective, it departs from those conventions in its hero's relation to nation. The American lone male detective is more heroically individual in his isolation, but "in Irish cultural traditions, the solitary male figure is generally both unusual and pitiable."[25] Accordingly, over the course of the series, Brady makes Swallow's personal life central to his professional and political identities, as the detective

22. Despite concerted unofficial efforts to keep Parnell out of the newspapers, *In the Dark River* brings the scandal to a public crisis; the wave of violence and chaos Mallon predicts first impacts the Irish families left fatherless by the murders of informant Pigott and Inspector Fleury.

23. Brady, *Eloquence*, 346.

24. Brady, *Eloquence*, 13.

25. Reddy, "Contradictions," 128.

marries and fathers two children. Swallow's feelings about Ireland stem from his attachment to home, and Brady charts his growing awareness of the need to protect his nation as well as his own family from imperial interference. Describing himself as uninterested in politics—he "cared nothing for it . . . and less for its practitioners"—Swallow at first holds that his commitment to Irish law is consistent with his opposition to Irish resistance efforts since "violence was futile, he believed."[26] In each novel, however, Brady returns to Swallow's roots in County Kildare and reminds the reader that "his own grandfather had joined the pikemen in the rising of '98," referencing an inherited capacity for revolt that lies dormant until awakened by the invasion of his home and privacy.[27]

Incensed by G Division's resistance to the request for the Parnell logs, Major Nigel Kelly forcibly enters the Exchange Court offices of the DMP with an armed escort of English detectives who, he declares, "will shoot anyone who resists their lawful authority."[28] This unprecedented act of dominance fires the Irish detectives to defend their territory, which functions simultaneously as a public workspace and a private repository for the gathering and interpretation of evidence. Dismissing Swallow's colleague Pat Mossop as a "stupid little Paddy," Kelly finds himself staring down the barrel of Mossop's Remington shotgun, as the G-men stand their ground and force an English retreat.[29] When English investigators return with a warrant, they claim a common police identity, declaring, "We're coppers, like you. Special Irish Branch, New Scotland Yard," but Swallow insists, "You're English. I'm Irish. . . . You've no clue about what's at stake."[30] The invasion of the workplace marks a turn in English-Irish relations, as Chief John Mallon makes plain: "It's open warfare now between us. The English are determined to find some way of taking Parnell down, even if it means bloodshed and mayhem here. . . . So there aren't any marks for

26. Brady, *Eloquence*, 47; Brady, *June*, 12.

27. Brady, *June*, 12. Similarly, the contrast between the apolitical Swallow and his politicized sister Harriet motivates the central murder in *A Hunt in Winter*.

28. Brady, *Hunt*, 123.

29. Brady, *Hunt*, 125.

30. Brady, *Hunt*, 181–82.

past efficiency or loyalty, or even an acknowledgement that Irishmen might know more about how to manage Ireland's affairs than wealthy blow-ins from Scotland."[31] Swallow's own political views become more partisan as tensions escalate between G Division and English colonial administrators, and the Irish home becomes the scene of the Irish host's transformation to hostage.

Infuriated by Swallow's resistance to his authority, Major Kelly takes the fight to the domestic arena, bursting in to search Swallow's home while he is out of the country following a lead. Swallow's home is a curious mixture of public and private Irish spheres. He lives with his wife in private quarters above M & M Grant's public house, which she manages. He is careful not to violate his professional position by stepping behind the bar, although all guests recognize him as a "bobby" whose presence helps to maintain order. The public house is a space with both domestic and national import since it serves both as a home and as a community gathering place where politics can be discussed. Since Swallow's family also owned a pub, he understands the running of the business and moves familiarly among the regular clientele, so Brady positions the pub as a professional space embedded in Irish cultural life, while at the same time the private quarters Swallow and Maria share above the pub offer a distinctly private domestic refuge.

Kelly invades the home when he knows that Swallow is away, unable to defend his quarters, his wife, or their business. The political strain between host and guest is dramatically underlined when Maria miscarries while trying to prevent Kelly's forcible entry into their home. Maria and Major Kelly offer differing accounts of the fall, a difference that underlines imperial authority to control the narrative around the invasion of domestic and personal privacy: "she says she was manhandled down the stairs," and "Kelly says she tripped."[32] Moreover, Kelly prevents their servant from calling for medical attention until the search is completed, thus taking command not

31. Brady, *Hunt*, 196–97.

32. Brady, *Hunt*, 271.

only of the Swallow family's business and their private home but also of Maria's body in a way that determines the fate of their unborn child. In this act of overt imperial invasion, Maria Swallow and her unborn child serve as hostages, demonstrating England's comprehensive control over Irish subjects, as Derrida reminds us that "the State cannot guarantee or claim to guarantee the private domain . . . other than by controlling it and trying to penetrate it to be sure of it."[33] This penetration of his secure home (extending to his wife's allegedly secure womb) radicalizes Swallow. Not only do his charges against the major go unanswered in this instance, but a formal charge of murdering an informant is also dropped at the order of the Chief Secretary for Ireland, Arthur Balfour.

Deprived of privacy, attacked and injured in the home, denied the justice of their own legal system, Detective Joe Swallow and his wife find their family broken by English powers of control and punishment, a "mechanism of objectification" that renders a pervasive sense of loss at the end of *A Hunt in Winter.*[34] As Mallon and Swallow commiserate over shots of Tullamore Dew, they can only console themselves by renewing their commitment to their homeland: "We're as Irish as any of the characters we chase and trace. . . . We can keep some sort of grip on things. Maybe save Ireland from the foolishness of the English."[35] The closing scene returns to the Irish home above the pub, where Joe and Maria Swallow sit together in subdued silence, and their losses bring their marriage close to a crisis in *In the Dark River.* In this most recent novel, Swallow angers Sir John McCartan, a prominent Queen's Counsel, whose influence forces him to leave G Division for a desk job.[36] Swallow's investigation of McCartan following a burglary provokes criticism of the inefficiency of the DMP, inflaming fears about public safety that, in turn, provide English law enforcement with a justification for more thorough surveillance. Although Mallon later offers him the opportunity to return as superintendent, Swallow appears

33. Derrida and Dufourmantelle, *Of Hospitality*, 55.

34. Foucault, *Discipline*, 187.

35. Brady, *Hunt*, 317.

36. Brady, *Dark*.

reluctant, believing that regular hours have helped to restore his marriage and family life. Brady concludes the novel with Maria's announcement of another pregnancy, potentially reactivating his detective's need to defend his home and therefore also to help "save Ireland" by reengaging in the unfolding political struggle. Observing the Irish family by turns radicalized and chastened by their colonial experience in the series, readers can only wait expectantly for Detective Inspector Swallow's inevitable rising.

Bibliography

Beyer, Charlotte. "'The Third Ireland': Inheritance and Postcolonialism in Irish Crime Writing." *Journal of Commonwealth and Postcolonial Studies* 4, no. 1 (2016): 61–81.

Brady, Conor. *In the Dark River.* Dublin: New Island, 2018.

———. *The Eloquence of the Dead.* Dublin: New Island, 2013.

———. *A Hunt in Winter.* Dublin: New Island, 2016.

———. "The Journalist and the Policeman: Seekers for Truth or Rivals in the Game?" *Éire-Ireland* 49, no. 1 (2014): 193–204.

———. *A June of Ordinary Murders.* Dublin: New Island, 2012.

Cawelti, John G. *Adventure, Mystery, and Romance: Formula Stories as Art and Popular Culture.* Chicago: Univ. of Chicago Press, 1976.

Clark, David. "Mean Streets, New Lives: The Representation of Non-Irish Immigrants in Recent Irish Crime Fiction." In *Literary Visions of Multicultural Ireland: The Immigrant in Contemporary Irish Literature*, edited by Pilar Villar-Argáiz, 255–67. Manchester: Manchester Univ. Press, 2013.

Derrida, Jacques, and Anne Dufourmantelle. *Of Hospitality: Anne Dufourmantelle Invites Jacques Derrida to Respond.* Translated by Rachel Bowlby. Stanford, CA: Stanford Univ. Press, 2000.

Foucault, Michel. *Discipline and Punish: The Birth of the Prison.* New York: Pantheon, 1977.

Kreilkamp, Vera. *The Anglo-Irish Novel and the Big House.* Syracuse: Syracuse Univ. Press, 1998.

Peach, Linden. *The Contemporary Irish Novel: Critical Readings.* London: Palgrave, 2004.

Reddy, Maureen T. "Contradictions in the Irish Hardboiled: Detective Fiction's Uneasy Portrayal of a New Ireland." *New Hibernia Review* 19, no. 4 (Winter 2015): 126–40.

Trotter, David. "Theory in Detective Fiction." *Critical Quarterly* 33, no. 2 (1991): 66–77.

Wallace, Arminta. "Conor Brady: Back on the Crime Beat." *Irish Times*, 16 November 2016. https://www.irishtimes.com/culture/books/conor-brady-back-on-the-crime-beat-1.2868989. Accessed 8 May 2017.

How History Helps

Michael Russell's Irish Thrillers

EUNAN O'HALPIN

In his *City* series, Michael Russell has produced four linked novels that span two genres: the police procedural detective story and the international thriller. Placed in order of the years they cover, from 1932 to 1941, they are *The City of Shadows* (2012), *The City of Strangers* (2013), *The City in Darkness* (2016), and *The City of Lies* (2017).

This essay does not attempt exploration of the purposes, nature, and limitations of contemporary historical fiction in general, but such issues lie at the core of Laurent Binet's extraordinary *HHhH*, based on the assassination of Reinhard Heydrich in Prague in May 1942. In a manner reminiscent of the eponymous author in Laurence Sterne's *The Life and Opinions of Tristram Shandy*, Binet—"a slave to my scruples"—engages in continuous dialogue with the reader and himself about how his narrative is progressing, writing and then challenging fictive dialogue and descriptive phrases for which he has no hard evidence.[1]

If not as avowedly intellectual as Binet's tour de force, and written with the different purpose of using historical personalities as a supporting cast in entirely fictional adventures, Russell's quartet of interconnected novels are considerably more than run-of-the-mill thrillers. They convincingly

1. Binet, *HHhH*, section 239 (this work is divided into sections but does not carry page numbers); Sterne, *Life and Opinions of Tristram Shandy*; Binet, *HHhH*, section 8.

evoke the atmosphere, sounds, and appearance of Dublin before and during World War II (or "the Emergency" as it was known in Ireland). Russell's narratives are located in a febrile political environment where basic loyalty—whose, and to what—is often in question. The pious public face of newly independent Ireland does not entirely conceal more interesting if problematic aspects of Irish life well known among those in authority if not among the general public. These include homosexual clergy; a Magdalene asylum where a chilly mother superior rules the roost over generations of "fallen" girls decaying through decades of incarceration into simple-minded old women; illegal abortions; the openly gay, behind-the-curtain culture of the Gate Theatre; and so on.

Furthermore, Russell's novels locate the experience of their fictional protagonist, Stefan Gillespie, a Garda Síochána detective, against the backdrop of the recent rebellion against British rule, the subsequent civil war of 1922–23, and the persistence of a militant republican strand in Irish life—a strand that would form alliances with any state or movement capable of defeating Britain. These are the forces that, along with German intrigue, frame the world within which Gillespie must solve his mysteries. Not the least of these concerns the drowning of his young wife while taking a solitary early morning swim, a matter that is only resolved in the third book of the series. In each volume, Gillespie's investigation of apparently straightforward private crimes leads him into areas where politics and international intrigue greatly complicate his inquiries, to the benefit of the reader if not of Russell's bemused protagonist.

This essay discusses Russell's *City* quartet primarily in terms of his use of historical events and personalities. The last twenty-five years have seen the release of huge tranches of British and Irish intelligence and security records, which historians have used to explore Irish radical politics and the intersection of Irish domestic and international affairs in the 1930s and 1940s. That work in turn has enabled Russell and other authors to produce well-grounded historical fiction with Irish security themes.[2] Maurice

2. For a now outdated discussion, see Jeffery and O'Halpin, "Ireland in Spy Fiction," 92–116.

Manning's *The Kilderry Files* (2018) accords an important role to the peerless intelligence officer Colonel Dan Bryan (1900–1985), whom I knew in his last years.[3] But Russell's work most closely resembles another recent Irish-themed series, Joe Joyce's troika of *Echo* thrillers set in Ireland during World War II, which also has some recourse to historical figures.[4] In style Russell's work can also be compared with the Canada-based John Brady's series of detective novels set in Ireland, beginning with the excellent *A Stone of the Heart* (1988), in which the Garda murder squad protagonist Matt Minogue, a County Clare man turned reluctant Dublin dweller, operates in a milieu where few colleagues and fewer superiors can be trusted.[5]

Stefan Gillespie, as a Protestant from a small farm in County Wicklow, has a slightly ambiguous status as a sort of "outside insider" in a very Catholic Ireland and an overwhelmingly Catholic police force. As a widower, he is obliged to allow his son to be raised in the Catholic faith due to that church's *Ne Temere* rule governing mixed marriages. Through his mother, Gillespie is also fluent in German. This enables the author to embroil the young detective in adventures involving IRA/German intrigue before and during the war, providing a reason why the Garda commissioner might entrust him with confidential tasks involving prewar trips to Danzig, New York, Lisbon, and civil war–torn Spain as well as a visit to wartime Germany.

In approach and ambition, the *City* series stands comparison with the writings of Philip Kerr and of Alan Furst. Russell can also be compared with Eric Ambler, whose prewar writings, particularly *The Mask of Dimitrios* (1939), did not simply evoke foreign and often exotic locales but described them through the eyes and experiences of the people who lived there as much as through those of his various British protagonists.[6] Furst has a similar talent, creating convincing characters—Poles, Spaniards, Bulgarians, Frenchmen—from across interwar and World War II Europe. Like

3. Manning, *Kilderry Files.*

4. Joyce, *Echoland*; Joyce, *Echobeat*; and Joyce, *Echowave.*

5. Brady, *Stone of the Heart.* For a full listing of Brady's works, see www.johnbradysbooks.com.

6. Ambler, *Mask of Dimitrios.*

Ambler's and Russell's works, Furst's novels vary in quality and depth, but all are underpinned by his convincing depiction of the places and peoples about whom he writes.

Russell's technique of populating his novels with real historical characters whom the protagonist encounters is hardly new. In recent decades the thriller writer Philip Kerr has used it repeatedly in his stories featuring the hard-boiled but essentially honest Bernie Gunther, World War I veteran and Berlin detective turned private eye turned intelligence officer turned postwar fugitive. Gunther makes his way through some thirteen novels, and in each of them he interacts with historical figures notorious for their Nazi links and deeds before, during, and after World War II.[7] Initially convincing, especially in the first three Gunther stories rebranded by Penguin as *Berlin Noir* (1993), this *diabolus ex machina* device becomes rather worn out over time. With each subsequent novel, the experienced reader of Kerr's Gunther books waits resignedly to see which real Nazi will turn up where, whether in full garb before and during the war, or behind shaded glasses and high walls somewhere in Central or South America after it.[8]

In some respects Russell has an easier task in that he can choose from a broader palette of historical figures rather than being confined mainly to notorious war criminals, their names known to posterity only through their villainy. He references various government ministers, politicians, judges, officials, lawyers, and public figures over the course of his four novels, and accords some of them quite significant roles in his narratives. The Gate Theatre's Micheál MacLiammóir (1899–1978) appears in two of the novels, portrayed in a very sympathetic light as a compassionate man who wears his homosexuality as a defiant badge of honor. Various real diplomats make appearances, displaying varying degrees of competence. These include Joseph Walshe (1886–1956), the punctilious, feline, and long-serving secretary of the Department of External Affairs from 1927 to 1946; Leo T. McCauley (1896–1979), consul general in New York from 1934 to 1946; Leopold Kerney (1881–1962), the hapless Irish minister in Spain from

7. Kerr's Bernie Gunther novels are listed and discussed at https://berniegunther.com/.

8. Kerr, *Berlin Noir.*

1935 to 1946; William Warnock (1911–86), the inexperienced Irish chargé d'affaires in Berlin from 1939 to 1943; Robert Brennan (1881–1964), the bumbling Irish minister in Washington from 1934 to 1947; and Séan Lester (1888–1959), who represented Ireland at the League of Nations before serving as League of Nations High Commissioner in Danzig from 1934 to 1937, and later became the last secretary-general of the League of Nations.[9] They are all well-drawn, though it is unlikely that any of these would have uttered so coarse an epithet as "fuck," particularly in the presence of a very junior Garda officer. Seán Russell and Frank Ryan, leading IRA men who became Nazi collaborators, are also accorded significant roles in two of the volumes. The writer and Nazi broadcaster Francis Stuart (1902–2000), who was on the margins of IRA/German intrigue in Berlin, also makes a brief appearance, as does Roger Casement's one-time assistant Robert Monteith.[10]

A handful of Germans also feature. These include the key agent Herman Goertz, who arrived by parachute in May 1940 and was at liberty until November 1941, the highpoint of whose Irish mission was a secret meeting with the fascist General Eoin O'Duffy. The intelligence officer Helmut Clissmann, who was involved in intrigues with the IRA and with Frank Ryan in Berlin and in Madrid, appears, as do two overbearing German Legation diplomats, Henning Thomsen and Dr. Carl Petersen, the latter a surprisingly louche figure whose amours and drinking were faithfully recorded by the Special Branch and G2 (Irish military intelligence). The loathsome Nazi judge Rudolf Freisler is accorded a brief cameo. The slippery Spanish lawyer Jaime Michels de Champourcin, who helped arrange Ryan's fake escape from a Burgos jail in 1940, is also portrayed.[11]

Russell's novels place appropriate emphasis on the external environment within which Gillespie's adventures take place. He reiterates the key point that the IRA's foreign links were important not simply for what they might actually deliver, but for how these relationships would be appraised,

9. Gageby, *Last Secretary General.*

10. Barrington, *Wartime Broadcasts of Francis Stuart*; Donoghue, *Hitler's Irish Voices.*

11. The activities of Goertz and Clissmann are discussed at length in Hull, *Irish Secrets*; O'Halpin, *Spying on Ireland*; and O'Halpin, *MI5 and Ireland.*

particularly by Britain and the United States. One of the key challenges facing the state from 1938—when the first evidence of German use of Ireland for intelligence purposes emerged—was not simply to control the IRA and to prevent foreign powers from using Ireland as a base to spy on Britain and her allies, but to demonstrate that this could best be done by the Irish government. The British (and from 1942 the Americans) took some convincing. On 29 May 1940, as France was crumbling in the face of Germany's assault, the newly appointed British prime minister Winston Churchill was informed that from a security point of view "the most urgent matter" was Ireland: "The War Office state categorically that the IRA is well-armed and well organised," whereas the Irish army was "little short of derisory . . . the Germans have plans to land troops by parachute and aircraft."[12] The danger was that Britain, having seen with what ruthless dispatch Hitler had gobbled up key Western European states in three short months, would immediately occupy Ireland, with the quiet support of the Roosevelt administration if not of the United States Congress. Britain's objectives would be to thwart any IRA-assisted German attack and to seize control of ports and airfields for Atlantic operations. But the Royal Ulster Constabulary inspector general, whose Special Branch had very close links with their Dublin equivalents, took a very different view of Irish security. He advised that the Garda Síochána were "quite expert" at dealing with the IRA, while the British security service MI5 also grew increasingly confident that G2 was a competent partner in counterespionage against German agents.[13] The highly effective and highly secret Irish management of security relations with Britain did as much as declared neutrality and the moral shield of international opinion to keep Ireland from combat, when so many other neutrals were overrun or otherwise drawn into the conflict.

Russell shows a commendable grasp of the curiosities of newly independent Ireland, where the political system was dominated by people who, having together rebelled against British rule, then fought a bitter though not very bloody civil war over the Anglo-Irish Treaty of December 1921,

12. Morton to Churchill, 29 May 1940, quoted in O'Halpin, *Spying on Ireland*, 93.

13. O'Halpin, *Spying on Ireland*, 100; O'Halpin, *MI5 and Ireland*, 51–76.

which granted twenty-six Irish counties practical independence within the British Empire, while the six northeastern counties remained within the United Kingdom as the self-governing province of Northern Ireland. The memory of this civil war lingered, although most of the losing side became grudgingly reconciled to the settlement under the leadership of Éamon de Valera, who in 1927 signaled acceptance of the new state and its constitutional arrangements by bringing his new party, Fianna Fáil, into Dáil Éireann. Within five years Fianna Fáil moved from the opposition benches into government through a peaceful transition of power following victory in the February 1932 general election.

Russell makes much use of two key figures from the years that followed, as de Valera saw off the challenges posed by the residual IRA and by the quasi-fascist Blueshirt movement. The charismatic but unbalanced Blueshirt leader General Eoin O'Duffy (1892–1944) had been an effective pro-Treaty army officer during the civil war, before becoming the inspiring leader and developer of the new police force, An Garda Síochána, in the autumn of 1922. But he was an erratic man. Although he was known to have planned a coup to prevent de Valera taking office, the Fianna Fáil government waited a full year before removing him as commissioner in 1933. Their patience was striking evidence of de Valera's decision not to conduct the wholesale purge of the machinery of state that many Fianna Fáil supporters had expected.[14] O'Duffy then built the Army Comrades Association, centered on discontented pro-Treaty veterans of the civil war, who soon became known simply as the Blueshirts.

But the new Ireland had little appetite for a self-made fascist generalissimo, or for the leftist republicans against whom he railed and who in the mid-1930s competed ineffectually with the mainstream IRA for ownership of the radical mantle.[15] The leftists included Frank Ryan, who made the ideologically curious journey from fighting in the International Brigade during the Spanish Civil War to working in Nazi Germany as an adviser on Irish matters. This romantic figure has received perhaps disproportionate

14. O'Halpin, *Defending Ireland*, 123.

15. For a balanced biography see McGarry, *Eoin O'Duffy*.

interest from biographers.[16] In 1936 O'Duffy led over 700 Blueshirts to fight against Godless communism alongside General Franco's mutineers in Spain, but this short-lived exercise in international Catholic and fascist solidarity proved a dismal, embarrassing failure. Thereafter the Blueshirt movement faded away with surprising suddenness. O'Duffy rotted on the political sidelines like an unused substitute pining for glory, secretly representing himself to German and Italian diplomats as the man who could bring Ireland into the Axis fold. He died a brandy-soaked death in 1944, coincidentally the same year that claimed the life of his would-be leftist nemesis Frank Ryan.[17]

Michael Russell is correct to depict the anti-Treaty IRA, bested in the field in 1923, as a significant force in Irish politics, a potential rival to the state's security organs and friend to whichever of Britain's enemies would pay it any attention. In the mid-1920s the IRA had acted as a kind of international espionage service for the Soviet Union, collecting intelligence in return for money, as is clear from the pioneering work of Thomas Mahon and Jim Gillogly in *Decoding the IRA*.[18] They show that the IRA used a very high grade Soviet coding system, as confirmed by Dan Bryan, who recalled supervising fruitless efforts to decode messages smuggled to and from IRA chief Maurice Twomey when he was in military custody in 1935.[19]

Fianna Fáil's ascent to power led to much apprehension in the Garda Síochána, its leadership full of men handpicked by O'Duffy, and in the skeletal army, which had to accept as their minister for defense Frank Aiken, who as the anti-Treaty IRA's chief of staff in May 1923 had issued the "dump arms" order that ended the civil war if not with a bang then at least with a faint whimper of defiance. Dan Bryan recalled that army concerns about a purge in 1932 soon dissipated: "This atmosphere fairly soon broke down . . . the creation of those good relations may have been due to

16. Cronin, *Frank Ryan*; O'Loughlin, *Frank Ryan*; McGarry, *Frank Ryan*; Hoar, *Red and Green.*

17. McGarry, *Eoin O'Duffy*, 339–48.

18. Mahon and Gillogly, *Decoding the IRA*.

19. Bryan, personal transcript, 16 February 1984, 2 (copy given by Colonel Bryan to the author in September 1984).

a considerable extent to the personality of the Minister for Defence, Mr Frank Aiken."[20]

Russell's depiction of the complexities of allegiance, loyalty, and duty within the Garda Síochána is particularly well-done. This is so both as regards Special Branch's antagonistic relationship with the rest of the force and tensions within the Special Branch itself. Faced with the growing street activism of both O'Duffy's preening Blueshirts and their IRA opponents, the new Garda Commissioner Éamon "Ned" Broy, a one-time agent of Michael Collins, recruited about fifty former anti-Treaty IRA men as armed detectives in a new Special Branch unit, quickly nicknamed the "Broy Harriers," to take on both the Blueshirts and the IRA. The Blueshirt bubble more or less burst in August 1934 when O'Duffy, faced with a state ban and the mobilization of military and police resources against him, abandoned plans for a Mussolini-style march on Leinster House (the seat of Dáil Éireann and Seanad Éireann). In contrast, the IRA threat became greater as time passed. The influx of Broy Harriers into the Special Branch caused particular bitterness among the IRA, who regarded the Harriers as traitors, but it also facilitated IRA penetration of the Special Branch. Events in 1939 and 1940 were to show that a handful of Harriers remained closet IRA supporters.

J. Bowyer Bell's uncritical oral history of militant republicanism, *The Secret Army* (1970), argues that the Broy Harriers were particularly hard on their former comrades. Russell provides a fictional instance of this in the brutal Garda Inspector Danny Skehan. On the other hand, the IRA veteran Christy Quearney (1918–2010), a lifelong anti-state militant arrested on various occasions in the 1930s and 1940s, and a republican diehard, never found the Special Branch unduly rough: he believed that this was precisely because many were Broy Harriers. On one occasion, after receiving a one-year jail term for the relatively anodyne offense of possession of seditious literature, a detective sergeant remarked: "God, Christy, that's an appalling sentence."[21]

20. Bryan, personal transcript, 16 February 1984, 1.

21. Bell, *Secret Army*, 187 and 227; O'Halpin, interview with Christopher Quearney.

One trope running through the *City* series is that of IRA sympathizers within the Broy Harriers. This was indeed a serious problem. Not long before the Magazine Fort raid of December 1939, "our Pearl Harbor" as Bryan termed it, in which the IRA briefly captured most of the army's ammunition stocks, G2 warned the Garda that "there was [*sic*] five wrong people in the police," and that the IRA appeared to be preparing for some major action in Dublin.[22] These warnings were ignored.[23] More embarrassing still, in April 1940 a bomb exploded inside the Special Branch office in Dublin Castle, wounding a number of officers. Russell uses this episode in *The City of Lies*. The ex–Broy Harrier who aided the IRA in this coup, Sergeant Jim Crofton, was eventually jailed after attempting to help the fugitive German agent Herman Goertz escape to France.[24]

As a writer of fiction is entitled to do, Russell somewhat overeggs the historical pudding in according G2 both the will and the capacity to send an officer abroad undercover in the 1930s: such a proposition would have been unthinkable, not only on financial grounds but lest the army be accused of threatening Ireland's friendly relations with other states. Furthermore, the G2 chief from 1930 to 1941, Colonel Liam Archer, was cautious by nature, and as the Irish Section of MI5 observed in 1946, "inclined to limit his co-operation rather strictly." The G2 officer Dan Bryan, by contrast, "was wrapped up in Intelligence work for its own sake."[25] He also had the advantage that, in the name of defending neutrality, the army expanded between 1939 and 1942 from about 7,000 to over 42,000 men, with a consequent growth in intelligence-gathering capacity throughout the state. This enabled G2 to make inquiries and to accumulate information not only on foreign intrigue but also on the republican movement, and to do so independently of the Garda Special Branch, who "were not happy"

22. Bryan, personal transcript, 7 March 1984, 49 (recorded in discussion with Eunan O'Halpin).

23. Bryan, personal transcript, 7 March 1984, 47 (recorded in discussion with Eunan O'Halpin).

24. O'Halpin, *Defending Ireland*, 205.

25. O'Halpin, *MI5 and Ireland*, 62.

but could do nothing about it.[26] This expansion also allowed the development of a highly efficient coastwatching and air movements reporting organization, which produced a continuous mass of information, shared with the relevant British fighting services.[27] Russell understands the importance of such sub rosa Anglo-Irish cooperation in maintaining relations between Irish and British professionals at a time when their respective political masters were publicly at odds, and in giving the lie to claims that neutral Ireland represented an unacceptable security risk to Britain and her allies.

Russell lays stress on the highly Catholic nature of independent Ireland and on the consequent chill in the air for religious minorities. He also explores undercurrents and subtexts relating to the precarious position of Jews. Among his dramatis personae is the Jewish Fianna Fáil TD Robert Briscoe, the son of a Lithuanian immigrant and an assiduous worker for Jewish interests internationally. Russell also picks up on the thread of anti-Semitism that ran through a good deal of semipublic discourse, particularly from the Catholic right and from O'Duffy's Blueshirt movement (and after 1939 in the IRA's underground propaganda bulletin *War News*). But he perhaps misrepresents the impact of the 1937 constitution. While it did indeed recognize the "special position" of the Catholic Church, it also protected religious freedom generally. It explicitly recognized various Protestant denominations and, most notable of all in the circumstances of the late 1930s, the Jewish community, a committee from which noted "with the greatest satisfaction and due appreciation that the 'Jewish Congregation' are included in the clause giving equal recognition to the religious bodies . . . and they respectfully tender congratulation on the production of such a fair and just comment."[28]

The one spiritual authority that signaled clear dissatisfaction was, ironically, the Vatican. When the hyper-pious Joseph Walshe of the Department of External Affairs visited the Vatican to brief them on the draft

26. Bryan, personal transcript, 7 March 1984, 4 (recorded in discussion with Eunan O'Halpin).

27. Kennedy, *Guarding Neutral Ireland*.

28. Rabbinate Committee of the Dublin Jewish Community to Éamon de Valera, 4 May 1937, in Hogan, *Origins of the Irish Constitution*, 547.

constitution, he was crestfallen to hear from the Cardinal Secretary of State—Eugenio Pacelli, later to be Pope Pius XII—"that the 'special position' given to the Catholic Church had no real value . . . the realisation given to the other churches mollified any advantage which might have been derived from exclusive recognition. He thought we should use the word 'tolerates' in regard to them." Pressed by Walshe for an assurance that the Pope himself did not object, Pacelli replied, "I do not approve, neither do I *not disapprove*; we shall maintain silence."[29]

A number of historical figures deployed by Russell were, like Gillespie, Protestant. In Danzig, Seán Lester—the County Antrim–born Presbyterian and one-time separatist propagandist turned international diplomat—and his wife prove themselves spirited, unflappable, and resourceful in saving Gillespie from a Nazi death squad. The Lesters' daughter Dorothy, who lived with them during their Danzig sojourn, later married Douglas Gageby, the legendary editor of the *Irish Times* in the 1960s and 1970s. Gageby, like Lester an Ulster Protestant, joined the Irish army in 1942. Being a German speaker, he served in G2 under Bryan, terming him "a remarkable man even in that remarkable generation."[30] William Warnock, who features fairly extensively in *The City of Lies*, was a member of the Church of Ireland. His disgraced anti-Semitic predecessor Charles Bewley, recalled from his position as minister to Germany in 1939, was the eccentric scion of a prominent Dublin Quaker family who had converted to Catholicism as a young man. He lived in Axis Europe throughout the war, pimping himself as a propaganda expert in both Berlin and Rome. After the war he settled in Italy, living the clichéd life of an affluent bachelor connoisseur and collector of fine art and porcelain. Another historical figure of Protestant stock who features briefly is Roger Casement's one-time assistant Robert Monteith, whom Russell nevertheless has blessing himself in distinctly Catholic fashion, while Judge Henry Hanna, quoted in *The City of Strangers*, was a northern Presbyterian. It is unclear whether or not

29. Walshe memorandum for de Valera, 22 April 1937, in Crowe, Fanning, Kennedy, Keogh, and O'Halpin, *Documents on Irish Foreign Policy*, 49–53.

30. Gageby, "Colonel Dan Bryan."

Russell's inclusion of so many non-Catholic employees of the overwhelmingly Catholic state is intentional, but in either case it serves to make the point that non-Catholics had found it possible to serve the new Ireland.

Russell's first Stefan Gillespie novel, *The City of Shadows*, opens in the summer of 1932, just months after Éamon de Valera peacefully assumed power. Taking place in Dublin to mark the 1,500th anniversary of St. Patrick's arrival in Ireland, the 31st Eucharistic Congress—the Catholic spiritual equivalent of the Olympic Games—had a calming influence on public life and discourse, diverting attention from partisan politics into fervent demonstrations of Catholic devotion and piety. It provided the army with an unparalleled opportunity to strut their stuff in wholly uncontroversial ceremonial duties.[31] The Congress also facilitated a spiritual reconciliation between the Church and the great majority of republicans, whose civil war campaign had been condemned out of hand by the Catholic hierarchy in October 1922. Russell contrasts the aromas of oils, incense, and piety swirling around the Eucharistic Congress with life in Dublin's small gay demimonde, sometimes tolerated and sometimes persecuted by the authorities. The intersection of these worlds provides the initial plot line for Stefan Gillespie's first set of adventures, which bring him all the way to Danzig.

In *The City of Strangers*, the suggestion that the New York Police Department's detective division was both corrupt and in the pockets of the IRA's American supporters is not at all fanciful: the partiality of many municipal and state police forces in the United States toward Irish republicanism remained a systemic problem as late as the first decade of the Northern Ireland troubles of 1969–98.[32] The issue also arose with federal agencies: the papers of the veteran Irish republican leader Ruairí Ó Brádaigh (1932–2013) contain material copied from Federal Bureau of Investigation (FBI) records relating to Irish republicanism between September 1973 and February 1975 leaked by "a decent senior FBI special agent sympathetic to Irish American activists."[33]

31. O'Halpin, *Defending Ireland*, 80 and 103.

32. O'Halpin, "British Intelligence," 180–85.

33. MacFhínin, Note; O'Halpin, "British Intelligence," 180–85.

Russell's treatment of Irish American republicanism focuses on the fictional Dominic Murray, whose actions very much resemble those of Joe McGarrity (1874–1940), who controlled the republican group Clan na Gael and who was at the center of Irish separatism's unfortunate German relationships in both world wars.[34] The ambiguity of McGarrity's relations with Dublin is reflected in how the Irish minister to the United States, Robert Brennan, described his warm reception at McGarrity's obsequies: "The Clan was in very strong force but they were all genial," and he was given "the place of honour at the funeral." He never picked up a whisper of McGarrity's German intrigues, an indictment of Brennan's competence rather than of McGarrity's loyalty to the state.[35] In Russell's novel, however, the problem is already well known in 1939 to Irish diplomats in America, to G2, and to the Garda Special Branch.[36]

The City in Darkness attempts a fictional reconstruction of Frank Ryan's last months with the International Brigade in the Spanish Civil War. He witnesses the brutality of both sides, and helps to hide a wounded young Irish member of O'Duffy's ill-fated Irish Brigade. In keeping with his reputation as a ladies' man, Ryan is also provided with a heroic Spanish lover. By the time Gillespie reaches Spain, his mission being to help the Irish minister to Spain Leopold Kerney, Frank Ryan is in a Burgos jail under threat of execution. Gillespie meets him before his staged escape, during which an uncommunicative Seán Russell, now working hand-in-glove with German intelligence, turns up, though in reality the two IRA leaders only met up in Berlin in June 1940. Gillespie works closely with Kerney, who was involved in the escape scheme. Ryan's whereabouts remained a mystery to his Irish friends and to G2 until 1941. Only after the war did some details emerge of his dealings with German intelligence. These included an abortive submarine journey to Ireland in August 1940 to lay the ground for a pro-German coup. Further activities included training agents, advising on Irish matters, and assisting Helmut Clissmann in an approach to the ever-gullible Kerney

34. For a sympathetic account of McGarrity, see Cronin, *McGarrity Papers*.

35. O'Halpin, "Endword," 835.

36. Brennan, correspondence with J. C. Walsh.

in 1942—"the Madrid betrayal" as Joseph Walshe later termed it—which could have had grave implications for neutrality and about which the British were very well informed through decoded German communications.[37] Ryan, weakened by his Spanish incarceration, died in Dresden in 1944. Gillespie naturally knows none of this in 1939, but when he visits Berlin less than a year later he encounters a somewhat cynical Ryan for one last time.

In *The City of Lies* Russell writes convincingly about the febrile atmosphere in Ireland during the spring and early summer of 1940, when it appeared likely that either the British—to preempt a German attack and to gain control of Irish ports and airfields—or the Germans and their IRA friends would attempt to seize the state. He compounds two separate incidents—the killing by the IRA's Paddy McGrath and Thomas Harte of two detectives in Rathgar, and the unsuccessful attempt to seize the British representative's mail from its Garda escort in May. McGrath had been released from detention in December 1939 after de Valera yielded to calls not to let a 1916 veteran die on a hunger strike, but the Rathgar killings changed the atmosphere radically. McGrath and Harte were sentenced to death by a military tribunal—itself composed of former War of Independence veterans now in military garb—and executed by firing squad. These deaths and those of four others convicted of murder or attempted murder between 1940 and 1944 were bitterly resented by republicans, but what was the state to do when the IRA started killing its servants?

The matter-of-fact way in which tough justice was administered thereafter is nicely captured in the cryptic daily diary entries of Colonel J. V. Joyce, a 1916 and War of Independence veteran, who sat on the Military Tribunal that dealt with serious political crime during the Emergency. In February 1942 he heard the case of George Plant, a respected IRA gunman and bank robber whom a fellow prisoner recalled as a quiet, pleasant, and studious man despite his colorful career, and two others charged with killing a suspected informer in 1940.[38] All three were sentenced to death:

37. O'Halpin, *Defending Ireland*, 196–97; and O'Halpin, *Spying on Ireland*, 186.

38. O'Halpin, interview with Christopher Quearney.

> Plant took it well & clicked his heels, Davern said "thank you," but Walsh seemed "shook". . . .
>
> Relief to get it all over.

In the event, only Plant, one of a handful of Protestant IRA men, was executed: Joyce noted that "he died, as I thought he would, without flinching."[39]

What remained of the IRA decided to get their own back in 1942, assassinating the former Broy Harrier Sergeant Denis O'Brien as he left his home. O'Brien had a very strong 1916, War of Independence, and civil war "record": in 1935 the militant republican Seán Dowling, himself to be involved in IRA/German intrigue in 1940, found "much pleasure" in providing the military pensions board with a glowing account of O'Brien's outstanding conduct during the 1916 Rising.[40] It is perhaps significant that his killers were young men without any 1916–23 experience.

The City of Lies brings Gillespie to Berlin, the heart of Nazi darkness. His mission is to bring new codes, as External Affairs suspects that their diplomatic traffic is being read in both London and Berlin. But in reality it was irrelevant what the Germans or British thought of Warnock's prognostications from Berlin. To complain of their contents would have revealed to the Irish the fact that they were being decoded. Furthermore, the highest-level Irish wartime code, *dearg* (red), was a one-time pad system that was extremely secure. British records show that for several months before the invasion of Normandy, when there were grave concerns that war information might leak out through Ireland, British codebreakers could not break *dearg* traffic between Dublin and Berlin.[41] The records also show that Churchill took a particular personal interest in Irish traffic from Rome in 1943, probably because the vastly experienced Irish minister Michael MacWhite—a much-decorated World War I French Foreign Legion veteran—produced well-informed, sophisticated political reports whereas the

39. J. V. Joyce, diary.

40. Dowling, letter to Pensions Board.

41. Memorandum, National Archives (London).

one-man Irish legation in Berlin had very little access to the higher levels of German bureaucracy.[42]

Writers of historical fiction have no particular duty to be either accurate or fair, but only to interest and to entertain. But an air of vérité and a clear understanding of wider political and international contexts undoubtedly adds authority to such works, and this Michael Russell certainly provides.

Bibliography

Ambler, Eric. *The Mask of Dimitrios*. London: Hodder & Stoughton, 1939.

Barrington, Brendan, ed. *The Wartime Broadcasts of Francis Stuart*. Dublin: Lilliput Press, 2001.

Bell, J. Bowyer. *The Secret Army: The IRA, 1916–1970*. London: Anthony Blond, 1970.

Binet, Laurent. *HHhH*. Grassit & Fasquelle: Paris, 2009; trans., London: Vintage, 2012.

Brady, John. *A Stone of the Heart*. Toronto: St. Martin's Press, 1988.

Brennan, Robert. Correspondence with J. C. Walsh, 12 August 1940. Box 1, fol. 2, Joseph Cyrillus Walsh papers, New York Public Library.

Bryan, Dan. Personal transcript, 16 February 1984. Private collection of the author.

———. Personal transcript, 7 March 1984. Private collection of the author.

Cronin, Séan. *Frank Ryan: The Search for the Republic*. Dublin: Repsol, 1980.

———. *The McGarrity Papers*. Tralee: Anvil Books, 1973.

Crowe, Catriona, Ronan Fanning, Michael Kennedy, Dermot Keogh, and Eunan O'Halpin, eds. *Documents on Irish Foreign Policy*. Vol. 5, *1937–1939*. Dublin: Royal Irish Academy, 2006.

Donoghue, David. *Hitler's Irish Voices: the Story of German Radio's Wartime Irish Service, 1941–44*. Belfast: Beyond the Pale, 1998.

Dowling, Sean. Letter to Pensions Board, 23 February 1935. Military Archives of Ireland (MAI), MSP, WMSP34REF1281DENISO'BRIEN.pdf. Accessed 29 June 2018 via http://mspcsearch.militaryarchives.ie/search.aspx.

Gageby, Douglas. "Colonel Dan Bryan: An Appreciation." *Irish Times*, 18 June 1985.

———. *The Last Secretary General: Séan Lester and the League of Nations*. Dublin: Townhouse, 1999.

42. O'Halpin, *Spying on Ireland*, 227–30; and O'Halpin, *Defending Ireland*, 184–85.

Hoar, Adrian. *In Red and Green: The Lives of Frank Ryan*. Tralee: Brandon Books, 2004.

Hogan, Gerard, ed. *The Origins of the Irish Constitution, 1928–1941*. Dublin: Royal Irish Academy, 2012.

Hull, Mark M. *Irish Secrets: German Espionage in Wartime Ireland, 1939–1945*. Dublin: Irish Academic Press, 2003.

Jeffery, Keith, and Eunan O'Halpin. "Ireland in Spy Fiction." In *Spy Fiction, Spy Film and Real Intelligence*, edited by Wesley Wark, 92–116. London: Frank Cass, 1991.

Joyce, Joe. *Echobeat*. Dublin: Liberties, 2016.

———. *Echoland*. Dublin: Liberties, 2014.

———. *Echowave*. Dublin: Liberties, 2017.

Joyce, J. V. Diary, 26 February and 6 March 1942. J. V. Joyce papers, Military Archives of Ireland (MAI).

Kennedy, Michael. *Guarding Neutral Ireland: The Coast Watching Service and Military Intelligence, 1939–1945*. Dublin: Four Courts Press, 2008.

Kerr, Philip. *Berlin Noir*. London: Penguin Books, 1993.

MacFhínin, Peadar. Note. Ó Brádaigh papers, POL28/89(2), undated (c. 2005 or later). Hardiman Library, National University of Ireland Galway.

Mahon, Thomas, and Jim Gillogly. *Decoding the IRA*. Cork: Mercier Press, 2008.

Manning, Maurice M. *The Kilderry Files*. Dublin: Columba Press, 2018.

McGarry, Fearghal. *Eoin O'Duffy: A Self-Made Hero*. Oxford: Oxford Univ. Press, 2005.

———. *Frank Ryan*. Dublin: UCD Press, 2002.

Memorandum to Miss Reid and A. G. Denniston re: unreadable Irish messages, 15 May 1944. HW53/56, National Archives, London (TNA).

O'Halpin, Eunan. "British Intelligence, PIRA, and the Early Years of the Northern Ireland Crisis: Remembering, Forgetting and Mythologising." In *The Image of the Enemy: Intelligence Analysis of Adversaries since 1945*, edited by Paul Maddrell, 180–85. Washington, DC: Georgetown Univ. Press, 2015.

———. *Defending Ireland: the Irish State and Its Enemies since 1922*. Oxford: Oxford Univ. Press, 1999.

———. "Endword: Ireland Looking Outwards, 1880–2016." In *The Cambridge History of Ireland*, vol. 4, *1880 to the Present*, edited by Thomas Bartlett, 835. Cambridge: Cambridge Univ. Press, 2018.

———. Interview with Christopher Quearney (1918–2010), Trinity College Dublin, 19 October 2008.

———, ed. *MI5 and Ireland, 1939–1945: The Official History.* Dublin: Irish Academic Press, 2003.

———. *Spying on Ireland: British Intelligence and Irish Neutrality during the Second World War.* Oxford: Oxford Univ. Press, 2008.

O'Loughlin, Michael. *Frank Ryan: Journey to the Centre.* Dublin: Raven Arts, 1987.

Russell, Michael. *The City in Darkness.* London: Constable, 2016.

———. *The City in Flames.* London: Constable, 2019.

———. *The City of Lies.* London: Constable, 2017.

———. *The City of Shadows.* London: Avon, 2012.

———. *The City of Strangers.* London: HarperCollins, 2013.

Sterne, Laurence. *The Life and Opinions of Tristram Shandy.* London: Robert Dodsley, 1759.

PART THREE

Novelists and Readers

7

Ren Bryce

Hiding in Plain Sight

DECLAN BURKE

Hiding in plain sight is a strategy more often pursued by the villains of crime and mystery fiction than by those who seek to bring them to justice. In public, such villains act in the way civilized human beings are supposed to act, obeying society's rules and mores and behaving in a manner perceived as normal. Where they wear masks, those masks are the antithesis of the Halloween variety: rather than disguise themselves with striking imagery designed to engender fear and revulsion, the chameleon-like villain adopts a physical persona—neat haircut, buttoned-down clothing, etc.—created to reassure and to project the impression of a person willing and eager to conform.

Ren Bryce is not a villain. But Ren Bryce hides in plain sight.

The protagonist of six Alex Barclay novels, Bryce is an FBI special agent working for the Safe Streets Task Force based in Denver, Colorado. Although not a private eye, Bryce is a direct lineal descendant of Sara Paretsky's V. I. Warshawski and Sue Grafton's Kinsey Millhone, complex women possessed of a razor-sharp intellect complemented by empathy and emotional intelligence. But Bryce, like Warshawski and Millhone, is the complete package as a hard-boiled heroine: when the action gets physical, she thrives on the challenge.

The first novel, *Blood Runs Cold* (2008), establishes Bryce as a fully integrated member of an effective team that investigates the murder of her FBI colleague. Her professionalism is only belatedly established, however.

Our first glimpse of Ren finds her sprawled across the white porcelain of a toilet bowl, "her blue dress, beautiful and complimented twelve hours earlier . . . open to the waist, limp and stained" with red wine. Her stockings, Ren discovers, are "in the corner by the toilet brush."[1]

The reader is immediately reminded of Raymond Chandler's introduction of Philip Marlowe in *The Big Sleep* (1939), a private investigator dapper in his "powder-blue suit, with dark blue shirt, tie and display handkerchief, black brogues, black wool socks with dark blue clocks on them."[2] No hangover for Mr. Marlowe, who doesn't care who knows that he is "neat, clean, shaved and sober." The very idea that those natty socks with their dark blue clocks would end up in the vicinity of a toilet brush verges on sacrilege.

The contrast—hungover versus sober, the wine-stained blue dress and the pristine powder-blue suit, the discarded stockings and the whimsically beclocked socks—is too sharp to be coincidental. Ren Bryce is not to be considered Philip Marlowe's polar opposite: they are both on the side of the angels, both professional investigators in pursuit of truth and justice, both tarnished or otherwise imperfect in their own way. But where Philip Marlowe is unconventionally conventional, a man's man in a patriarchal world where it was not uncommon for a woman to be referred to as a "frail," Ren Bryce has *conventional* thrust upon her, obliged to don a mask of conformity as a consequence of being a woman living in a world that is still a man's world. Its patriarchal hierarchy is confirmed by the fact that Ren not only answers to a male boss, Gary Dettling, but is the protégé of her Quantico physical training instructor, Paul Louderback. She may not be a "frail," and scoffs when a colleague requests her assistance for her "feminine presence," but Ren Bryce is nevertheless emotionally fragile, constantly struggling with the manic highs and lows of a bipolar disorder. She embraces this condition for the short-term hyperintensive focus it provides her with, even as it—or, more accurately, Ren's self-neglect, as she

1. Barclay, *Blood*, 9.

2. Chandler, *Big Sleep*, 7.

refuses to take her medication and repeatedly engages in self-destructive behavior—threatens to destroy her long-term mental health.

Ren Bryce, however, hides in plain sight. In the depths of her hangover, having hauled herself off her porcelain crutch, "she walked past her dressing table, a wave of nausea sweeping over her at the thought of makeup."[3] Nevertheless, moments later she is seated before the mirror, her face "a blank canvas. . . . She dragged her makeup toward her and applied a calm surface."[4] Later, "Ren went to the bathroom with her makeup bag. One day she would put these trips on a résumé to signify her ambition."[5]

For Ren, makeup is more weapon than shield. When her colleague Robbie Truax suggests that he has been busy investigating a criminal while Ren was "fixing her makeup," Ren retorts, "That's crime-fighting in itself."[6] It's a recurring motif all the way through the six novels, to the extent that, in *The Drowning Child* (2016), Ren, rushing out to take a meeting, grabs her bag to do "a quick no-makeup makeup job."[7]

It's a simple, everyday routine for millions of women, the subtle application of foundation, mascara, and lipstick. This mask of nuance and accentuation is designed to camouflage and conceal, and noticeable only in its absence, a sacrament of the invisible that is—when Ren Bryce sits down before her mirror—akin to Spartan warriors grooming themselves before going into battle.

▪ ▪ ▪

She's an Everywoman, Ren Bryce. An all-dancing, all-boxing woman's woman who likes men, loves shoes, and would no more consider facing the world without makeup than without clothes. She's a fragile-but-strong latter-day Amazonian battling men—overbearing bosses, unworthy lovers, savage killers—on all fronts. Right? Well, mostly. Or partly, at least. Some of the time, anyway.

3. Barclay, *Blood*, 10.

4. Barclay, *Blood*, 10.

5. Barclay, *Blood*, 45.

6. Barclay, *Blood*, 260.

7. Barclay, *Child*, 76.

In fact, Ren Bryce would be a nightmare subject for the psychological profiling unit based at Quantico. A strong, independent feminist, she isn't above a little private snark: "When God was handing out good looks, this lady was in line at the bar. And the all-you-can-eat buffet,"[8] Ren remarks, observing later that a "mother and three blonde identicoiffed daughters bumped past her, confident that high hair, Fake Bake and miniskirts worked well across a forty-year age spread."[9] A traffic jam is caused by "another idiot lady driver in an SUV without chains."[10]

Women, we are given to understand, are not necessarily perfect, although few are less perfect, in Ren's eyes, than Ren Bryce herself. "*I am a loser. I am a terrible human being. I'm not human, in fact.*"[11] By her sixth outing in *The Drowning Child*—having resisted the urge to take her own life at the conclusion of the fifth novel, *Killing Ways* (2015)—Ren, blaming herself for multiple murders, is so traumatized by her own behavior that she is locked into a vicious dialogue with her inner demon:

> *I am taking [my meds], and I will continue to take them for the rest of my life, because I believe that not taking them killed my friends, and killed my boyfriend. There's the reality: my friends, my boyfriend, my loved ones, are dead because I didn't open a packet of pills and swallow them down with a glass of water like a good mental patient. Because I was too busy being mental. And wanting to feel good.*[12]

Suicidal ideation, manic highs and lows, alcohol abuse, reckless actions endangering colleagues—these, to put it mildly, are not characteristics of the conventional Everywoman law enforcement heroine. Not that Ren is unaware of her flaws. When she belatedly discovers that her psychiatrist, Dr. Helen Wheeler, was planning to write a book about her patients, Ren refuses to believe that she would have been one of Wheeler's subjects. "I

8. Barclay, *Blood*, 184.
9. Barclay, *Blood*, 398.
10. Barclay, *Blood*, 123.
11. Barclay, *Blood*, 245.
12. Barclay, *Child*, 74.

mean, it's not like I'm relatable to in the grand scheme of things. My case study is too unusual."[13]

Relatable? Certainly Ren Bryce is not the "likable" protagonist many contemporary crime fiction publishers seem to believe readers prefer—those heroes and heroines who, unburdened by moral or philosophical complexities, see the world as black-and-white as any chessboard. Their parameters are firmly established, their progress governed by rules and conventions, their conclusions inevitable, preordained, and limited.

Ren Bryce doesn't play chess. She is a mass of contradictions, a complex character of multiple complexes—assertive yet insecure, capable of great kindnesses and brutal violence, smart when it comes to saving others' lives but dumb as a hard-drinking post in managing her own health. She is intuitive when solving crimes and sociopathic when tracking criminals but utterly deaf to her inner guardian angel when it pleads for mercy on her own behalf.

In short, Ren Bryce is so frustratingly contradictory, so maddeningly and realistically multifaceted a character, that the reader is frequently moved to wonder what—or who—it is Ren Bryce actually sees as she sits in front of the mirror each morning applying her mask. Nothing worth celebrating, according to Ren:

> She stood in front of the mirror.
>
> *Here we go again.*
>
> *No pride to be found in that reflection. Don't waste your time.*[14]

Ren Bryce has very little in common with most of her peers in contemporary crime and mystery fiction, who deliver the illusion of justice that the genre peddles as a corrective to the scarcity of justice available in the real world (although the apprehending and incarceration of a killer, either in the real world or the realms of fiction, is itself an illusion of justice). Instead she is made of the good stuff, the messily toxic stuff, the hell-in-a-burning-handcart stuff, the stuff of ambition exceeding grasp, and the heroic

13. Barclay, *Death*, 117.

14. Barclay, *Child*, 229.

impulse doomed from the off by predestined flaw. The stuff of which truly great fiction has always been made.

▪ ▪ ▪

> Until Ren was diagnosed bipolar at twenty-six, she had never guessed that there was anything wrong with her. Mental illnesses were for the mentally ill. It seemed like one minute she was the youngest FBI agent to go under deep cover and blow apart an organized crime operation and the next, she was lying in her pyjamas on the sofa, eating junk food, crying, not answering her phone, drinking, obsessing about all the regrets she had in her life, wondering what point there was in doing anything again. Ever.[15]

It may well be that Bryce's bipolar condition is hereditary. Her parents don't seem to be affected, nor does her long-suffering brother, Matt, but we know that her younger brother, Beau, suffering from depression, took his own life. Perhaps Ren was genetically predisposed to the condition; perhaps not. But a crucial factor in its emergence was the undercover operation Ren took part in, before we first meet her in *Blood Runs Cold*, when she infiltrated the cartel run by Domenica Val Pando, playing the part of a children's nanny. It exacted an emotional toll: "She had spent one year looking after six-year-old Gavino Val Pando and trying to deny how much she really cared about him."[16]

In the Val Pando case and in general, we learn very quickly that Ren doesn't do half-measures. In *Blood Runs Cold*, she risked her career by falling in love with confidential informant Billy Waites; by the conclusion of the fifth novel, *Killing Ways*, her all-or-nothing approach to medicating her condition—in this case, nothing—persuades Ren that she is responsible for the death of friends and colleagues. In *Time of Death* (2010), we discover that Ren's inability to suppress her affection for young Gavino Val Pando undermined her professionalism in the undercover operation. When the assignment concludes in a hail of gunfire, Ren somehow manages to escape unharmed from the Val Pando compound, but she subsequently discovers that the invisible scars of betrayal and guilt will take significantly longer to

15. Barclay, *Death*, 18.

16. Barclay, *Death*, 17.

heal, if they ever do, especially as they are entirely incompatible with her "overwhelming compulsion to fix things"[17] and her unrealistic need for "everything to be perfect."[18]

Ren's skull is a pressure-cooker, her mind constantly simmering, boiling over, hissing steam, invective, and profanity. Diagnosed as bipolar in the wake of the Val Pando assignment, Ren occasionally wishes that she was back in the Val Pando compound, "because I was oblivious, I didn't know how lucky I was to be sane. Or at least to think I was sane."[19] But if there are times when Ren tries to ignore her condition, there are others when she embraces it, willfully abandoning her medication in order to accentuate the manic high: "*I can't afford to be numb. I need a sharp mind, I need to solve things, make connections, have clarity. I need to find a killer.*"[20]

Perhaps the undiagnosed Ren was already hiding in plain sight, managing the condition as best she could, unaware that her experience of highs and lows was not everyone's experience of the world. Doubling down by going undercover with a Mexican cartel—a rather extreme version of hiding in plain sight—caused the pressure-cooker to crack, the lid to blow. And even if she occasionally thinks she might prefer a blissful ignorance, the diagnosis at least allows Ren to own her condition, and—perhaps more importantly—question the world's negative perception of mental illness. "Sanity is bullshit," she tells Gary Dettling. "Sanity is like happiness; it comes, it goes, it feels good, it means one thing to me, something else to someone else."[21]

Ren might balk at the idea of being anyone's role model—waaaay too much pressure—besides, she believes she is not relatable, her case study too unusual. But it remains the case that she is a high-functioning FBI special agent, a trusted and admired member of her team, an attractive woman with a host of firm friends who is loved by men and admired by women.

17. Barclay, *Death*, 80.
18. Barclay, *Blood*, 279.
19. Barclay, *Death*, 20.
20. Barclay, *Killing Ways*, 174.
21. Barclay, *Blood*, 459.

She, better than anyone else, appreciates her flaws, the damage caused by her risky behavior(s), the chaos she leaves in her wake as she careers wildly up and down the roller coaster of her bipolar condition. Ultimately, however, Ren comes to an understanding with herself, an acceptance of her failings, an appreciation that things can never be perfect and, such being the case, she cannot hold herself uniquely responsible for fixing a broken world: "*Is that it? Do we all just aspire to be one thing, the best person who ever lived, when really, as we move through life, we realize that all we can be is the best flawed human being under the circumstances.*"[22]

> *Am I actually funny or do people just laugh because they're expecting Clarice Starling? I'm funny too, people. No screaming lambs, but lots of fucking voices.*[23]

Told in the third-person, the Ren Bryce novels provide the reader with the conventional narrative two-step: Ren's public engagement with the wider world as expressed through dialogue, and an interiority explored by way of internal monologue. Yet the novels are remarkably intimate and revealing as a consequence of Barclay employing a narrative third way—Ren's frequent mental interjections—delivered in italics on the page.

The target audience for these observations, commentaries, and contradictions is never made clear. Are they asides to the reader? Is Ren entertaining herself with funny quips as she waits for the rest of the world to catch up with the manic pace of her thinking? Are they the unfiltered wailing of a Greek chorus delivering a demented and often contradictory commentary on events as they unfold?

Early on in *Blood Runs Cold*, Ren is introduced to Tiny Gressett, a colleague of murdered FBI agent Jean Transom. Gressett makes a snide comment about Ren being parachuted into what he considers his investigation:

> "Oh," said Gressett. "Being that you're familiar with the area and all that." He smiled and laughed alone.

22. Barclay, *Child*, 380.
23. Barclay, *Child*, 124.

> "Nope, just being that I'm familiar with homicide investigation. . . ."
> *And being patronized by men who aren't.*
> "Well, good for you," said Gressett.
> "Yes, sir," said Ren. *Now can we please stop this bullshit?*[24]

It's a tactic that will serve Ren well throughout the six novels, saying one thing—particularly to overbearing men who don't take kindly to being challenged, queried, or interrogated by a woman—and meaning another. The unvoiced commentary allows her to blow off a little of that ever-hissing steam while also reminding the reader of the kind of casual, everyday sexism women are obliged to endure.

The italics serve many purposes, however, chief among them the regular reminder that Ren is not fully in control of her emotional and mental health. Talking over coffee with her friend, Janine, about a new love in Ren's life, Janine advises Ren against overthinking things:

> "Stop. Be kind to yourself."
> *I don't deserve kindness.*
> *Joe is kind.*
> *Fuck him.*[25]

In three very short, spare lines, Ren tumbles all the way from superego down to id, her instinctive, brutal verdict on Joe in particular and kindness in general entirely unnoticed and wholly unsuspected by Janine, even though Janine is at this point Ren's most trusted friend. Ren Bryce, hiding in plain sight, doesn't just don a mask; she silences the very words that reveal the true, unvarnished Ren Bryce. It is a conceit reminiscent of Brian Friel's Public Gar/Private Gar in *Philadelphia, Here I Come!*, although Public Ren and Private Ren are engaged in a vicious struggle for supremacy that might well conclude with Public Ren concurring with Private Ren's assessment that she does not deserve the privilege of being alive, not when her rash actions and reckless behavior caused the death of her friends, colleagues, and lover:

24. Barclay, *Blood*, 55.
25. Barclay, *Child*, 285.

I am louder than your kindest thought. I win. I always win. You're a mess, you always will be, you'll always feel, in your soul, that everything is about to go wrong and it's all your fault. Because it is your fault. . . .

Ren started to cry. *I'm so tired. I'm just so tired.*

Kill yourself, then. What's the point? End it.[26]

She does not, of course, and so the voices continue to screech and shriek. Not so much a Greek chorus as a flock of Furies, who relentlessly pursue Ren Bryce, demanding the ultimate vengeance for all the wrongs—real and imagined—that she has perpetrated.

▪ ▪ ▪

At some point, the reader feels, one of Ren Bryce's many good friends needs to take her to one side and gently break it to her that the role of FBI special agent may not be the ideal one for her. Unusually sensitive to others' pain as a consequence of her own experience of mental torment, Ren—despite her fondness for working the gym's punchbag—never really learns to roll with the punches. Each death is taken personally; her vivid imagination allows her to place herself in every victim's shoes; every mutilated corpse and dead child becomes a stick with which to beat her already fragile sense of self-esteem.

Ren is entirely bound up in what she is. *Blood Runs Cold* begins two years after she "had transferred to Denver from the high-intensity of Washington D.C. . . . She felt she was where she should have been from the moment she graduated."[27] It's not just the place, though, or the people she meets on the Safe Streets team; it's the job itself, the investigation of killers, the bringing them to justice. "I love my job," Ren tells Dr. Wheeler. "There's nothing else I can do."[28] Not that that should be a problem, because she's a top-notch professional, even though she won't allow herself to accept it: "'Look, you're good at your job,' said Paul [Louderback]. 'There it is. The thing you can't believe in.'"[29]

26. Barclay, *Killing Ways*, 398.

27. Barclay, *Blood*, 48.

28. Barclay, *Blood*, 257.

29. Barclay, *Blood*, 71.

Ren's devotion to her role begins to become an issue, however, when she fails to divorce what she is from who she is. It's not even that the two are inextricably linked; the job appears to have effaced her sense of her own identity: "After her own deep-cover assignment, Ren had gone the other way. Once it was all over, she wanted to reinforce who she was more than ever. The problem was, she had never worked out who Ren Bryce was. And somewhere along the way, she had given up."[30]

This is an issue that Ren never fully resolves. In the final novel, *The Drowning Child*, Louderback tries again to persuade Ren of her professional worth, and that her peers trust her to get the job done. "'Thanks,' said Ren. 'I love this job.' *I love being able to escape. Even though I keep showing up wherever I go.*"[31]

Near the close of that novel, in a conversation with Janine, Ren confesses that "'I don't know what's going on. I guess I'm finding it hard to process who I should be after all this.' She laughed. 'I don't know who I am any more.'"[32] The tone might be self-mocking, and the conversation about the suitability of a potential boyfriend rather than the job, but "all this" refers to the potential boyfriend being caught up in Ren's professional life, a reminder of the horrors she has seen, and the guilt she believes she bears for causing her friends' and colleagues' deaths. As always, the personal and professional are intertwined; as always, professional Ren, the public Ren, ultimately gets to call the shots, to define and negate the personal, private Ren Bryce.

But even as Ren loses sight of herself, she never forgets her primary goal; the more cynical and experienced she becomes, the more her focus turns to the young, the vulnerable, and the innocent. *Blood Runs Cold* opens as a conventional murder-mystery investigation into the killing of one of Ren's FBI colleagues, but *Time of Death*, while exploring Ren's backstory in terms of her undercover assignment with the Val Pando cartel, revolves around the whereabouts of two missing teenagers and the psychological damage

30. Barclay, *Death*, 11.
31. Barclay, *Child*, 229.
32. Barclay, *Child*, 284.

wrought on young Gavino Val Pando. *Blood Loss* (2012)—Barclay's most overtly political novel—takes Big Pharma to task, particularly in terms of the epidemic of children being prescribed antidepressants and antipsychotics. In *Harm's Reach* (2014), Ren investigates a cold case brought to light by the murder of a young pregnant woman near a ranch for troubled teenagers. *Killing Ways* finds Ren pursuing a brutal serial murderer of women, but at the novel's emotional core is a young girl who is the sadistic killer's ultimate target. Finally, *The Drowning Child* revolves around an investigation into suspicious deaths by drowning—although by then the title could just as easily refer to Ren herself:

> She inhaled the fresh smell of the water, the grass, the soil. She jammed her hands into her pockets, stared out across the surface.
>
> *God, I love lakes.*
>
> She was drawn to the water's edge, mesmerized by the rippling water. She walked closer.
>
> *I want to be down there.*
>
> *I want to be swallowed up.*[33]

She won't do it, of course. She's tougher than she looks, Ren Bryce; tougher than she thinks she is. Sure, she might wake up from a nightmare slick with sweat and wanting, childishly, nothing more than "someone to tell me it will all work out."[34] Maybe, okay, she's nowhere near as perfect as she seems to think she should be, and yes, she failed to save all those women and children she might have saved if only she'd been exactly that perfect. Maybe she hears more voices than any one person should; maybe she's not even the best flawed human being she can be.

But she's still there, hanging in, toughing it out at the end of the investigation, doing what she does best—catching killers, taking the depraved and the twisted off the board, and saving more lives than she loses—despite it all.

Ren Bryce may have never worked out who she is, but the reader instinctively understands what it is she represents.

33. Barclay, *Child*, 90.

34. Barclay, *Child*, 333.

If Ren Bryce, despite her myriad flaws, self-doubts, and self-sabotaging behaviors, can not only find her place in the world but also play a small but crucial part in changing that world for good, then perhaps we the readers—all of us struggling in our own way, all invisible men and women hiding in plain sight as we seek to negotiate our private path through the world—can take heart.

Bibliography

Barclay, Alex. *Blood Runs Cold*. London: Harper, 2008.

———. *The Drowning Child*. London: HarperCollins, 2016.

———. *Killing Ways*. London: HarperCollins, 2015.

———. *Time of Death*. London: Harper, 2010.

Chandler, Raymond. *The Big Sleep*. New York: Knopf, 1939.

8

The Ties That Bind

Arlene Hunt's QuicK Investigations

JOE LONG

Irish crime fiction owes a debt to Arlene Hunt. Together with work by Julie Parsons and Gemma O'Connor, Hunt's QuicK Investigations series—*False Intentions* (2005), *Black Sheep* (2006), *Missing Presumed Dead* (2007), *Undertow* (2008), and *Blood Money* (2010)—helped pave the way for many contemporary Irish crime writers, and it set a high bar from which the genre continues to benefit. The series, centering on QuicK partners John Quigley and Sarah Kenny, takes the characters on a journey that explores the underbelly of human existence. At the same time, Hunt writes with "a deceptive ease, a fluidity and a breezy wit that can veil some of the narratives' increasingly bleak matters."[1] The result is an engrossing, haunting, and heartful ride through a Dublin that, when the series first launched, was seldom explored.

Even as the series takes its unnerving journey through Dublin, the novels also draw readers into the relationship between the partners. Sarah and John keep us hoping for a happy ending, which the series has yet to provide: the most recent book, *Blood Money*, concludes with John leaving Dublin to find Sarah, who has gone into hiding. This hope carries over into the cases that each novel investigates, as Hunt's nuanced attention to the tenuous threads that connect us to each other becomes an interrogation of secrets

1. Cliff, *Irish Crime Fiction*, 126.

kept and lies told among those who love each other most. The result is a series that questions the courage it takes to risk bonds of intimacy and the obstacles that challenge that courage, all in turn explored through relationships between family and friends. As we will see, family structures are central to each case in the series as well as to the principal characters.

Through these structures and cases, Hunt both drives the plot and develops her primary characters, often indirectly, as through some of the criminals and their own families. Many aging gangsters lament where they went wrong, but few more grimly so than expat Patrick York in *False Intentions*. Forced back to Dublin when a drug deal he's overseen from Holland goes wrong, he finds Dublin's underworld has gone soft from easy Celtic Tiger money and a sense of entitlement: the younger criminals don't honor relationships, their extravagant lifestyles draw attention from the law, and they use their own product. He finds no honor among these thieves, most of all his son, who he has to remind to "at least brush the fucking nose candy out of your beard before you leave the house."[2] Other old criminals in the series, like Darren Wallace in *Undertow*, with his "quick temper and low tolerance for stupidity," are forced to clean up the messes of errant sons.[3] Though he had gone legit, Wallace has to reconnect with former associates to get his son off a hit list, but it pains him to see how a young man with every advantage on offer would turn to playing gangster. Both Wallace's and York's knucklehead nouveau-riche sons survive at the end of the novels in which they appear, unlike the series' young working-class men, who rarely fare so well. The ones who get caught up in circumstances largely beyond their control, like Mick Quinn in *Black Sheep*, are bathed in a sweeter light by Hunt.

Through Quinn, Hunt illustrates John's character, much as Sarah's deep concern for those around her shapes her character over the course of the series. Because he sees Mick as "a plucky kid with a good heart,"[4] worth so much more than the rich guys who work the system and have

2. Hunt, *False Intentions*, 445.

3. Hunt, *Undertow*, 173.

4. Hunt, *Black Sheep*, 390.

a chance to hide behind a veil of respectability, John does everything he can to give the kid comfort as he faces the prospect of prison. John's heart breaks a little at Mick's lost future, reflecting his tendency to wear his heart on his sleeve. As such moments suggest, John may be "a little rough around the edges, scruffy, impatient and he likes to bend things to suit himself,"[5] but even his nemesis, Sarah's sister Helen, comes around to seeing the good that's in him.

Helen, to be fair, has her reasons for mistrusting John: QuicK Investigations was set up when Sarah came home to Dublin after years in England, where she had moved after her relationship with John collapsed when he cheated on her. These are years about which no one in Sarah's Dublin circles—neither John nor her friends, siblings, or mother—knows much at all. As the series gradually reveals, Sarah was in a long, horrifically abusive relationship with Victor, a relationship that ended only when she set him up for a drug bust and fled to Dublin. These years are a kind of depth charge at the heart of the QuicK series, in no small part because Sarah has drawn such a dark veil over them, hiding her life in Manchester from family and friends alike. Though he doesn't yet know about Victor or the abuse, John can see how Sarah has changed: once open and direct, she is now closed and private, even secretive. When she first returns to Dublin, for her father's funeral, she "had looked a shadow of her former self. Her long dark hair was limp and ragged down her back and she was deathly pale."[6] He recognizes that Sarah's physical state reflects something beyond her immediate grief, but John—this self-professed embodiment of "dumb luck and quick reflexes"[7]—never pushes for an explanation. Though John and her family notice the changes, only her mother, Deirdre—despite her rapidly progressing Alzheimer's—seems to understand that Sarah is hiding from something or someone.

Sarah's arc—with her departure, return, and secrets—highlights the complex importance of family to the series: relationships here are at once

5. Hunt, *Missing*, 107.

6. Hunt, *False Intentions*, 109.

7. Hunt, *Missing*, 175.

necessary and vigilantly guarded. That fragile but loved air extends to the building that houses QuicK Investigations, a building that shelters John and Sarah's own odd little extended family. Their shabby office is "little more than a cold, damp, gloomy room at the top of a building on Wexford Street—a building that should probably have been pulled down years before, but which, by dint of having an original Georgian façade, had avoided the wrecker's ball."[8] It is part of the fabric of old Dublin set amidst a block transformed multiple times, "as the Celtic Tiger roared, spluttered and meowed."[9] Its tenants—the Freak FM pirate radio station, the struggling solicitor Rodney Mitchell, and a small neighborhood grocery that, like its aging proprietor, has seen better days—comprise a de facto family that represents both Dublin's past and its present. The series establishes the hospitably ramshackle nature of this setting from the moment John first arrives at work: "The pungent sea breeze blankets the city in wet, damp air, interwoven with the molasses tang from the Guinness factory. At the first whiff the nose revolts, struggling to separate the sweet from the sour and fetid but after a few breaths the heavy, contrary air is oddly reassuring, pure Dublin."[10] This "contrary" air permeates those who work on Wexford Street, and helps define the tenor and focus of the books.

Among the building's tenants, Rodney models the way Hunt frequently delivers some of her most tender prose through her secondary characters. Rodney is able to provide John and Sarah with work—like catching insurance scammers and fake injury claimants—that helps pay the bills, all the while falling head over heels for Sarah. Rodney wears his heart on his sleeve, an exposed nerve of adoration, but is unable to act on his desire. Like his professional life, his personal ambitions are cocooned in a haze of booze. A minor character, he nonetheless proves pivotal in uncovering the abuse that Sarah suffered while living with Victor: although she has hidden it all from her family, both biological and extended, from within his own alcoholic fog Rodney recognizes her use of secrecy's protective veil.

8. Hunt, *False Intentions*, 15.

9. Hunt, *Black Sheep*, 16.

10. Hunt, *False Intentions*, 35.

Each book runs on dual rails: the case QuicK has been hired to investigate, and the relationship between Sarah and John. Indeed, although the QuicK agency may be in theory an equal partnership, Hunt makes Sarah—and her deflection of intimate bonds—the heart of the series, and deftly uses each of these dual rails to amplify the other. Each novel draws attention to how a different one of her relationships has been compromised by the abuse she endured in Manchester, where Victor capitalized on her isolation from her family, compromising all of her intimate relationships going forward.

Sarah's is not the only life marked by such ruptures: reflecting the series' investment in families and relationships, QuicK's clients are often tenaciously trying to fill missing pages in the stories of their loved ones. When the Gardaí won't dig deeper, the families hire QuicK, risking disappointment or disillusionment in their attempts to honor love. Parents (*False Intentions*, *Blood Money*), siblings (*Black Sheep*, *Missing Presumed Dead*), and naïve young lovers (*Undertow*) summon the courage to confront the fact, as one grieving mother states, that "none of us ever really knows what's going on in another person's life."[11] While these desperate family members take action to locate their missing and unpack the circumstances of their dead, and while QuicK works to help them, John bides his time in gradually solving the mystery of Sarah, the woman he loves, one who is physically present but often mentally miles away. Like many of his clients, whose grief at their familial losses is equaled by their guilt for not being able to protect loved ones, John remorsefully wonders how things would be different if he hadn't cheated on Sarah, ending their romance and motivating her to leave Dublin for Manchester.

Through these ruptures, Sarah distills one of the series' key patterns: despite being unambiguously a crime fiction series, the QuicK novels contain fewer murder victims than they do characters whose very presence is enigmatic to those to whom they are theoretically closest. This dynamic largely revolves around families here, both biological and extended, both innocent and guilty. Through them, Hunt both illustrates the novels'

11. Hunt, *Blood Money*, 37.

thematic concerns and develops her protagonists, as is particularly clear with Sarah's long arc across the series. Much as Sarah is simultaneously back in her family members' lives and more distant than ever, and much as Deirdre's daughters are confronted with their mother's Alzheimer's making her at once present and absent, many of QuicK's clients are painfully forced to acknowledge the gulfs that suddenly separate them from their family members.

Sarah's unease is framed gently from the start of the series, laying the ground for gradual revelations in later books, which eventually make her motivations clear. She will, for example, only join QuicK Investigations as a silent partner, with "her name on nothing."[12] Through the first three novels, she is also something of a silent daughter and sibling. Hunt depicts this secrecy with a persuasive sense of a rounded character's ambivalent psychology. Although Sarah recognizes that her secrets frustrate those around her —John in particular struggles to understand why she would "hide anything from him of all people"[13]—she cannot or will not bring herself to disclose them. She also seems to understand that the secrecy is eroding her sense of self, mirroring her response to her mother's Alzheimer's, which she was slow to accept or discuss: "I thought if I didn't say it [aloud], then it wouldn't be true."[14] She is equally unable to give voice to her own circumstances. Despite all of this, Sarah takes only tentative steps in articulating to her family the truth of what drove her back to Dublin, but those steps stop in *Missing Presumed Dead*, when Victor tracks her to the home city that she hoped would provide her with sanctuary.

Sarah, of course, has her reasons—including shame and safety—for hiding: she "couldn't risk exposing herself to" John, she thought, because "he'd never understand."[15] This is the same rationale she uses to justify not sharing her burden with her sisters or seeking professional help. Despite her efforts, by the closing pages of *Blood Money*, John has nonetheless learned of her relationship with Victor and—because he was told about it by police

12. Hunt, *False Intentions*, 118.

13. Hunt, *Undertow*, 56.

14. Hunt, *Black Sheep*, 331.

15. Hunt, *Undertow*, 59.

investigating Victor's death—suspects she killed him before disappearing at the end of *Undertow*. As *Blood Money* ends, John is dropping his dog off with his sister, packing a bag, and heading off to England to find her. With this, the series leaves one of its central questions open, revealing Sarah's secrets but not resolving their effect on the characters' lives.

Building up to *Blood Money*, Sarah is the central figure in the series' exploration of being simultaneously present and missing, but that exploration also works through the QuicK agency's cases. Sarah's development and her deep ambivalence about her own actions, her past, and her relationships are both magnified by QuicK's cases and magnify those cases in turn. This is particularly so with *Missing Presumed Dead* and *Undertow*, both of which track female vulnerability across varied sinister operations: the theft of children and the exploitation of couples desperate to have a child; Eastern European girls sold into prostitution; a pregnant teenager being abused by a lover who'd hidden his criminality from her. With distinct echoes of Sarah's trauma at Victor's hands, these cases repeatedly feature characters who are victimized as a direct result of either misguided or betrayed trust. Random acts of violence are few and far between.

In *Missing Presumed Dead*, QuicK takes a case that concerns the sudden reappearance of a young woman, Katie Jones, who had been abducted as a child two decades earlier. Like Sarah's mother, Deirdre, Katie—in a coma after a shooting—is simultaneously present and not present. Her childhood disappearance during a family beach outing has haunted her older brother and parents, who have been consumed with guilt about not being able to protect her. (In an elegant narrative juxtaposition, this parallels Sarah's constant worry that she is not doing enough to care for her mother, a bold portrayal of the role reversal adult children confront when caring for an aging parent.) Much as Katie's brother and mother relive their imagining of the fear and confusion a young Katie must have experienced after being taken away from her family, Sarah's traumatized anxiety is playing out in her dreams. This anxiety intensifies dramatically with Victor's return to Dublin.

By the time Victor is named on the page, the plot tension has built up like something out of a Hitchcock film, for as much as Victor serves to illuminate Sarah's past, he also accelerates the plot, and his terror-spree through Dublin shows Hunt stepping on the gas harder and harder. Making his presence violently known to Sarah, he smashes the windows of her car; steals her address book from her apartment; runs Sarah's sister's car off the road, leaving her in the hospital; and beats Rodney nearly to death. These moments build to the final terrifying confrontation between Sarah and Victor.

Amidst all of this violence, Hunt manages to continue developing Sarah's character through her relationships to the other characters. The scene where Sarah finds Rodney in the wake of Victor's attack, for example, is heartbreaking. He does not fully comprehend what has happened to him but understands that it connects to Sarah, a woman he's put on a pedestal, but by whom his love is unrequited. Though he gives her a note left by Victor, Rodney can't "meet her eyes, and when she reached to wipe the tears off his face, he moved his head away," closing his eyes and leaving Sarah to wonder "if he had passed out again or if he just couldn't bear the sight of her."[16] She calls an ambulance for her fallen friend, but rather than calling the police she instead draws even more deeply on her own diminishing reserves: "Rodney, listen to me. I'll get him. . . . I'll handle it . . . just say you disturbed a break-in, a robbery. I promise, Rod, I'll take care of it."[17] As these brutal events make clear, there is no doubt about the lengths she will go to save her family and friends: she's gone out of her way to keep them—and vulnerable clients—safe throughout the series. We see here that she has a survival instinct for herself too, but flight turns to fight only when Victor harms others, not when she alone is a target of his brutality.

Though she fled Victor in England, where her emotional reserves were limited far from home, far from family and friends, she now holds her ground when he finds her in Dublin, where she chooses to defend the bonds she's forging with her sisters, John, and QuicK neighbors like Rodney. These bonds, like caring for her mother, have made her realize that "she wasn't a kid any more—she'd changed."[18] She's stronger because of the

16. Hunt, *Missing*, 267.

17. Hunt, *Missing*, 267.

18. Hunt, *Missing*, 193.

skills she's developed as a private investigator, but she's also emboldened by her oldest relationships, because she has begun to accept the love that John and her family have for her. She's ready to champion herself as strongly as she champions the disenfranchised—like Katie's family—who seek the services of QuicK.

Accordingly, Sarah agrees to meet Victor, because she knows what he "could do to Helen or her mother if she disobeyed him" and because she sees no alternative to ending the abuse herself, even though she understands that, without a doubt, "he was planning to kill her."[19] As she heads out to meet him, "she wondered why she no longer felt afraid. Perhaps this was how soldiers felt before they went into battle. When there was no hope of a good outcome, calm descended. Maybe it would hold, maybe not, but whatever happened, she had decided, she would no longer allow Victor any power over her life."[20] Instead, when Victor tries to justify his abuse, Sarah emphatically rejects his version of their past: "You gave me black eyes, a broken rib. I lost two teeth and I've got a scar on my arm longer than my index finger."[21] As he beats her in response, she waits until "she had a free swing, and . . . buried her mother's good carving knife as deep as she could in the side of Victor's exposed neck and twisted it."[22] She empties his pockets, pushes his body into the ocean, and walks her battered body back to her mother's house in the rain.

As Victor's body floats away into the Irish sea, so too does a part of Sarah Kenny. Whatever solace she finds in knowing that she and her loved ones are safe is mitigated by the horror of what she was driven to do. Although she makes herself physically safe by killing him, he still haunts her on two levels: as the man who destroyed her life; and as the man responsible for driving her to premeditated murder, an act that continues to trouble her through the subsequent novels. By juxtaposing this continual traumatized unease with the guilt and uncertainty swirling around Katie's case, Hunt

19. Hunt, *Missing*, 281.
20. Hunt, *Missing*, 282.
21. Hunt, *Missing*, 284.
22. Hunt, *Missing*, 287.

sharply depicts the limits of vigilance in the face of randomness and chance: even eventual safety, the series suggests, does not guarantee peace.

That horror and that disrupted peace bleed across the series, drawing in other families, as when Victor's body washes up on a Wales beach, considerably dampening the family outing of the father and son who find him. But then, "Victor had that effect on people."[23] Such gallows humor is a hallmark of Hunt's writing, providing breathing room in a series that addresses some very grim, serious issues. Across five books in six years, the QuicK series challenges us to confront some major topics. Hunt explores such horrors as human trafficking, the impact of civil wars, the buying and selling of human organs, and the cruelty that people can inflict on each other. But she also stresses that love, family, and friendship contain the promise to get us through what the world throws at us. She leaves us hanging in *Blood Money*, but we've come to see that John has grown up as much as Sarah has and we believe that he will bring her back, that we can rely on the ties that bind—however flawed we all are—to have our backs, if we just let them.

Bibliography

Cliff, Brian. *Irish Crime Fiction*. London: Palgrave Macmillan, 2018.

Hunt, Arlene. *Black Sheep*. Dublin: Hodder Headline, 2006.

———. *Blood Money*. Dublin: Hachette, 2010.

———. *False Intentions*. Dublin: Hodder Headline, 2005.

———. *Missing Presumed Dead*. Dublin: Hodder Headline, 2007.

———. *Undertow*. Dublin: Hachette, 2008.

23. Hunt, *Missing*, 302.

9

The Touch

Steve Cavanagh's Eddie Flynn Series

GERARD BRENNAN

Steve Cavanagh is the pen name of Stephen Mearns, a Belfast-born writer who is also one of Northern Ireland's most highly accomplished civil rights lawyers. It is not a stretch to posit that he knows a thing or two about burning the candle at both ends and blowtorching the middle, having already published four novels in his Eddie Flynn series—*The Defence* (2015), *The Plea* (2016), *The Liar* (2017), and *Thirteen* (2018)—as well as an e-novella prequel, *The Cross* (2015), and a standalone novel, *Twisted* (2019). As exhausting as his workload must be, the pace of his books, which are usually driven by high-stakes deadlines and double-dealing twists, seem to benefit from his hectic lifestyle. This assessment of high-speed plot driving does not preclude acknowledging the emotional content of the work. There is heart at play here too. Cavanagh chose his mother's maiden name as his pseudonym to honor her after she passed away. His debut novel, *The Defence*, is dedicated to his parents, referring to them by their first names, Bridie and Sam, and he has created a character in Eddie Flynn who often thinks about his own parents in the rare quiet moments of the series.

Cavanagh's pen name places his novels on the bookstore shelf near some of the writers who influenced his style: Michael Connelly, Lee Child, and John Connolly. Like Connolly, author of the Charlie Parker series, Cavanagh identifies as Irish (not always the case for Northern Irish natives), but has chosen to place his series in an American setting. Other than a short story that appears in the Akashic Press anthology, *Belfast Noir* (2016), and his most recent novel *Twisted*, all of his work takes place in and around New York City, making him a relative and intriguing rarity in the current crop of crime fiction authors from either side of the border. Perhaps on similar grounds, Stuart Neville even went so far as to openly rebrand as Haylen Beck when he departed from his Belfast novels to set *Here and Gone* (2017) in the States in the hope that it would attract a newer, wider audience while maintaining his established following. (Doing so also affords freedoms such as a separation from the baggage of Troubles history and politics.) Cavanagh is ahead of the curve in this respect, and so immersed in Americanism that even though his novels were first published in the United Kingdom and Ireland, he wrote them using American spelling.[1]

Series protagonist Eddie Flynn, like his creator, works on the side of justice. But in the course of his work, Flynn operates on both sides and upsets many players in the legal game. Throughout the New York–based series, it is difficult to determine if Flynn is too good to be a crook or too crooked to be a lawyer.

The Defence introduces Flynn with a merciless and tense line of dialogue: "Do exactly as I tell you or I'll put a bullet in your spine."[2] Flynn's first reaction to this predicament is to fight back, an instinctual characteristic that runs through the series, usually to the detriment of his well-being. His initial thoughts are cool and considered, revealing the calculating mind of an accomplished survivor who has been at the wrong end of a gun before. As quickly as this initial resistance surfaces, it melts away with the realization that—since trading in his old life as a con artist for that of a New York lawyer—Flynn has become sloppy and can no longer count on his body to follow the whip-crack commands of his mind. He is forced to relent to his unknown assailant, whom he identifies as a killer with the same self-aware calm that advises him to hold steady and to play things by ear.

1. The edition of *The Defence* to which this chapter refers uses the traditional British version of the word whereas the US edition spells it *The Defense*. Perhaps a mass market UK readership would find an Americanized title—for a book written by an Irish equal rights solicitor, from the point of view of a New York lawyer—a step too far, even before the days of the Brexit referendum.

2. Cavanagh, *Defence*, 1.

These opening pages are mostly concerned with Flynn's attempts to keep panic at bay—"I took in a sharp gulp of metallic air and forced myself to breathe it out slowly"[3]—and this ability to keep his head in a crisis, honed by his criminal background, serves him well in and out of the courtroom. This establishes a defining tension in the series: Flynn would not be such an effective protagonist without his shady origin story. His criminal experiences have made him a greater good guy, a more heroic hero, than could be found in a run-of-the-mill lawyer.

By the end of chapter 2 of *The Defence*, the stakes are ramped up to gargantuan proportions. Flynn is forced to don a coat with a bomb stitched into it, shown the decapitated head of his former law partner stuffed into a gym bag, and told that his daughter has been kidnapped. From this point, the novel tracks Flynn through forty-eight hours of personal hell in which he is forced to do the bidding of a Russian crime boss, Olek Volchek, by relying on his skills as both a lawyer and a con artist. Flynn's brief as the replacement to his now headless ex-colleague Jack Halloran is to assassinate a snitch who is set to testify against Volchek in a murder trial, and to do so by smuggling the bomb that he has been forced to wear into the Chambers Street Courthouse. The threat of an explosion is a surefire way to inject suspense into any story, and suggests a cheeky hat-tip to Cavanagh's Belfast roots. The setting of that particular courthouse at 52 Chambers Street contains another hat-tip of sorts, this time to New York City's Irish American roots: the graft involved in its construction ultimately led to the downfall of Tammany Hall's notorious Boss Tweed.

At his book launch in Belfast's No Alibis Bookstore in 2015, Cavanagh was asked where the idea for his character had come from. He joked about the similarities they shared, in that they were both lawyers who enjoyed an occasional drink, and while Flynn spent most of the first book with a bomb strapped to him, Cavanagh had grown up in Belfast, a city that was no stranger to incendiary devices. His punchline hit the spot, and the remark was met with a good-natured laugh. However, when Cavanagh related the

3. Cavanagh, *Defence*, 3.

same story a year later on an Irish Noir panel at the Old Peculier Crime Writing Festival in Harrogate, the joke was met with an uncomfortable silence. The English audience didn't seem to get the black humor in the anecdote, which acutely demonstrated the difference in the two societies. The whistling-past-the-graveyard humor that has seen the Northern Irish through decades of hardship had no real place in the polite Yorkshire town. Perhaps they thought it would be rude to laugh at such a hideous idea. Or maybe there was a sense of guilt in the room, a recognition that English colonization had created the Irish conflict. Mercifully, Cavanagh was able to charm the audience out of this silence and to squeeze a few laughs out of them before the end of the discussion. This sense of humor has served him well, both in creating a wiseacre protagonist and in cohosting the entertaining podcast, *Two Crime Writers and a Microphone*, with fellow crime writer Luca Veste.[4]

Throughout Flynn's backstory, he identifies as a con artist, not a killer. This means that even though it might put his daughter's life at risk, Flynn must use all his skills of persuasion to deter Volchek from this ham-fisted assassination plan. He negotiates for an opportunity to win the case as a lawyer rather than overturn it with a murder. Flynn is able to sell the idea, not just because he has attended law school and served his time as a practicing attorney, but because his past allows him to relate to the likes of Volchek on a criminal level: "There was no denying it; every time I put on a suit and looked in a mirror, I didn't see a lawyer. I saw a con man."[5] This leads to the familial insight that a young Eddie Flynn had learned his first criminal skill from his father at the age of eight. Pat Flynn taught little Eddie the ways of the pickpocket, or "cannon" in his preferred parlance, under the strict condition that he keep this tutelage a secret from Eddie's mother, Isabella. She earned her money legally as a waitress, while Pat contributed to the household as a small-time crook. When this backstory is retold in *The Liar*, Cavanagh adds the detail that Pat Flynn referred to

4. See https://twocrimewritersandamicrophone.libsyn.com/.

5. Cavanagh, *Defence*, 31.

his son's natural gift for picking pockets and sleight-of-hand tricks as "*the touch*," giving it an almost supernatural dimension.[6] Each novel makes references to Flynn's past in brief snippets like these, which are relevant to the main plot and allow for the books to be enjoyed as standalone thrillers.

The recurring elements of Flynn's backstory throughout the series include references to his childhood in the West Side Manhattan neighborhood Hell's Kitchen, and a portrait of his father as a small-time crook with connections to bigger fish in the murky pond. These are connections that Flynn can often call upon for favors thanks to the goodwill built by his father, who recognized the importance of maintaining solid relationships with his dangerous colleagues. The first family flashback in *The Defence* also reveals that only a few years after the beginning of Eddie's underworld apprenticeship Pat died from a form of cancer that was not covered by the health insurance for which he had faithfully paid. Young Eddie blamed the American legal and insurance system representatives for the loophole that swindled his father out of necessary medical treatment and for the resulting heartbreak suffered by his mother. With his father's St. Christopher medal around his neck serving as a constant reminder of what he'd lost, Flynn's plan for vengeance was forged and financed by the illegal boxing circuit and the side scams he developed along the way. His ambition to fight back against all comers on behalf of his father not only became a focus but also became a character-defining habit. In his own words, "they hadn't stood a chance."[7] Reflecting this mindset, the novels usually find Flynn working for a high-profile client—rich and successful in their chosen field, whether it be legitimate or illegitimate—but approaching that work with the mentality of an advocate who looks after the little guy. When he has the ability to choose his clients more freely, he shows a level of loyalty rare in the caricatures usually applied to the profession in pop culture.

Despite his fierce loyalty to the memory of his parents and to his duty of care for his clients, Flynn's characterization is ambivalent. The front cover of the first edition of *The Defence* invites you to "Meet Eddie Flynn . . .

6. Cavanagh, *Liar*, 59.

7. Cavanagh, *Defence*, 33.

con artist/lawyer, liar/husband, drunk/father." This indicates the failure to properly attend to his own wife and child that is explored throughout the series. With each novel, his actions expand the chasm between him, his wife, Christine, and their daughter, Amy. In the e-novella prequel, *The Cross*, a phone call between Flynn and Christine reveals that Amy does not want to speak to her father because another late night in the office has cost him the chance to see her music recital:

> The last few months had put a strain on an already fraught home life. Money was tight, Christine didn't see much of me and my nine-year-old daughter was beginning to wonder where the man in the wedding photo with her mom had gone. I would catch glimpses of Amy, early in the morning when she was eating her cereal or asleep in bed at night when I got home. I knew this had to stop sooner or later.[8]

By the time Amy is ten, it seems that Flynn has been unable to learn his lesson, despite the early signs. He has separated from Christine and only sees his daughter on arranged outings away from his old family home. During one of these outings Flynn agrees to Amy's plan to synchronize the matching digital watches Flynn purchases for their shared birthday: "Well, I thought if we both got these watches, we could set the alarms for eight o'clock. Then you would remember to call me and we could like, talk, or you could, like, read me a story or something."[9]

Flynn attributes the stability of being accountable to his daughter and her timetable in this way with giving him the strength to get through rehab, so at the very least he can now cross drunkenness off his list of vices. That cheap watch was instrumental to his redemption. Tragically, it later serves as a reminder that his daughter is being held hostage and that her life depends on his ability to navigate the obstacles Volchek set out in front of him: the watch explicitly counts down the minutes to his daughter's execution, should he fail to earn Volchek's freedom. This is not the only time that Flynn can be accused of getting in his own way when trying to maintain

8. Cavanagh, *Cross*, chap. 1.

9. Cavanagh, *Defence*, 56.

a relationship with his daughter. Like numerous classically hard-boiled characters, especially those inspired by Raymond Chandler's wisecracking Philip Marlowe, Flynn wears his many flaws—his drinking and his weakness for smartassery among them—like a suit of armor. But despite his habit of merciless internal self-assessment, he can be frustratingly stupid in his decision making. Although Flynn seems to prefer to believe that his habit of falling off the wagon is the real culprit, his obsession with doing the right thing—his white knight mentality—is probably the greater cause of his family's broken status. Rather than examining this mentality with any stoicism, however, Flynn redirects blame so he can keep riding that white horse into battle. And so, he fits neatly into the character mold of the mean streets hero that Chandler champions: "If there were enough like him, the world would be a very safe place to live in, without becoming too dull to be worth living in."[10]

Following our protagonist into battle, *The Plea* checks back in with Flynn a little over half a year after his Volchek case. In another hat-tip to Cavanagh's Irish heritage, this novel is set during the hours leading up to St. Patrick's Day. Although Christine tells Flynn near the end of *The Defence* that she'll never forgive him for putting their daughter in danger, *The Plea* sees her in a precarious situation that requires her to place faith in Flynn's ability to keep her out of jail. In the time between the two books, Flynn has negotiated a more harmonious relationship with his family. He has been allowed to maintain contact with his daughter while repairing some of the damage done to his marriage, although he is still living separately from Christine.

This progress toward a happy life is jeopardized by Christine's professional involvement with a law firm that has committed a colossal act of global fraud. As she unwittingly becomes entwined in Flynn's case, the reader gets a closer look at their relationship dynamic. Christine is afforded more attention in this novel than in the others, where her status is relegated to that of a recurring side-character. But this closer examination of the relationship proves that there is little hope of a reconciliation between the

10. Chandler, *Simple Art*, 18.

two any time soon, and "she'd stopped wearing her ring a long time ago."[11] Given Flynn's pigheadedness in his quest to do the right thing, this is not surprising. When he is able to ensure that she is removed from danger, he insists on sending her away so that he can work on proving his client, David Child, is also innocent of the murder of his girlfriend and the global fraud for which he has been framed. It's his natural instinct to see the case through to the end—to be the hero when all Christine wants him to be is a husband and father—that makes it seem unlikely that he can repair their broken relationship.

The Liar hints that Christine has moved on. Her first appearance doesn't occur until chapter twenty-two, and it is in the form of a phone call. She isn't even physically present. Flynn has phoned to apologize because, upon his admittance to the hospital following another act of heroics gone wrong, a nurse has contacted his ex-wife, still listed as his next of kin. Flynn detects another voice in the background and Christine admits that she is with her new "friend" Kevin. This obviously bothers Flynn, but he talks himself out of making a fuss about it. In his mind, Christine is entitled to some happiness, but he is not the man who can provide it for her. Their separation may also suit his needs somewhat. He seems to recognize that he has carved out a life that, while not conducive to a happy wife, he doesn't plan to change. It's difficult to be a lawyer and an action hero of sorts when your significant other expects you home at a certain time each night.

While Flynn may be at peace with definitively losing Christine, what cuts him deeper is the realization that Amy, his now thirteen-year-old daughter, has also moved on in her own way. He learns that rather than spend time with him over the summer, she has opted to go to camp with her friends. When he asks her about it, careful not to lay on a guilt trip, Amy references an old arrangement: "I was going to tell you. It's okay, Dad, I'll call you most nights, at eight. Like we used to do. I get to see my friends and hang out and stuff. I can still see you when I get back."[12] This eight o'clock arrangement, first concocted in *The Defence*, was originally intended to

11. Cavanagh, *Plea*, 106.

12. Cavanagh, *Liar*, 119.

keep the relationship between father and daughter alive. At that stage, it was the daughter who needed it more than the father. Now, though, the dynamic has shifted, and the proposition is a way for Amy to indulge her father, rather than a routine for the child to feel more secure in their long-distance relationship. It's very much a "Cat's in the Cradle" moment, and—in his own mind—probably no more than the deadbeat father deserves. His daughter needs him less now, and it's too late for him to claw back the years he missed while drinking, working, and taking on high-risk clients. Again, he accepts this development with little resistance, as if he believes that he warrants no better and recognizes it will make his job a little easier. After all, it's usually Amy and Christine's association with the con artist/lawyer in their life that causes the worst of their problems.

But as these familial relationships become less prominent in Flynn's life, he's not quite allowed to become a total loner. An uneasy alliance is initiated in *The Liar* with FBI Special Agent Harper, a character whose first name is, curiously, never revealed. Perhaps this marks a relationship barrier that she is not willing to cross with the likes of Flynn any time soon. She dislikes and distrusts Cavanagh's protagonist at first, but by the end of the novel, she begins to respect him. When she reappears in *Thirteen* in the guise of a security consultant, having given up her post at the Bureau, Flynn and Harper could be described as friends as well as colleagues. Despite the occasional flirtation, there seems to be no real potential for a romantic relationship. Flynn is satisfied to live in a separation limbo—having built an amicable but nonromantic relationship with Christine—and Harper is involved with another man. But the connection between them is strong enough that she becomes a target for Flynn's latest and greatest nemesis, Joshua Kane.

Introduced in *Thirteen*, Kane is an intriguing creation. A master of deceit and disguise, he is a man who feels no physical pain due to a rare medical condition that affects his nerve endings. He's also an outright psychopath and serial killer, and therefore experiences mental anguish in a nonconventional way. Usually the deaths that occur in the Flynn series are a byproduct of crimes fueled by greed or revenge, but Kane simply enjoys killing, and then finding inventive ways to frame other people for his murders.

Through Kane's point-of-view (a break from the series' usual strict first-person narrative), Cavanagh affords the first external evaluation of his protagonist, Flynn. This also gives the villain greater depth of character, something that is somewhat missing in the previous installments of the series. Usually the antagonists are subject to Flynn's judgment and presented to the reader through his lens. In *Thirteen*, in contrast, Kane gets to present his own thoughts, feelings, backstory, and motives, as twisted as they may be. This narrative decision to juxtapose the main players in the story shows that they bear a startling similarity to each other. Although morally poles apart, they both rely on their masterful abilities to deceive in meeting their personal goals. In Kane, Flynn has met his most worthy opponent. A true match, and a serious threat.

The juxtaposition of these characters confirms that Eddie Flynn is too good to be a criminal. His skills and mindset are much better suited to the courtroom, especially when he puts them to use defending those innocent of the crimes of which they stand accused. Flynn has lines that he is unwilling to cross, chief among them the unbreakable rule of not committing murder. Kane has no such moral lines. It is well within his modus operandi to, at the toss of a coin, extinguish a life like he's blowing out a birthday candle. His only worry is whether or not he can get away with the crime, rather than any moral philosophy about the act of murder itself. While Kane feels no pain, and certainly no guilt, Flynn is the polar opposite. He feels pain, he suffers guilt like a true Catholic, and he has a burning desire to protect others rather than end their lives for sport, personal gain, or convenience. These characteristics, while admirable in a protagonist, manifest as a personal code that does little to make his life easier; instead, it ensures that he will always find himself running toward danger, whatever the personal cost. Eddie Flynn is an excellent lawyer and a master of deception and misdirection, but more importantly, and despite his many failings, he is a good man. Too good to be a career criminal. Wherever Cavanagh takes Flynn in future novels, his moral compass will always set him on the path of the hero.

Bibliography

Cavanagh, Steve. *The Cross*. London: Orion, 2015.

———. *The Defence*. London: Orion, 2015.

———. *The Liar.* London: Orion, 2017.
———. *The Plea.* London: Orion, 2016.
———. *Thirteen.* London: Orion, 2018.
Chandler, Raymond. *The Simple Art of Murder.* New York: Vintage Crime, 1988.

PART FOUR

Adapting Hard-Boiled Models

10

Troubling the Genre

Declan Burke's Harry Rigby Novels

MAUREEN T. REDDY

To include an essay about Declan Burke's Harry Rigby novels in a collection focused on Irish crime fiction series may seem perverse. After all, Burke has written just two Rigby books and the chances of there being a third are quite slim, given both the passage of time since the second was published and the way it ends. Two books do not a series make. However, treating the two books as a series offers a symmetry with the novels themselves, which break some rules of detective fiction so thoroughly that one could reasonably argue that the Rigby books do not in fact belong to the genre. Of course, one would be wrong, because although Burke's Harry Rigby books trouble the genre and push its boundaries, they simultaneously establish themselves as inheritors of the hard-boiled tradition begun in American pulp magazines like *Black Mask* nearly a century earlier.

In order to situate the Rigby books in the specific context that best illuminates them, I want to consider briefly the distinctive features of the hard-boiled form in order to demonstrate why the currently popular label "noir" is misleading, flattening important differences among types of crime fiction. There is certainly a close association between the hard-boiled and noir, dating back to the film noir movement. Those films were frequently based on hard-boiled fiction and/or fiction by writers known for the hard-boiled (e.g., *The Maltese Falcon* [Dashiell Hammett, 1930; directed by John Huston, 1941], *The Big Sleep* [Raymond Chandler, 1939; directed by Howard Hawks, 1946], *Time to Kill* [directed by Herbert I. Leeds, 1942], and *The Brasher Doubloon* [directed by John Brahm, 1947], the last two both adaptations of Raymond Chandler's *The High Window* [1942]). However, film noir postdates the hard-boiled by a full decade and is a *movement*, while the hard-boiled is best thought of as a *form* or a *subgenre* (in film, a *genre*), a distinction that points to important differences. As Janey Place points out in "Women in Film Noir," "movements occur in specific historical periods—at times of national stress and focus of energy. They express a consistency of both thematic and formal elements which makes them particularly expressive of those times, and are uniquely able to express the homogenous hopes . . . and fears . . . brought to the fore by, for example, the upheaval of war."[1] Genres, in contrast, exist across multiple periods. Noir, as Place further explains, can be seen in many film genres in the 1940s–50s. Movements in literature are much like movements in film in their being expressive of the concerns and dominant mood (or energy, as Place puts it) of a particular moment. "Noir," when applied to crime fiction now, is often used quite loosely to mean any work that offers a bleak or pessimistic view of humanity; the term no longer designates a movement, but instead describes a mood. Even so, it continues to share some characteristics of a movement, such as manifesting itself across many subgenres of crime fiction. There are "noir" thrillers, detective novels, amateur whodunits, police procedurals, and so on, which limits the utility of the term for anyone interested in understanding genre or tradition in crime fiction.

The early hard-boiled defined itself against classical detective fiction and positioned its central characters as loners who stood outside official centers of power.[2] They were "hard men," in Raymond Chandler's oft-quoted formulation, doing "hard, dangerous work" in the "mean streets" of cities where the "law was something to be manipulated for profit and power."[3] Among the significant generic features of the hard-boiled, the most important is the shared ideological orientation of those texts, which Bethany Ogdon has dubbed "hard-boiled ideology": a commitment to a

1. Place, "Women in Film Noir," 49.

2. See Reddy, *Traces, Codes*, 6–40.

3. Chandler, *Trouble Is My Business*, viii and vii.

value system in which whiteness, maleness, and heterosexuality reign supreme and in which their supremacy, when threatened, must be defended with violence, even extreme violence.[4] A quintessentially American form, the hard-boiled metaphorically spits in the face of seemingly more polite, civilized, British, and faux-British forms of crime fiction popular at the time it came into being. Every element of hard-boiled fiction is presented to readers from the perspective of the protagonist, who is also usually the narrator, whose white/male/heterosexual consciousness shapes the reader's understanding of the text. That consciousness finds expression in a voice that is cool, detached, a bit self-mocking, given to slang and to tough talk, a voice so distinctive that it is easily parodied, as it has been countless times in multiple media.

Easy as it is to parody, the hard-boiled is far more difficult to revise. The many writers who have tried to reinvent the hard-boiled while deliberately rejecting the ideology at its core have sometimes written brilliant books—among American writers, Sara Paretsky and Walter Mosley spring immediately to mind—but those books have not actually been hard-boiled. The ideology, repugnant as it is, is *the* essential element of the form. The Irish writers who took to crime fiction in large numbers in the late twentieth and early twenty-first centuries were often drawn to the hard-boiled, perhaps partly because of its persistent critique of the established order and of official power. That critical attitude may have seemed perfectly suited to the moment in Irish history when corruption was being exposed in virtually every part of society, from church to government to business to banking. However, the critique in the hard-boiled comes from a deeply conservative position, whereas—with the notable exception of Benjamin Black (John Banville)—the Irish writers who have taken up the form have for the most part instead sought to criticize the valorization of whiteness, maleness, and heterosexuality itself. As a consequence, their work has frequently foundered, with their protagonists so trapped in ideological contradictions that the series descend into confusion.[5]

4. See Ogdon, "Hard-Boiled Ideology."

5. See Reddy, "Contradictions," 126–40 for a more detailed version of this case.

Declan Burke's Harry Rigby books belong in the company of other Irish series indebted to the hard-boiled tradition. However, even though the Rigby series does seem to founder by the end of the second book, a closer analysis suggests that the apparent foundering actually is purposeful, a deliberate consequence of the extremely bleak worldview the novels incorporate. Although the traditional hard-boiled detective is often thought of as cynical, that cynicism is rooted in thwarted idealism, a belief that some things have transcendent value and are worth trying to preserve or recuperate (high on the list: the American preference for and anxiety about whiteness, maleness, heterosexuality). The detective has his own moral code that is inviolable; that code may or may not coincide with the law, but in any case the law matters less than the detective's code, which is what makes him "not mean," to return to Chandler's essay. In a move that mirrors the standard advice offered to writers of speculative fiction—begin with a realistic world and alter just one thing to trace the far-reaching consequences—Burke's Rigby novels change just one key element of the hard-boiled by making the detective *not* a detective. That one shift, from professional detective to accidental (not amateur) detective, is the origin of all else in the Rigby novels that pulls them ever further from their hard-boiled predecessors and into a universe in which nothing at all is worth preserving.

Burke is not only a writer of crime fiction but also something of a scholar of the genre, with a popular blog *Crime Always Pays* on which he reviews crime fiction and interviews writers,[6] a regular column on crime fiction in the *Irish Times*, and several essays to his credit. His awareness of generic requirements and of the original hard-boiled writers is quite sharp, as we can see in *Slaughter's Hound* (2012), which has multiple direct references to Chandler's *The Big Sleep* (1939). None of this is meant to imply that a writer must specifically indicate or even be conscious of influences for readers to trace those influences in the writer's work, but the explicit use of Chandler's novel in Burke's *invites* readers to consider the two novels, and the two writers, together. The most obvious similarity between the two novels may be their labyrinthine plots, which are so convoluted that even

6. Burke, *Crime Always Pays*.

the authors seem to lose track of them. A famous but evidently apocryphal anecdote has Howard Hawks and Humphrey Bogart, the director and star of the film adaptation of *The Big Sleep*, asking Chandler who killed Owen Taylor, the chauffeur whose death seems to be forgotten partway through the novel, and Chandler replying, "How the hell would I know?" Whether true or not—and it does seem to be mostly urban legend—the anecdote underscores the plot's messiness while implying that the plot is not the point, anyhow. Although Declan Burke is presumably clear about who kills whom and why in *Slaughter's Hound*, readers might be less so, but that does not much matter as the plot is secondary to the characters.

In *The Big Sleep*, the house to which Marlowe is summoned by General Sternwood is like a character itself: an imposing faux-castle featuring stained-glass depictions of knights and ladies among other extraordinary features. Similarly, the Hamilton house, The Grange, in *Slaughter's Hound* is "a faux-Georgian pile, of course, although to be fair to the Hamiltons, it was only faux because the original had been torched back in 1921 during the IRA campaign to ethnically cleanse Ireland of Protestants."[7] Saoirse Hamilton, the owner, is protected by a faithful manservant much like the Sternwood butler. Both houses hold the dangerous secrets of the troubled, bizarre families that live there. Most ominously, Grainne Hamilton, the daughter of the house, behaves very much like Carmen Sternwood at first meeting, appearing "vacant," giggling bizarrely, behaving seductively toward Harry, and then assaulting him when he doesn't do what she wants, clawing his cheek and kicking him.[8] The next time he sees her, Harry decides he won't stop "to discover which Carmen she was today, the vicious Miss Sternwood or the gypsy lover driven to operatic hysterics by unrequited arias."[9]

How are Philip Marlowe and Harry Rigby, the protagonists, connected? In myriad ways, it turns out, some of which are typical of the hard-boiled genre but others of which are specific to these two characters and

7. Burke, *Slaughter's Hound*, 60.

8. Burke, *Slaughter's Hound*, 89–90.

9. Burke, *Slaughter's Hound*, 233.

the two novels through which they are linked. Harry Rigby—like all protagonists of the traditional hard-boiled—is a white, heterosexual man with a distinctive voice that could belong only to someone secure in his high position in the hierarchy that matters to him, if not to everyone around him. The two opening paragraphs of the first Rigby novel, *Eight Ball Boogie* (2003), describe the stabbing death of a woman. The third paragraph goes like this: "These things happen, although not usually in shiny new towns on the Atlantic seaboard, and rarely to the middle-aged wife of an independent politician that's keeping the government in clover. But they happen. It's a crying shame, yeah, so have a cry, feel ashamed and get over it. The rest of the week is coming on hard and its brakes are shot to hell."[10] The flat, matter-of-fact tone in reporting a gruesome murder, the detachment, the slanginess ("clover"), and the use of metaphor with a revival of a dead metaphor through literalization ("crying shame" and "have a cry") put Harry in the same company as Philip Marlowe and other hard-boiled detectives through his voice.

The very next sentence, however, establishes his chief difference from them: "My job was to find out who and why, at twelve cent per word for the right facts in the right order."[11] Harry is paid for his *words*, his writing, not for detective work; he does the detective work in order to be able to write a news story, not as the actual activity for which he is paid. That difference—unlike his American hard-boiled predecessors, Burke's detective did not set out to be a detective and is not trained to do detective work—makes all the other differences possible. Most importantly, it explains why the father of a young child would go into such dangerous work, as it shows that he falls into that work and does not choose it or prepare for it. The traditional hard-boiled detectives are loners with no family on the scene and no continuing romantic relationships. That solitariness both sets them apart from ordinary people and makes their choice of potentially dangerous work palatable to readers, as they are risking only their own lives, not

10. Burke, *Eight Ball Boogie*, 7.

11. Burke, *Eight Ball Boogie*, 7.

the lives of others who have no say in that work. Harry does have family, but only one family member who really matters to him and with whom he wants to maintain a close relationship—his son, Ben.

From the beginning of *Eight Ball Boogie*, Harry assumes that his brother, Gonzo, is involved in the murder with which the novel opens. Gonzo has been gone for four years—he has been in prison for at least some of that time, although Harry doesn't know that yet—but has recently contacted Harry's girlfriend/Ben's mother, Dee, to say he will be back by Christmas, which is just a few days away. Harry is right about Gonzo's involvement, but it takes the rest of the novel for him to figure out exactly how and why Gonzo is involved. Imelda Sheridan's murder ultimately is far less important to the plot than are the other crimes to which it is related. Indeed, Imelda herself is a cypher, a plot device, about whom the reader is never led to care, another link to the traditional hard-boiled in which the murder victims are often more or less incidental, such as Miles Archer and Captain Jacobi in *The Maltese Falcon* (1930) or Owen Taylor and Arthur Geiger in *The Big Sleep*. Similarly, the first violent death in *Slaughter's Hound*, the person Harry at first thinks is his friend Finn but later learns is another man, is less important in the novel than the art forgery/insurance scam to which that death is related.

In both Rigby novels, women are dangerous, whether through their own criminality (Helen Conway in *Eight Ball Boogie*) or through their sexuality, which they deploy against men in order to get what they want (Katie in *Eight Ball Boogie*), or through both (Saoirse and Grainne Hamilton in *Slaughter's Hound*). As do the traditional hard-boiled, the novels also include a few "good girls," such as Pam, a nurse in *Slaughter's Hound* who helps Harry at a critical moment. The most dangerous woman to Harry is Dee, who is not criminally inclined but who betrayed Harry by having an affair with his brother, who is in fact the biological father of Harry's son, Ben. Although it is true that Harry is betrayed by virtually everyone he knows in the course of the two novels, this betrayal hurts him the most and cuts him loose from all ordinary human relationships, other than the one with his son. That betrayal hurts even more because it was the second time Gonzo had a sexual relationship with a girlfriend of Harry's.

Traditional hard-boiled detectives are *never* hurt by betrayals, which they always expect and generally see as confirmation of their rightness in choosing solitary lives.

In common with the traditional hard-boiled, Burke's Rigby novels portray the criminal justice system as fundamentally unjust, with those sworn to uphold the law instead more interested in their own personal access to money and power. Both novels feature crooked cops whose illegal machinations offer a justification for independent investigation of crime. The police as a whole cannot be trusted because no one can be certain which of them is honest and which is corrupt. Further, the entire policing system is suspect anyhow, given its fealty to the wealthy and powerful over the interests of ordinary citizens. As is often true in the traditional hard-boiled, the most dangerous criminals are not the gangsters on the streets but their masters in the mansions and government buildings.

As is also often true of the plots of hard-boiled novels, greed is the primary motive for the crimes in both novels, with the exception of those Harry himself commits, and the greediest of all are those who already have considerable wealth. The criminal enterprise in *Eight Ball Boogie* brings together property development and drug dealing, with a car importer's wife in league with a crooked TD (a local representative to the national legislature) to smuggle drugs and to launder the drug money via the funds from property development in a booming Celtic Tiger economy. Harry is not averse to smoking pot or opposed to small-time sellers (his friend and partner in journalism, Herbie, is one), but he objects to hard drugs and those who profit from the misery of others. In *Slaughter's Hound*, the crimes are all connected to a massive scam in which a family cheats individual art investors and the government itself (via the National Asset Management Agency, NAMA) by copying paintings and selling both the copy and the original to unsuspecting but certainly unethical people, many of whom seem to be trying to hide their assets by buying art and allowing it to be displayed in various public buildings. In both novels, the dirtiest work involved in the main crimes, especially the violence, is handled mostly by gangland members and small-time criminals, while the profits go mainly to respectable, socially prominent, and powerful people. The people at the top of each criminal conspiracy engage directly in violence only when desperate and unable to assign it to underlings, as for example when Helen Conway is cornered in *Eight Ball Boogie* or when Finn Hamilton thinks Harry is getting too close to the truth of his supposed suicide in *Slaughter's Hound.*

Violence, including extreme violence, is a standard feature of hard-boiled fiction, with the detective both enduring such violence and meting it out. The detective's willingness to engage in violence is an important component of his status as a "hard man." Although parodies of the hard-boiled often imply that the hard-boiled detective is impervious to such violence, shrugging it off and somehow always avoiding real pain, that characterization is inaccurate. The detective's ability to endure serious pain and his refusal to give up regardless of whatever violence comes his way are evidence of his authentic toughness, which would be undermined by superhero-like strength. In this way, Harry is virtually indistinguishable from the hard-boiled protagonists, as he is regularly beaten and shot at (with some bullets finding their mark) in both novels, but is not dissuaded from his mission to find the truth and hold the guilty accountable.

Harry also inflicts violent damage on others, on some occasions behaving precisely as the villains do. One of the clearest parallels drawn between Harry and criminals involves a journalist of sorts, Katie, in *Eight Ball Boogie*. Katie is held hostage by Helen Conway, who breaks Katie's fingers one by one when Harry does not reveal where Helen can find the camera that has incriminating pictures stored on it. Helen is monstrous in her cool approach to hurting Katie, noting after breaking the first finger that "this is not torture. Every time I break a bone, the agony subsides to a level that can be tolerated. Even now, Katie's body has forgotten the intensity of the pain, because our bodies have no physical recollection process."[12] Katie's howls of agony and sobbing punctuate these remarks. Helen continues, "Ideally, torture should involve the gradual increase of pain, to the point that the victim will do anything to be released. This isn't ideal, but. . . ."[13] After she breaks the fourth finger, Harry claims to have the camera in his car. Throughout this not-torture, Tony Sheridan—the crooked TD and

12. Burke, *Eight Ball Boogie*, 245.

13. Burke, *Eight Ball Boogie*, 245. Ellipses in original.

Helen's lover/partner in crime—cannot even look at what is going on, although he shows "grim satisfaction" once Harry says he has the camera.[14] Helen, then, is more masculine in hard-boiled terms than Tony, who can order that violence be done but does not have the stomach to do it or even observe it himself. Once Harry and Katie get away from the abandoned theater where the violence is carried out, Harry tortures Katie in the exact same way for the exact same reason as Helen: to get information she has that he does not. The narrative underscores these parallels by using the same phrases; like Helen, Harry holds Katie's hand and "stroke[s] it gently," for example.[15] Harry does not give readers a finger-by-finger commentary, as he does when Helen is the perpetrator, but asks Katie questions and then says, "It took maybe ten minutes and a few more broken fingers, but in the end she told me what I wanted to know," at which point he leaves her at the driveway to a hospital, where she can "hardly stand up, fainting from pain."[16]

What, then, separates Harry from the villains? Just two things: the larger motive, with Harry on the side of justice if not law; and his feelings about his behavior. We have seen that Helen is emotionless as she hurts Katie while Tony is too cowardly to look at what she is doing despite his approval of it, but Harry "concentrated on the self-loathing, feeding off it. If I'd thought for a second about what Katie was enduring, I'd never had the strength to do what I was going to have to do."[17] Afterward, Harry works to "keep down the rising gorge of bile and self-disgust."[18] Motive and feelings are not much to counterbalance the similarity of behavior of hero and villain; that similarity is also an element of the traditional hard-boiled, in which the detectives often behave in ways that make clear they are not "good guys" in any simple or absolute sense.

The departure from the hard-boiled that Burke incorporates in his series—the protagonist's commitment to his son, fully believable in context

14. Burke, *Eight Ball Boogie*, 246.

15. Burke, *Eight Ball Boogie*, 260.

16. Burke, *Eight Ball Boogie*, 262.

17. Burke, *Eight Ball Boogie*, 262.

18. Burke, *Eight Ball Boogie*, 261.

because Harry is not a detective by choice—is highlighted in the paragraph immediately following the scene in which Harry tortures Katie in *Eight Ball Boogie*. As Harry drives away from the hospital, trying to keep down that nauseated self-disgust, he says that the other thing on his mind "was also a nauseous sensation, this one driven by fear, a primal instinct I had never experienced before. . . . This was a fear for someone else, a sleepy-eyed kid who wouldn't even know he was in danger until it was too late, for whom it was maybe already too late."[19] Harry's assertion that he has never experienced fear before is an extraordinary claim, as surely all human beings feel fear sometimes. Indeed, the inability to feel fear is associated with brain damage, specifically the destruction of the amygdala. Even psychopaths feel fear, as do sociopaths, although the latter's feelings of all kinds are weaker than normal people's. Harry is capable of feeling fear, as this passage shows, so he must mean something else. The *type* and *depth* of the fear he feels are new to him, as he loves Ben more than he loves himself or anyone else and therefore his fears for Ben are more intense than any fear he has previously felt. The "primal instinct," then, is not fear itself linked to self-preservation, but fear specifically *for Ben*, a paternal instinct.

Love of Ben makes Harry infinitely more vulnerable than hard-boiled detectives normally are. In both novels, Harry's adversaries capitalize on that vulnerability by threatening Ben in order to control Harry. They fail, instead bringing about their own destruction at Harry's hands. In *Eight Ball Boogie*, Harry kills Gonzo in order to stop the latter from taking Ben. The extremity of that action—killing his brother to keep his son away from a dreadful influence—appalls even the cop, Brady, who has seen the ugliest of human behavior and has little respect for anyone or anything. Brady, who knows what Gonzo was up to and his plan to take Ben, tells Harry he is a "cold bastard" because he is not destroyed emotionally by killing his brother.[20] Brady plans to lie about who did what, reporting that a crooked cop, Galway, shot Gonzo, but Harry doesn't much care. Brady says, "I'm ten years on the force and I've shot a gun in anger twice. Never came near

19. Burke, *Eight Ball Boogie*, 262.

20. Burke, *Eight Ball Boogie*, 279.

hitting the target either time and you better believe I'm twice as happy as they were that I didn't." Weighing Ben's future against Gonzo's continued existence presents no such difficulty to Harry, who reflects a bit later that he feels "no remorse for killing him, no regret that he was dead. I felt nothing, numb. All I knew was that the world was one sociopath fewer."[21] In *Slaughter's Hound*, we learn that Harry was tried for his brother's murder and spent six years locked up in a hospital ward for the criminally insane, a sentence suspiciously lighter than one might expect and perhaps indicative of his collaborating with the police.[22]

Slaughter's Hound intensifies the focus on the difference Ben's existence makes in Harry's acting as a detective. After witnessing his friend Finn's apparent suicide, Harry is asked by Finn's mother to search for a suicide note, a request that is meant to obscure what she is really looking for and that pulls Harry ever deeper into a sprawling array of linked criminal activities. Ben, now an adolescent, is the passenger in a car Harry is driving when he is forced off the road and crashes. While Ben is in a coma, an investigator from the Criminal Assets Bureau (CAB), Toohill, interrogates Harry, threatening him with Ben's arrest and prosecution for hash possession if Harry doesn't go along with Toohill's plans for Harry to perjure himself in order to advance the CAB investigation. When Ben dies as the result of his injuries in the car crash, Harry loses all interest in life except for the desire for revenge. He is determined to find out who was driving the car that caused the crash and annihilate them. At this point in the book, Harry ceases to be a hard-boiled detective in the Chandler/Hammett mode and instead metamorphoses into a more violent and frightening version of those detectives, like the vigilante types created by Mickey Spillane in the 1940s–50s.

Like Spillane's investigator, Mike Hammer, Harry's name is obviously symbolic, but we don't learn that until late in *Slaughter's Hound*. It turns out that Harry was not named Harry at birth, but Archú. In Irish mythology, the archú are "war hounds feared for their love of slaughter," as an

21. Burke, *Eight Ball Boogie*, 282.

22. Burke, *Slaughter's Hound*, 19.

author's note at the start of the novel states.[23] In that mythology, though, the archú are associated with the great Irish hero, Cú Chulainn, the Hound of Culann; therefore, being a slaughter-loving war hound is not necessarily a bad thing. But whatever else it is, a war hound is not a human being, and we see Harry shedding his humanity in the pages after Ben's death, as if to demonstrate that Ben alone tethered him to the ordinary human world. Soon after learning that Ben has died, Harry tortures a man, first telling him that "I've got nothing left to live for."[24] The body count in the last quarter of the book is quite high, with most of the dead killed by Harry. On the last page, a seventeen-year-old girl shoots Harry and leaves him bleeding in a remote area. The final paragraph suggests that Harry is dying, as "it all started to fade away, the world bleeding dark from the edges in."[25] Harry imagines seeing Ben, who morphs into Gonzo, "waiting for me and saying put it down, just let it go, you can't go on, you'll go on, and the leaves faintly rustling, whispering, yes, I will, yes, yes."[26] The echo of the final words of James Joyce's *Ulysses* could not be accidental, but instead of Molly Bloom's affirmation of life, here the "yes" comes not from a person but from nature and implies that Harry's body is returning to nature through death, to the dirt and the leaves in which he lies. Harry is closer to the immobile narrator of Samuel Beckett's *The Unnamable*, whose last words Harry's also echo.[27]

The death of the detective is not entirely new in crime fiction; even Sherlock Holmes dies in that series (but, of course, is eventually resurrected). However, it does break the tacit rule of hard-boiled fiction that the detective must ultimately prevail, even if only by outliving his adversaries. In the traditional hard-boiled, readers are meant to admire the detective and want him to succeed. It is not clear what readers are meant to think at the end of the Rigby series. The absence of hard-boiled ideology, apart from

23. Burke, *Slaughter's Hound*, 5.

24. Burke, *Slaughter's Hound*, 332.

25. Burke, *Slaughter's Hound*, 383.

26. Burke, *Slaughter's Hound*, 383.

27. Thanks to Brian Cliff for drawing the Beckett reference to my attention.

casual misogyny and heterosexism,[28] creates a sort of ideological vacuum in which nothing has transcendent value. Once he has achieved some vengeance for his son, Harry has no reason to live, and readers are not encouraged to imagine that he might find one. At the end of *Slaughter's Hound*, the man responsible for Ben's death and his closest associates are all dead, his house left burning to the ground. Harry's final purpose is achieved. That purpose, significantly, is entirely personal, which perhaps could have been predicted from the moment the first Rigby novel mentions his fatherhood, a role infinitely more important to Harry than detective. In the traditional hard-boiled, there is no man more admirable than the detective; in Burke's revision, there is no actual detective and no one admirable at all.

Bibliography

Burke, Declan. *Eight Ball Boogie*. 2003. Reprint, Dublin: Liberties Press, 2012.

———. *Crime Always Pays* blog. http://crimealwayspays.blogspot.com. Accessed 10 September 2019.

———. *Slaughter's Hound*. Dublin: Liberties Press, 2012.

Chandler, Raymond. *Trouble Is My Business*. New York: Random House, 1992.

Ogdon, Bethany. "Hard-Boiled Ideology." *Critical Quarterly* 34, no. 1 (1999): 71–87.

Place, Janey. "Women in Film Noir." In *Women in Film Noir*, edited by E. Ann Kaplan, 47–68. London: British Film Institute, 1998.

Reddy, Maureen T. "Contradictions in the Irish Hardboiled: Detective Fiction's Uneasy Portrayal of a New Ireland." *New Hibernian Review* 19, no. 4 (Winter 2015): 126–40.

———. *Traces, Codes, and Clues: Reading Race in Crime Fiction*. New Brunswick: Rutgers Univ. Press, 2003.

28. Harry describes the crooked cop, Galway, who is evidently a semicloseted gay man, as a "fruit" and a "fairy" at several points in *Eight Ball Boogie*. See, for instance, 100 and 270.

11

"A Spanner in the Works"

Metaphysical Detection in Colin Bateman's Dan Starkey Series

BRANDI BYRD

In *Divorcing Jack* (1995), the first novel in Colin Bateman's darkly comic thriller series featuring Unionist newspaper-columnist-turned-private-detective Dan Starkey, Starkey finds the single piece of evidence that both explains why his friend Margaret was murdered and exposes a political cover-up on the eve of a major election. This evidence is a tape-recorded conversation wherein Mark Brinn, the favored Alliance Party candidate for prime minister of Northern Ireland, confesses that he was not the victim of a decades-old sectarian bombing, but rather the one who planted the bomb and inadvertently got caught in the blast. Starkey discusses the tape with a friend who muses on the indeterminacy of the recording as proof of anything: "That is presuming it's authentic. . . . I believe they can do wonderful things with tapes these days. I mean they could make an authentic tape sound like a fake as well, couldn't they?"[1] Starkey ultimately decides that what is more important than what the tape *says* is what kind of narrative is scripted around it: "Whoever had the tape had the power, but only if they knew how to use it."[2] In this moment as throughout the series, Bateman complicates the generic expectations of the detective novel,

1. Bateman, *Divorcing Jack*, 221.

2. Bateman, *Divorcing Jack*, 223.

primarily the expectation that the detective is the one who finds the truth by sifting through evidence and making the right connections. Instead, Bateman draws attention to the ways that the narrative construction of meaning—both in the specific stories used to narrate past events and in the narrative schemata used to organize individual and communal experience—is a highly complex and subjective enterprise, one open to revision and reinterpretation.

John Scaggs provocatively claims, "Crime narratives that are structured around the investigation of a crime are, by default, metanarratives. They are narratives about narratives, or stories about reconstructing and interpreting the story of a crime."[3] While all detective novels might thus be read in terms of their narrative engagements, the subgenre of "metaphysical detective stories" foregrounds these textual and epistemological preoccupations through metafictional strategies, thus performing a specific type of narrative work. Patricia Merivale and Susan Elizabeth Sweeney have defined the metaphysical detective story as "a text that parodies or subverts traditional detective-story conventions . . . with the intention, or at least the effect, of asking questions about mysteries of being or knowing which transcend the mere machinations of the mystery plot."[4] Because "the work of the detective mirrors not only the work of reading . . . but also . . . the work of writing,"[5] such stories often feature a writer as detective, relying on intertextual references, parody, and pastiche in order to "speculate about the workings of language, the structure of narrative, the limitations of genre, the meanings of prior texts, and the nature of reading."[6] Additionally, the metaphysical detective very often "fail[s] to solve the crime altogether—or do[es] so only by accident."[7] These components add up to a radical deconstruction of meaning; as Merivale and Sweeney argue, the metaphysical detective story asks, "What, if anything, can we know? . . . How, if at all, can we rely on anything besides our own constructions of

3. Scaggs, *Crime Fiction*, 142–43.

4. Merivale and Sweeney, "Game's Afoot," 2.

5. Nealon, "Work of the Detective," 118.

6. Merivale and Sweeney, "Game's Afoot," 7.

7. Merivale and Sweeney, "Game's Afoot," 2.

reality?"[8] The metaphysical detective, then, overturns the primary generic expectation of the conventional detective novel, the idea "that patterns *do* cohere behind the confusing surface of reality, and that there exists a specialized group, detectives, who can read them."[9]

As one such metaphysical detective, Dan Starkey seeks to disrupt the existing order rather than to create order out of chaos. Throughout the series, Starkey describes his investigative strategy as "put[ting] a spanner in the works."[10] Given Starkey's propensity for parody and the consistent parallels between his detective work and his writing projects,[11] Bateman's Starkey novels clearly fit the parameters of the metaphysical detective genre. This generic classification is all the more significant given the series' uneasy positioning within the broader categories of Northern Irish crime fiction and Troubles novels. The Starkey novels represent a significant departure from "Troubles trash," those "sensationalist journalistic thrillers" that propagate "a stereotypical and reductive vision of a society divided in two monolithic identities."[12] They are also formally and stylistically distinct from later Northern Irish thrillers that explore the "moral, psychological, and social preoccupations that were ignored in the most popular and traditional mode."[13] Such novels, like Brian McGilloway's *The Nameless Dead* (2012) and Stuart Neville's *The Twelve* (2009), complicate the clichés of Troubles discourse by humanizing rather than stereotyping their characters. McGilloway, for example, emphasizes the value of empathy in building cross-community relations, and Neville explores the legacy of the Troubles through the lens of psychological trauma. Bateman's novels, meanwhile, accomplish their critique through satire, which, as John Connolly notes, is something of a double-edged sword: "Colin Bateman . . .

8. Merivale and Sweeney, "Game's Afoot," 4.

9. Bernstein, "Story Itself," 138.

10. Bateman, *Turbulent Priests*, 162.

11. Dan describes his career shift from newspaper columnist to "something like a private detective" as follows: "I was, as you know, one of this country's leading journalists. That's still what I do, except I don't publish . . . I get answers" (Bateman, *Nine Inches*, 5).

12. Morales-Ladrón, "'Troubling' Thrillers," 59.

13. Morales-Ladrón, "'Troubling' Thrillers," 60.

recognised the tragic absurdity of what was taking place, with the emphasis on the absurd, and used that recognition to power his fiction. As with all satirists, there were times when the balance between rage and humour, between the need to confront the reality of violence and the satirist's desire to mock all involved in it, were less than perfect in Bateman's work, but it was brave and untypical nonetheless, and he has never received the critical acknowledgement that he deserves."[14]

While these novels have been read as "comedy thrillers"[15] and "Troubles thrillers,"[16] reading them as metaphysical detective stories clarifies the parameters of Bateman's ethico-political vision. Stephanie Schwerter, for example, makes the important argument that Bateman uses the carnivalesque in order to "ridicule . . . traditional value systems . . . reject[ing] the elevation of one ideological position above all others," while "the humorous tone in which [*Belfast Confidential* (2005)] is written and the explicit description of the city's positive development offer an optimistic perspective on the city's future."[17] By tracing the ways that the Starkey novels complicate narrative conventions through the lens of metaphysical detective fiction, I suggest that this optimism resides in the plasticity of traditional social narratives: Starkey not only ridicules these narratives but also routinely revises them.

As I have mentioned, one of the important components of the metaphysical detective story is the complication of the investigator's attempts to create a meaningful narrative to explain that which others cannot, gesturing toward a broader deconstruction of meaning. Throughout the series, Starkey's investigative projects are routinely resolved without, and even despite, his intellectual input. In *Turbulent Priests* (1999), for example, Starkey is searching for a rumored cache of alcohol when he accidentally uncovers a mass grave,[18] evidence of the darker agenda of the church on

14. Connolly, "No Blacks, No Dogs, No Crime Writers: Ireland and the Mystery Genre," 51–52.

15. Smyth, *Novel and the Nation,* 123.

16. Morales-Ladrón, "'Troubling' Thrillers"; Schwerter, "Peacefire."

17. Schwerter, "Peacefire," 20, 26.

18. Bateman, *Turbulent Priests*, 214.

Wrathlin Island that he has been charged to investigate. In *Shooting Sean* (2001), he is used as a pawn in someone else's investigation: "We've been watching right from the start," an undercover policeman tells him near the novel's conclusion. "This is an Interpol operation. We had agents on set . . . we had agents at the party, we had agents at your hotel."[19] And at the end of *Divorcing Jack*, he dejectedly reflects on the role that he has played in investigating Margaret's murder and uncovering evidence of political corruption: "I was not privy to any secrets; I was not involved for any reason other than my own stupidity; I was a fool first and a journalist second and neither had overlapped during the whole episode."[20] Despite Starkey's apparent failures as an investigator, however, the fact that each of the ten novels in this series concludes with a neat resolution—and one in which Starkey plays a central, though unconventional, part—suggests at the same time both an optimistic sense that meaning *can* be found in chaos, and a sense that Starkey's disruptive strategies for creating or revealing that meaning are more effective than they may initially seem.

In particular, as Schwerter points out, Bateman's carnivalesque subversions perform a social critique whereby traditional social narratives are devalued. This ideological stance is mirrored in Starkey's self-identification as a "punk rocker . . . Anarchy. No respect for authority. And vaguely silly with it."[21] He routinely subverts the ideological frameworks of the politicians, gangsters, businessmen, and priests he investigates, reflecting his own insistent views as he does so. In explaining Belfast's political violence to an American journalist, for example, Starkey insists that "it's long past the political stage, the Nationalist or Loyalist stage, for most of them. Now it's down to money."[22] And though he considers himself a Protestant, he also believes that "Protestantism never has been and never will be about religion. It's about property and culture and spitting at Catholics."[23]

19. Bateman, *Shooting Sean*, 212.

20. Bateman, *Divorcing Jack*, 275.

21. Bateman, *Driving Big Davie*, 351.

22. Bateman, *Divorcing Jack*, 88.

23. Bateman, *Turbulent Priests*, 8.

Bateman uses Starkey's disruptive tendencies not only to effect social critique, however, but as a critical component in solving mysteries. Starkey's "spanner in the works" does not simply function as a devaluation of others' narrative schemata, it actually contributes to the creation of meaning. In keeping with the generic conventions of the thriller, each novel sees Starkey enmeshed in an impossibly elaborate and far-reaching conspiracy. He resolves these cases not by untangling the complex networks of secret alliances and schemes, but by revealing an altogether different type of organizational framework behind each mystery. As he observes, "Twenty years of journalism has taught me that . . . conspiracies are in the crossed eyes of the easily convinced beholder; that most crimes are domestic in origin."[24] At the heart of all this political intrigue and gang warfare, Starkey disrupts the conspiracy narrative to uncover a family drama. For instance, in *Belfast Confidential*, he begins looking into the deaths of people expecting to be included in that year's "Power List": "Belfast's top fifty movers and shakers. A canny mix of multi-millionaire industrialists, TV chat-show hosts, pop stars, gangsters and politicians."[25] What he discovers, however, is that someone is murdering these influential people—not as some kind of power play but in revenge for an act of cruelty perpetrated on another character. In *Nine Inches* (2011), radio-show host Jack Caramac's son is kidnapped and returned a few hours later with a vaguely threatening note in his pocket. While Jack believes the incident to be connected to one of his many controversial public opinions, Starkey learns that the nanny and her partner want a baby of their own and, in a brief moment of desperation, they kidnapped the child.

These family narratives, however, are not simply a different organizational framework upon which Starkey creates meaning out of chaos; they are narratives that defy merely rational logic and resist stability. As Starkey says in attempting to explain his own complicated family dynamics, "Love isn't quite as clear-cut as that."[26] Starkey's anarchic investigations, in other

24. Bateman, *Nine Inches*, 243.

25. Bateman, *Belfast Confidential*, 9.

26. Bateman, *Divorcing Jack*, 256.

words, deconstruct rigid social frameworks in order to reveal the messiness of everyday life. He subverts authoritative narratives not to expose a lack of meaning, or even to substitute a different meaning, but to attest to the plasticity of the narratives that structure the human experience.

Given the centrality of chaotic family narratives to the cases Dan investigates, the development of Starkey's own family throughout the series becomes key to making sense of Bateman's optimistic anarchy. Like the other traditional social narratives that Bateman subverts and questions, Starkey's familial relationships parody the conventional family unit. *Divorcing Jack* begins with his wife, Trish, catching him with another woman and kicking him out of the house. Throughout the novel, as well as the rest of the series, Starkey fights to save their family, both from external threats as well as their own constant disagreements, infidelities, and trials. In *Of Wee Sweetie Mice and Men* (1996), Trish has an affair and becomes pregnant; she and Starkey eventually decide to raise the baby as their own, although his lingering jealousy troubles his attempts to bond with Stevie and reconcile with Trish. When Trish and Stevie are kidnapped in connection with one of Starkey's cases in *Shooting Sean*, Stevie dies from hypothermia. Starkey and Trish eventually go through a lengthy separation culminating in a divorce, though the official termination of their marriage coincides with their unofficial adoption of Bobby, a fourteen-year-old boy whose single mother was murdered during another of Starkey's investigations. Trish and Starkey help each other to take care of Bobby, thinking all the while about their own lost son: "Our boy might have been like him," Trish muses, "But I don't want to project *that* . . . on to Bobby."[27] A few years later, when Bobby and his girlfriend have a baby, Trish calls Starkey from the hospital to tell him, "Well, you're a grandad,"[28] a position that he begrudgingly but happily accepts: "It was a lie, a damn lie, but I knew it meant I had to drag myself over to the hospital to make smiley at a barely sixteen-year-old Lolita with a bouncing babe, and her proud ex-druggie one-legged teenage lover, and the ex–Mrs S . . . and wonder how the hell I'd

27. Bateman, *Nine Inches*, 364–65.

28. Bateman, *Dead Pass*, 5.

ended up outside of but eternally connected to any of them. . . . He wasn't my flesh, or blood . . . but I felt a little moist in the eye."[29]

What Starkey's unusual family demonstrates is that while the traditional family "script" has failed to function, the bonds of love and necessity that hold them together have not. Their complicated dynamics do not fit any conventional family framework, but that does not mean that their relationships do not work—they just have to revise the parameters of the family narrative. If the work of the literary detective is "deriving order from the seeming chaos of conflicting signals and motives,"[30] and the work of the metaphysical literary detective is to question the possibility of finding order, then Starkey finds meaning precisely in the chaos of everyday life. Starkey's family, like the cases he investigates, somehow works out in the end, despite his failures to make sense of everything and the lack of conventional "closure." Trish and Starkey never stop loving one another, but they also never get back together. He structures his meaningful relationships within a constantly changing, chaotic social narrative—one that is open to revision when the circumstances necessitate.

Of course, this kind of narrative revision is not without risk. In fact, throughout the series, many of Starkey's investigations focus not only on uncovering a crime but also on the ways that powerful individuals seek to bolster their own authority—and cover up or mitigate their own crimes—by revising the way that the story is told. Given the political dimensions of many of these cases, this kind of revisionary storytelling is hardly surprising; a Northern Irish audience would be very familiar with Starkey's frequent arguments about whether some Troubles-era killing ought to be understood as murder or a casualty of war. Starkey repeatedly encounters a number of former paramilitaries who manipulate the way their stories are narrated—and the social schemata by which they are structured—in order to exercise social or political power. In *Belfast Confidential*, for example, Starkey is kidnapped by the "West Belfast hard man"[31] turned painter Con-

29. Bateman, *Dead Pass*, 5–6, 21.

30. Nealon, "Work of the Detective," 117.

31. Bateman, *Belfast Confidential*, 147.

crete Corcoran. Corcoran wants to convince Starkey that he is "a different man now . . . a born-again painter!"[32] so that Starkey's feature about him in his magazine's Power List will "be about my art, about how important it is. . . . Nothing to do with the old stuff, okay? Nothing at all."[33] Although this scenario is treated as a comic interlude in the novel, Bateman is satirizing the dangerous lengths to which some people will go in order to manipulate their narrative. When Mark Brinn gains political power by recasting himself as a victim rather than a perpetrator, several people are murdered in the attempt to control the public narrative. What is problematic in each of these cases, though, is not so much the plasticity of the narratives, but rather the violent efforts of some to hide their own narrative revisions by silencing other versions of the story. This kind of narrative work is dangerous both because it is performed in secret and because its goal is to cement the explanatory power of one particular narrative.

Bateman thus does not simply advocate a singular revision of social narratives, but a general, and ongoing, willingness to revise. In *Driving Big Davie* (2004), Starkey has a telling encounter with a childhood friend who has lately been acting suspiciously. Davie has invited Starkey on holiday, though his behavior on the trip—lying about his previous relationships, sneaking away to a nearby hotel, and illegally procuring a gun without telling him—forces Starkey into treating Davie like the subject of one of his investigations. "I was coming up with a different theory every day," he remarks, "one to suit every move Davie made . . . but where did I fit in?"[34] He no longer knows how to make sense of Davie, or how to understand their relationship. When Davie invites him out to a nice dinner, Starkey leaves the restaurant a number of times to get a break from his friend; each time he returns, he finds Davie sitting at a different table, without a word of explanation. When he finally confronts his friend about his strange behavior, Davie reveals what Starkey has failed to notice, in no small part because of his heavy drinking: "It's a revolving restaurant. I haven't

32. Bateman, *Belfast Confidential*, 242.

33. Bateman, *Belfast Confidential*, 242.

34. Bateman, *Driving Big Davie*, 138.

moved tables. The restaurant has just revolved."[35] Moreover, Davie says that *he* has been worried about *Starkey*, offering an alternate perspective on Starkey's antics—"getting drunk like you were determined to damage yourself"[36]—which make them seem as disturbing as Davie's own behavior. What Bateman illustrates in this comically poignant scene is that the work of interpreting the other is a constantly shifting endeavor. Given both the fundamental divide between self and other, along with the subtle changes to our own perspectives and situations—"No, Dan, it doesn't feel like we're revolving. . . . It's gradual. You'd hardly notice"[37]—the narratives structuring our relationships with others must, by necessity, be provisional and open to change. While the conventional detective novel is very often "conservative, almost compulsive in the belief . . . that one may in truth trace cause and effect, may place responsibility just *here*, may pass judgment, may even assess blame,"[38] Bateman here destabilizes the notion of objective knowledge in favor of subjective reinterpretation.

While Starkey routinely faces failures, both as a writer and as a detective, Bateman recuperates the explanatory power of narrative even as he complicates it, indicating his unique positioning within the metaphysical detective subgenre. In the quintessential metaphysical detective novel, Paul Auster's *City of Glass* (1985), the protagonist, Daniel Quinn, is a mystery writer who finds himself working as a private detective. As Quinn "devolve[s] into fragmentation and madness,"[39] Auster's novel explores the failure of narrative to adequately capture "a reality that has no coherent structure."[40] Similarly, one of the touchstones throughout Bateman's series is the failure of all of Starkey's writing projects. As his career at the newspaper goes downhill—"The cease-fire was good news for everyone but journalists"[41]—he takes on other commissions. He writes a biography of Irish boxer Bobby

35. Bateman, *Driving Big Davie*, 127.
36. Bateman, *Driving Big Davie*, 124.
37. Bateman, *Driving Big Davie*, 127.
38. Winks, *Detective Fiction*, 10.
39. Bernstein, "Story Itself," 137.
40. Bernstein, "Story Itself," 137.
41. Bateman, *Turbulent Priests*, 14.

McMaster, but the publisher gets hit with a libel suit and he never gets paid;[42] he writes a book about a bizarre cult on Wrathlin Island, which was "remaindered within six weeks";[43] and he becomes the editor of the hugely successful magazine *Belfast Confidential* only to drive it into bankruptcy soon thereafter.[44] Alongside all of these professional disasters, he describes his continuing effort to write "the Great Ulster novel";[45] decades later, he's still "working on a novel, which I knew would never be finished."[46] In keeping with the optimism of the series, however, Starkey's literary failures do not gesture toward the failure of narrative, but rather suggest that the genre—the structure of that narrative—has to change with the times. As Starkey muses, "Perhaps journalism was dying in cyberspace. Or maybe it was just becoming something else."[47] In much the same way that Starkey resolves his cases by adjusting the "genre" through which they are read, revealing apparent political conspiracies to be better understood as family dramas, so too his own writing career is a constant flux of generic lenses; he writes everything from newspaper columns to tourism literature to "the sequel to the Bible."[48] When each of these projects fails, he simply changes gear and begins again. Like the novel Starkey seems destined never to finish, Bateman suggests that the task of narrating "a reality that has no coherent structure"[49] is by necessity an unending project, never finally settled but continually requiring narrative work.

Colin Bateman's Dan Starkey novels not only utilize the work of the detective as a metaphor for the narrative construction of meaning but also consistently upset the generic convention that the detective's narrative work enables access to the truth. Kelly suggests that the mystery thriller in Northern Ireland is formally suited to radical social critique: "What the

42. Bateman, *Shooting Sean*, 4.

43. Bateman, *Horse with My Name*, 3.

44. Bateman, *Nine Inches*, 4.

45. Bateman, *Divorcing Jack*, 5.

46. Bateman, *Fire and Brimstone*, 21.

47. Bateman, *Shooting Sean*, 22.

48. Bateman, *Turbulent Priests*, 64.

49. Bernstein, "Story Itself," 137.

organic, filiative ideologies and communities of both Irish Nationalism and Unionism encounter in the thriller . . . are traces of their own contradictions, the breakdown of their imagined nation. . . . The thriller . . . fractures the ideological mirage of the organic, knowable whole, and crime becomes a . . . means of not only expressing social insecurity but also of mapping the seemingly indecipherable reaches of society itself."[50] The Starkey novels certainly participate in this deconstruction of accepted ideologies, but with the important distinction that Starkey does not provide a "map" of society so much as reveal the malleability of any such narrative schemata. These characteristics locate Bateman's novels within the tradition of the "metaphysical detective story," although rather than "indicat[ing] that 'reality' is ultimately unknowable,"[51] the novels suggest that the *knowing* is a complex process, requiring both narrative construction and deconstruction. Though Starkey might bemoan his failures as an investigator, he also states at the end of *Divorcing Jack*: "Oh, I'm still confused, but so's everyone else. It's nice to have company."[52] By revealing the inadequacy and flexibility of others' narratives—as Starkey describes it, putting a spanner in the works—Bateman highlights how the narratives we use to structure and explain our world are always open to revision. While these narrative revisions are not without danger, Bateman imagines that hope for the future might be negotiated through "reread[ing] tradition . . . as a palimpsest of creative possibilities."[53]

Bibliography

Auster, Paul. *City of Glass*. New York: Penguin, 1987.

Bateman, Colin. *Belfast Confidential*. London: Headline, 2005.

———. *The Dead Pass*. London: Headline, 2014.

———. *Divorcing Jack*. London: Harper Collins, 1995.

———. *Driving Big Davie*. London: Headline, 2004.

———. *Fire and Brimstone*. London: Headline, 2013.

50. Kelly, *Thriller and Northern Ireland*, 22–23.

51. Merivale and Sweeney, "Game's Afoot," 4.

52. Bateman, *Divorcing Jack*, 256.

53. Kearney, *Transitions*, 280.

———. *The Horse with My Name.* London: Headline, 2002.

———. *Nine Inches.* London: Headline, 2011.

———. *Shooting Sean.* London: Harper Collins, 2001.

———. *Turbulent Priests.* London: Harper Collins, 1999.

———. *Of Wee Sweetie Mice and Men.* London: Harper Collins, 1996.

Bernstein, Stephen. "'The Question Is the Story Itself': Postmodernism and Intertextuality in Auster's *New York Trilogy.*" In Merivale and Sweeney, eds., 134–53.

Cliff, Brian. *Irish Crime Fiction.* London: Palgrave Macmillan, 2018.

Connolly, John. "No Blacks, No Dogs, No Crime Writers: Ireland and the Mystery Genre." In *Down These Green Streets: Irish Crime Writing in the 21st Century*, edited by Declan Burke, 39–57. Dublin: Liberties, 2011.

Kearney, Richard. *Transitions: Narratives of Modern Irish Culture.* Dublin: Wolfhound, 1988.

Kelly, Aaron. *The Thriller and Northern Ireland since 1969: Utterly Resigned Terror.* Aldershot: Ashgate, 2005.

McGilloway, Brian. *The Nameless Dead.* London: Macmillan, 2012.

Merivale, Patricia, and Susan Elizabeth Sweeney. "The Game's Afoot: On the Trail of the Metaphysical Detective Story." In Merivale and Sweeney, eds., 1–24.

———, eds. *Detecting Texts: The Metaphysical Detective Story from Poe to Postmodernism.* Philadelphia: Univ. of Pennsylvania Press, 1999.

Morales-Ladrón, Marisol. "'Troubling' Thrillers: Between Politics and Popular Fiction in the Novels of Benedict Kiely, Brian Moore and Colin Bateman." *Estudios Irlandeses* 1, no. 1 (2006): 58–66. Accessed 26 July 2017.

Nealon, Jeffrey T. "Work of the Detective, Work of the Writer: Auster's *City of Glass.*" In Merivale and Sweeney, eds., 117–33.

Neville, Stuart. *The Twelve.* London: Harvill Secker, 2009.

Scaggs, John. *Crime Fiction.* Abingdon: Routledge, 2005.

Schwerter, Stephanie. "Peacefire: Belfast between Reality and Fiction." *Canadian Journal of Irish Studies* 33, no. 2 (Fall 2007): 19–27.

Smyth, Gerry. *The Novel and the Nation: Studies in the New Irish Fiction.* London: Pluto Press, 1997.

Winks, Robin W. *Detective Fiction: A Collection of Critical Essays.* Woodstock, VT: Foul Play Press, 1988.

12

"This Isn't Fucking *Miss Marple*, Mate"

Intertextuality in Adrian McKinty's Sean Duffy Series

ANJILI BABBAR

In *Rain Dogs* (2015), the fifth novel of Adrian McKinty's Sean Duffy series, Detective Inspector Duffy of the Royal Ulster Constabulary (RUC) remarks that music "can lift you out of the present, or perhaps take you into an alternative present."[1] Trapped as a participant in the Troubles by his sense of moral responsibility, Duffy turns to music, coupled with alcohol and drugs, as a form of periodic emotional escapism. At the same time, his reliance on the transformative qualities of music underscores McKinty's strategy in titling each novel in the series with reference to the lyrics of Tom Waits. Through the backdrop of Waits's songs, McKinty creates a discomfiting mood of danger, mistrust, and entrapment to envelop his audience in the reality of Troubles-era Belfast. McKinty also establishes tone cinematically, describing characters' resemblance to recognizable film and television personae to outline their appearances and personalities. With tongue in cheek, Duffy compares himself to familiar actors, such as Cary Grant, John Wayne, and Clint Eastwood, both emphasizing and ridiculing his fantasies of heroism and masculinity. More often, though, Duffy is sardonically described (by himself and others) in terms of fictional detectives. In this

1. McKinty, *Rain Dogs*, 315.

way, McKinty both utilizes and subverts hard-boiled and procedural standards, adapting them to a Northern Irish context to contextualize his narratives, while simultaneously highlighting crime fiction's divergence from reality and its limited ability to represent experiences of sustained violence.

McKinty's incorporation of Waits's song titles and lyrics has much the same effect as the soundtrack of a film, and the author stresses that it is vital to his process, beyond what his readers might see: "I would listen to the whole album, listen to various cuts. I did way more on this than I should have. Like, I spent a week listening to about thirty different versions of 'Cold Cold Ground' to see which one I really wanted, even though it's never going to be referred to at all."[2] This emphasis is especially remarkable in that Waits is not an obvious choice for the series. Waits's songs are not precisely contemporaneous with McKinty's settings; "Cold Cold Ground," for example, was released in 1987, while its namesake, the first novel of the Duffy series, is set in 1981. More to the point, Waits is an American musician, highly influenced by the blues, jazz, and gospel genres of his own country. Of his anachronistic and culturally transcendent selection, McKinty notes that theme and tone ultimately outweighed considerations of temporal and spatial context: "My first temptation was to do new wave music, 'cause that's the music of the time. . . . I [wanted] one consistent voice throughout all the titles. And I couldn't get The Jam to work, I couldn't get The Smiths to work, I couldn't get New Order to work. Joy Division almost worked, but I just couldn't quite get it, and then I thought, well, it's got to be Tom Waits."[3] McKinty became so determined to use Waits's songs as a running theme in the Duffy series that he disregarded the advice of his publisher—who would have preferred a more commercially recognizable artist—and wrote a four-page plea to Waits and his manager to reconsider their initial refusal of usage rights. The letter had its desired effect.[4]

McKinty's choice of Waits is reflective of a tendency among Irish crime writers to both incorporate and destabilize the standards affiliated with

2. McKinty, interview.

3. McKinty, interview.

4. McKinty, interview.

subgenres established by British and American authors. John Connolly, author of the Charlie Parker series, notes that "the absence of any recognisable Irish models" led him to the study of American and British detective fiction, in the hopes of both using and subverting the form: "For me, the choice was either to import genre conventions from the UK or the US to an Irish context, which I felt was neither appropriate nor, indeed, interesting; or to apply a European, outsider's perspective to those conventions, to try 'to change the system from within,' to borrow a line from Leonard Cohen."[5] McKinty approaches this change to "the system" in part by applying American hard-boiled tropes to a procedural context: while Duffy is technically a police officer who works with a team of trusted colleagues, the seamy urbanity of the settings, the emphasis on corrupt institutions, and the wise-cracking, nonconformist protagonist of the Duffy series are distinctly hard-boiled. Waits's lyrics serve to highlight this adoption of the American postwar PI (private investigator) atmosphere, drawing on its use of dark humor and witty repartee and its themes of criminality, alcoholism, and the dangerous underbelly of city life. Unsurprisingly, Waits has repeatedly noted the influence of American authors who incorporate modified versions of these tropes, such as the Beat poets and Charles Bukowski, on his lyrics. Waits's praise of Bukowski, in particular, might as easily be an excerpt from Chandler's delineation of hard-boiled ideals in "The Simple Art of Murder": "[Bukowski] seemed to be a writer of the common people and the street people, looking in the dark corners where no one seems to want to go . . . he was the writer for the dispossessed and the people who didn't *have* a voice."[6]

Waits's music includes some convenient parallels to Irish crime fiction, and to McKinty's work in particular, in that it is simultaneously respectful, challenging, and self-deprecating in its use of tradition: Waits's dramatic adoption and adaptation of various forms and personae has been described as "*very* deliberate, pushing the boundaries and genres that he had come out

5. Connolly, "No Blacks, No Dogs, No Crime Writers: Ireland and the Mystery Genre," 43–44.

6. Waits, quoted in Hoskyns, *Lowside of the Road*, 73.

of."[7] Waits frequently personifies cities, especially Los Angeles, thus conjuring the anthropomorphized "mean streets" of Hammett and Chandler; his lyrics emphasize anonymity and the idiosyncratic, focusing on peculiar characters, nightlife, and death. In this sense, they establish an appropriate mood for the Duffy series, in which the dystopian, "Gap-toothed"[8] Belfast of the Troubles plays as central a role as Duffy himself. This mood is clear when Duffy describes Belfast as mired in its own horror, angst, and tragedy: "City of dreadful night. City of the damned. City of no escape. Rain hisses onto the cobbles and the open drains. The city hums and seethes. The black Farset bubbles to the surface of High Street, oozing human filth. The rusting giant cranes droop over the empty docks like the bones of dead gods. Army helicopters sweep the city with a sick white light."[9]

While enamored with the pulse and heterogeneity of cities, Waits's music is equally concerned with the devaluation of human life that results from overpopulation and urban violence. McKinty employs these same themes, adapting them to the context of ideological extremism and civil war.

In *The Cold Cold Ground* (2012), Duffy outlines his situation as a Catholic detective in the RUC, detailing the constant threats of riots, bombings, and the IRA bounty on Catholic cops. He also introduces his motivation for joining the police as a dream of being "some small part of ending this madness."[10] This optimism slowly erodes, however, as little progress results from his efforts. In this novel, Duffy investigates what appear to be the serial murders of gay men and is hindered as much by his society's homophobia as by the obstructionism of paramilitaries on both sides. From the beginning, then, each of the Duffy titles alludes to a Waits song, which provides a central premise for the novel. Waits's "Cold Cold Ground" sets the scene for the series, with references to religion, gun violence, property damage, bigotry, annihilated dreams, and the inevitability of death. Subsequent titles allude to stages in Duffy's efforts to come to terms with his surroundings and responsibilities, which closely resemble the controversial

7. Walker, quoted in Maher, *Tom Waits on Tom Waits*, chap. 1.

8. McKinty, *Rain Dogs*, 319.

9. McKinty, *Rain Dogs*, 307.

10. McKinty, *Cold Ground*, 31.

Kübler-Ross model of the progression of grief (1969): Duffy begins with the conviction that he can change the course of the Troubles, becomes angry and frustrated when he grasps the depth of the corruption that underlies them, considers compromising his ethics in an effort to ameliorate his personal and professional circumstances, sinks into despondency when his plans are thwarted, and finally learns to accept the limits of his ability to improve the state of his community.

Waits's "A Sweet Little Bullet from a Pretty Blue Gun" considers the scores of young women who arrive in Hollywood with fantasies of fame, vulnerable to exploitation and suicide. The most striking aspect of the song is its depiction of one such woman's death as unremarkable in a town habituated to such stories. The second Duffy novel, *I Hear the Sirens in the Street* (2013), references a line from this song to underscore the commonness of human injuries and premature death. Set during the Falklands War, the plot follows Duffy's increasing agitation as the British government and media turn their focus to a meaningless display of power in a faraway land, rather than concerning themselves with the daily casualties in Northern Ireland. When a body is discovered in a suitcase, Duffy is given a lead on a suspect, only to discover that the suspect has been dead for months. Although he was a member of the security forces, the man's death had been overlooked, prompting a scornful reaction from his widow: "This is why this country is going down the drain. Nobody cares."[11] When he retrieves the patrolman's file, Duffy is shocked at the inattention to detail: "*That's it?. . . . A man gets blown away and that's bloody it?*"[12] Duffy's interest in the case provokes Dougherty, the lead officer, to investigate more thoroughly. For his meddling, Dougherty is subsequently killed with a car bomb, an event dismissed as a random, par-for-the-course, unsolvable IRA hit in a chapter ironically titled "A Very Ordinary Assassination." In Duffy's Belfast, like Waits's Hollywood, life has become cheap, murders routine, and the populace anesthetized to human loss.

11. McKinty, *Sirens*, 51.

12. McKinty, *Sirens*, 66.

In the Morning I'll Be Gone (2014) takes its title from a Waits song that conflates travel and death as means of escape. The first two chapters—"The Great Escape" and "The Little Escape"—describe a breakout of IRA prisoners at the Maze, including Duffy's former schoolmate, Dermot McCann. Duffy's own situation is the inverse of McCann's: having been wrongfully dismissed from the RUC, he contemplates escape through emigration and suicide but is unable to follow through with either. MI5 then enlists his help in tracking Dermot, promising to reinstate him to his former position in exchange for his cooperation. By the end of the novel, after two near-death experiences, he is "seized by a wild impulse" to "get on [a] boat and escape to Britain and leave . . . all this madness behind,"[13] but feelings of obligation overwhelm him, and he returns home to prepare for "what [is] evidently going to be a long, long war."[14]

Waits's "Gun Street Girl" describes problems with the law and life on the run following an unspecified encounter with a femme fatale. In McKinty's novel of the same name (2015), Duffy is tempted, both romantically and professionally, by Kate, an MI5 agent with a family home on Gun Street in Oxford. At the same time, the governmental forces with which Kate is entangled work to undermine Duffy's current investigation: the case of a murdered couple, the apparent suicide of their son, and the disappearance of missiles from a warehouse with which the son was connected. The plot is a reimagining of the Iran-Contra affair, in which McKinty assigns more weight to British involvement than has been avowed and offers his strongest critique of governmental obfuscation. Duffy's ill-advised flirtation with working for this government is attributed to his fascination with Kate, a kind of Eve in Duffy's dystopian Garden of Eden: alluring, representative of new avenues for the future, but potentially destructive to his soul. Duffy is spared from both the MI5 job and death only by accident or the intervention of fate: a broken arm and foot from a domestic incident prevent him from joining Kate and other intelligence agents aboard a

13. McKinty, *Morning*, 313.

14. McKinty, *Morning*, 314.

helicopter that crashes on the Mull of Kintyre, resulting in the deaths of all of its passengers.

Morbidly fortuitous, Kate's death abruptly puts an end to Duffy's plans for his future. McKinty emphasizes this loss of purpose through Waits's "Rain Dogs," which ruminates on people who have become directionless due to social and moral conflict. *Rain Dogs* (2015) gives the impression that Duffy is consigned to readdressing familiar conflicts instead of making professional progress. Convinced that the deaths of a young woman in Carrickfergus Castle and his chief superintendent are both connected to a foreign businessman considering opening a plant in Northern Ireland, Duffy's inquiries are hampered by the government's desperation for foreign investment. This is a turning point in the series. Already dismayed that the government is willing to overlook crimes for the sake of diplomacy, Duffy now discovers that it is willing to do so for economic advantages as well, and he begins to question his own loyalty. Duffy's personal and professional lives careen off course due to the chaos in which he is engulfed: his girlfriend leaves him, and his faith in trusted allies—and in his own judgment—falters when a former colleague, McIlroy, turns out to be complicit in the murders.

The sixth novel of the series, *Police at the Station and They Don't Look Friendly* (2017), takes a line from Waits's "Cold Water," a reflection on poverty, ostracization, aging, and, obviously, the dubious benevolence of the police. Until this point, Duffy has justified working for an untrustworthy government, which has historically oppressed his fellow Catholics, by persuading himself that he is "doing bad . . . for the greater good."[15] The British may be imperfect, so his logic went, but the paramilitary vigilantism Duffy fights is self-serving, hypocritical, and costly in terms of human casualties. Investigating the death of a drug dealer and the disappearance of the dealer's wife, Duffy is framed as an IRA mole by his superintendent and is subject to suspicion, bigotry, and verbal abuse from Special Branch. Although he clears his name and solves the case, Duffy's faith in the RUC has been permanently undermined by the corruption and bigotry.

15. McKinty, *Gun Street*, 130.

At the end of the novel, Duffy is resigned to his limitations in effecting change under these circumstances; he moves to Scotland and scales down his involvement with the RUC to a part-time position.

The straightforward use of Waits's songs to provide context and atmosphere serves as a counterpoint to McKinty's ambivalent treatment of other intertextual sources. In particular, Duffy's habitual references to detective television shows from the seventies and eighties highlight his yearning for a simpler path to justice and heroism while underscoring popular culture's misrepresentation of police work. In contrast to these televised narratives, the resolution of cases does not, for Duffy, imply a restoration of social order. On the contrary, each investigation increases his awareness of the political corruption that perverts justice, and heightens his conviction that, regardless of dedication and intellect, individuals are largely powerless in the face of such structural chicanery. Duffy brags about his "*Starsky and Hutch* moves"[16] and, when offering classical denouements, warns culprits not to "interrupt Columbo when he's doing his final fucking speech."[17] However, these conflations are clearly self-mocking: Duffy lampoons his own belief that he can make a difference in the pursuit of justice, and McKinty exploits his own self-consciousness about using a traditionally unrealistic form to convey a realistic sense of history.

"There was a brand new cop show on called *Magnum P.I.*," explains Duffy in *The Cold Cold Ground*. "He was a PI. He was called Magnum. Like Serpico he had an impressive moustache. This, I realized, was my problem."[18] Duffy's real "problem," of course, is that criminal investigations are neither as linear nor as prone to satisfactory resolution as implied by certain tropes of crime fiction. Although he clearly recognizes this, there is a sense of earnest self-laceration throughout the series, as he fails to live up to the popular detective standards by which he is besieged. He watches *Murder, She Wrote*, attempting to "[solve] the murder before Jessica, [solve] the numbers before Carol,"[19] and opines that "A better detective" would

16. McKinty, *Sirens*, 229.
17. McKinty, *Police*, 300.
18. McKinty, *Cold Ground*, 210.
19. McKinty, *Gun Street*, 274.

put clues together more effectively than him: "Where was Miss Marple when you needed her?"[20] While he maintains that crime fiction has little in common with real detective work, particularly in a war zone, he is unable to fully distance himself from these characters and their situations, which at times are relatable to him: "You had to like the fact that Rockford got shat on all the time and was living in penury. . . . Seemed about right for a detective."[21] Likewise, when debating the relative values of compassion and professionalism in his field, he looks to fiction as a reflection of his own circumstances: "The policeman, like the doctor and the paramedic, treads a fine line between distance and humanity. . . . Like old Inspector Laidlaw across the sheugh you found yourself in the dilemma of either indulging in grief by proxy or imitating a stone."[22]

A similar dichotomy exists in Duffy's approach to solving cases. *In the Morning I'll Be Gone* has Duffy turn to a series of locked-room mystery novels in order to gain insight into his own case; in an instance of life mimicking art, it is eventually revealed that the killer referred to these same texts in formulating the crime.[23] When faced with the second locked-room mystery of his career in *Rain Dogs*, Duffy contends that there must be a mistake: "Surely it would be stretching the confidence limits to suggest that an incident like that could ever occur again to the same peeler. I was not the brilliant but exceptionally statistically unlucky Dr. Gideon Fell, nor was I the equally unlucky Hercule Poirot; no, I was the plodding, *ordinary*, Detective Inspector Sean Duffy of the humdrum RUC."[24] Unlike the first locked-room murderer, who relied on traditional crime stories as sources, this criminal has familiarized himself with Duffy's own previous situations in order to taunt, confuse, and mislead him. The killer is ultimately foiled by his own presumption, developed from a crime fiction trope, that the whole truth is always brought to light for the audience. In a prideful rage, Duffy ridicules the murderer for believing the public reports that his first

20. McKinty, *Police*, 245.

21. McKinty, *Sirens*, 177.

22. McKinty, *Police*, 107.

23. McKinty, *Morning*, 255.

24. McKinty, *Rain Dogs*, 62.

locked-room case was never solved and assuming that it was consequently a sore point for him.[25]

McKinty thus weaves a self-reflective pattern, lampooning his own use of form and standards, and highlighting his awareness that certain of his plotlines are inevitably "like an episode of fucking *Columbo*."[26] Certainly, he does nothing to disguise his reformulation of historical events for the sake of narrative structure. To offer an expedient conclusion to Duffy's relationship with Kate and MI5, for example, the helicopter crash at the end of *Gun Street Girl* displaces by seven years the 1994 crash that killed key agents from MI5, the RUC, and the British army. At the same time, McKinty exploits crime fiction clichés in order to underscore the differences between Duffy's experiences and those of traditional fictional detectives: a "dead blonde" is not a beautiful woman but "some chubby guy with yellow tips in a denim AC/DC jacket";[27] a stakeout of a graffiti artist is "hardly *The French Connection*";[28] the messy resolution to a case is not "*The Mystery of the Yellow Room* but it was a case solved and it kept the Chief off our backs for a couple of days."[29] Moreover, Duffy is robbed of the opportunity to deal with criminal masterminds, as, in reality, "Most crooks are bloody eejits."[30] He is also frequently denied the closure of evoking a confession through conscience and evidence alone; as one suspect asserts, "This isn't fucking *Miss Marple*, mate. I'm not confessing to anything." Indeed, as Duffy begins to outline the details of the case, the suspect taunts him—and possibly McKinty as well—with the suggestion that he "should write a novel."[31]

It is perhaps not surprising that the most recurrent references in the series are to Colin Dexter's Inspector Morse; having completed his graduate studies at Oxford, McKinty would have been inundated with allusions to

25. McKinty, *Rain Dogs*, 274.
26. McKinty, *Morning*, 116.
27. McKinty, *Cold Ground*, 21.
28. McKinty, *Sirens*, 125.
29. McKinty, *Sirens*, 200.
30. McKinty, *Sirens*, 39.
31. McKinty, *Morning*, 247–48.

the city's ubiquitous inspector. Moreover, the central tension of the Morse series arises from the displacement of a traditional fictional detective, who prioritizes moral responsibility over status and economic concerns, into a realistic Thatcher-era criminal justice system.[32] Dexter's series, like McKinty's, is thus particularly concerned with disparities between actual police procedure and the way it is often presented in popular media: "*Morse* does not look to real history for its prelapsarian idyll. . . . What we see in *Inspector Morse* is a nostalgia dependent on an audience's familiarity with other police fictions."[33] While McKinty loosely applies Dexter's model—emphasizing the distinction between real and fictional police work through a detective whose ideals, derived from fiction, are at odds with the reality of his vocation—he nevertheless identifies the ways in which the earlier series falls short of the authenticity he wishes to convey. McKinty's most obvious homage to Morse, in *Gun Street Girl*, is largely parodic. When Duffy and his colleague Lawson travel to Oxford to follow a lead, Duffy is full of bitterness at the tranquility of the station and the city where Morse was ostensibly run off his feet solving crimes: "A quiet little police station. No one wearing body armor, no one wearing side arms, no stench of fear. This was what policing was like over the water. This was policing in civilization. These guys didn't know how lucky they had it. Burglaries, stolen bicycles, the odd rape, a murder every five or ten years—the real Morse World."[34]

At the heart of McKinty's intertextual and metatextual considerations are a desire to challenge crime fiction conventions (again, like Connolly, to "apply a European, outsider's perspective to those conventions") and a concurrent acknowledgment of the difficulty in rejecting clichés for even the most self-aware of authors. Ultimately, his solution—satirizing characters and tropes—allows him to explore the absurd pretense of crime-solving as puzzle-game and to edify readers about the complexities of Troubles-era Northern Ireland without resorting to pedantry. "I wasn't going to bang my head against a wall," Duffy muses about his acceptance of imperfect

32. Davis, "*Inspector Morse*," 137.

33. Davis, "*Inspector Morse*," 146.

34. McKinty, *Gun Street*, 141.

conclusions to cases. "Magnum PI did that on TV and other cops in books. But few people in the RUC ever banged their head against a wall about a case. We conserved our psychic energy for the day-to-day. We were all too busy trying to stay alive."[35]

McKinty thus establishes a casual communication with his readers, hinting that he understands the temptations of tidy endings and absolute good and evil precisely because he shares them, despite his determination to give an accurate representation of the Troubles and to tell the story of those involved "more or less the way it was."[36] In this way, he encourages his audience to join him in a quest for truth that, after all, has at least nominally been at the center of crime fiction since its inception.

Throughout the series, McKinty unravels the way the Troubles, and Irish society more broadly, have been misrepresented, particularly by American media. References to *The Quiet Man* and Liam Neeson as an ex-paramilitary in *Miami Vice* are introduced with a combination of humor, frustration, and comprehension.[37] Duffy is not unsympathetic to the reductive Irish American narrative of the Troubles, the "simple story of peace-loving Irish patriots starving themselves to drive out the evil British imperialists," conceding that it "would have been my view too if I'd gone to New York and stayed there."[38] Duffy further meets American idealists on their own ground by confessing that he once shared their perceptions and considered joining the IRA.[39] Literary references in the series reinforce Duffy's aversion to the disenfranchisement of Catholics, which he views as ongoing fuel for the Troubles, both because it evokes international sympathy for the IRA and because it limits the nonviolent options for Catholics in pursuit of civil rights. In *I Hear the Sirens*, Duffy's ambivalence about his only act of murder leads him to the parish of Kilroot for solace, absolution, and a reinforcement of his pacifistic ideals.[40] In reality, of course, such support would

35. McKinty, *Morning*, 218.
36. McKinty, interview.
37. McKinty, *Police*, 67.
38. McKinty, *Cold Ground*, 130.
39. McKinty, *Cold Ground*, 30.
40. McKinty, *Sirens*, 258–59.

likely not be forthcoming for a repentant Catholic at Kilroot, a Protestant parish reputed for Jonathan Swift's tenure there, hardly a place catering to the spiritual needs of local Catholics and dissenters.[41]

By contextualizing his commentaries with familiar references, McKinty effectively communicates his own points of concern while avoiding an alienating sanctimony. Understanding the American view of the Troubles as a battle between freedom fighters and fascists (and the media from whence this view springs), Duffy is able to secure the attention of his readers by contrasting this outlook with his own experienced reality. In particular, he subtly discredits dramatic delineations of good and evil, framing both Catholic and Protestant characters as complex individuals—with personal motivations, capable of both compassionate and cruel behavior—rather than as reductive symbols of opposing political, social, or religious philosophies. Duffy suggests that while the IRA's apparent objective—the pursuit of civil rights for Northern Ireland's Catholics—may situate it on the right side of history, the organization's violence complicates the narrative exponentially, and he appeals for a recognition of violence as a destructive, dehumanizing force, regardless of its underlying ideology. Having conceded his initial attraction to the IRA, Duffy strives sincerely to be objective as he juxtaposes the reality of Northern Ireland's civil war with the way it is portrayed in popular culture: "When the IRA take a policeman or a soldier hostage in the pictures," he remarks, "what follows is an often philosophical and historical argument about the British presence in Ireland and the crimes the Brits have committed against Irish rebels." The truth, he suggests, is considerably bleaker, comprising beatings, killings, and torture: "I had seen bodies where the paramilitaries had drilled into victims' kneecaps, wrists, and ankles. I'd seen bodies where the eyeballs had been gouged out, where the victim's feet had been blowtorched, or where the victim had been castrated and forced to eat their own genitalia until they'd choked to death."[42]

Ultimately, McKinty's use of intertextuality in the Duffy series tends neither toward obsequiousness nor condemnation. Rather, McKinty

41. McKinty, interview.

42. McKinty, *Police*, 205.

acknowledges both the value and limitations of crime fiction standards and reductive ideologies, positions himself as a searcher for truth as fallible as any other, and suggests improvements in discourse about justice and human nature. McKinty parodically (and self-parodically) comments on the potential of crime fiction to generate such discourse by honestly considering various personal, social, and cultural perspectives, by recognizing the complexities of detective work and the improbability of satisfying conclusions to investigations, and by acknowledging the multifaceted characters of individuals. The series' tendency toward self-mockery and black humor also offers a snapshot of a society's awkward attempts to contend emotionally with the violence, terror, and injustice of civil war. McKinty has confessed a kind of regret at his hesitance to fully embrace this tone at the outset of the series, due to a concern that it would be misunderstood: "I was unsure I could convince readers of the tone. . . . If you want to be at least partly mimetic you need to capture the mood. . . . I remember very clearly people using humor as a response to the nightmare that was happening all around us and because I was worried that readers might think I was being glib, I cut that from book one and to some extent from book two."[43] The metatextual comedy of the later books in the series, then, represents a redoubling of efforts at realism, regardless of the discomfort it might cause. Like Duffy, even as McKinty ridicules his own resort to cliché and theatricality,[44] he vehemently maintains that "out here, on the edge of the dying British Empire, farce is the only mode of narrative discourse that makes any sense at all."[45]

Bibliography

Connolly, John. "No Blacks, No Dogs, No Crime Writers: Ireland and the Mystery Genre." In *Down These Green Streets: Irish Crime Writing in the 21st Century*, edited by Declan Burke, 39–57. Dublin: Liberties Press, 2011. Kindle edition.

Davis, Helen. "*Inspector Morse* and the Business of Crime." *Television and New Media* 58, no. 4 (2001): 133–48.

43. McKinty, interview.
44. McKinty, *Police*, 277–79.
45. McKinty, *Gun Street*, 14.

Hoskyns, Barney. *Lowside of the Road: A Life of Tom Waits.* New York: Crown Archetype, 2009.

Maher, Paul Jr., ed. *Tom Waits on Tom Waits: Interviews and Encounters.* Chicago: Chicago Review Press, 2011. Kindle edition.

McKinty, Adrian. *The Cold Cold Ground.* Amherst, NY: Seventh Street Books, 2012.

———. *Gun Street Girl.* Amherst, NY: Seventh Street Books, 2015.

———. *I Hear the Sirens in the Street.* Amherst, NY: Seventh Street Books, 2013.

———. *In the Morning I'll Be Gone.* Amherst, NY: Seventh Street Books, 2014.

———. Personal interview. Digital recording. Belfast, 28 October 2017.

———. *Police at the Station and They Don't Look Friendly.* Amherst, NY: Seventh Street Books, 2017.

———. *Rain Dogs.* Amherst, NY: Seventh Street Books, 2016.

13

The Radical and the Unrepresentable in Gene Kerrigan's Dublin Tetralogy

RICHARD HOWARD

At a writing festival in Dublin in 2008, the Irish crime writer Gene Kerrigan remarked that while he personally subscribed to "radical politics," he wrote "conservative novels."[1] Although Kerrigan never articulated whether he was referring to his novels in a formal or structural sense, these terms offer a starting point for an interrogation of his work. Kerrigan's politics are evident to anyone who has read his weekly column in the *Irish Independent* or his polemical nonfiction works such as *This Great Little Nation* (1999) and *The Big Lie* (2012). The author's categorization of his own fictional work as conservative seems to stem from critical appraisals of detective fiction from the Golden Age onward as working in favor of the status quo.

This view of the genre is contested by critics such as Lee Horsley, who suggests that even classic detective fiction can serve to expose "abuses of power and callous greed," and Martin Priestman, who attributes to the genre "a stance of ironic detachment from the world depicted which suggests a sub-Marxist or absurdist critique of bourgeois society in general."[2] Robert P. Winston and Nancy C. Mellerski elaborate on this, arguing that

1. Burke, "Great Meeting."

2. Horsley, *Twentieth-Century Crime Fiction*, 19; Priestman, "Post-War British Crime Fiction," 175.

certain strands of crime fiction, including the police procedural, have been utilized to critique society from a more progressive position rather than merely reproducing the culture from which they originated. Winston and Mellerski discuss the work of Maj Sjöwall and Per Wahlöö as "police procedurals with a social conscience" that examine urban alienation and corruption, and question the foundations for the laws that the police uphold. They conclude that such fictions constitute Sjöwall and Wahlöö "subverting a popular formula to their overtly ideological aims," and this essay will reflect on the extent to which Kerrigan's work performs a similar maneuver.[3]

In doing so, this essay will attempt to interrogate Kerrigan's crime fiction within the broad categories of conservative and radical that the author invokes, while also taking into account the postcolonial status of his works. Kerrigan is among a number of writers involved in a resurgence of Irish crime writing that Charlotte Beyer—addressing John Connolly and Jane Casey in particular—links specifically to a postcolonial "commitment to the richness and significance of home-grown literature that represents and reflects Irish locations."[4] With that "commitment" in mind, this essay defines Kerrigan's novels as vernacular crime fiction, dependent upon their Dublin location in regard to setting and language.

This essay will also consider Kerrigan's use of objects as a critique of commodity fetishism, and show how Kerrigan marks out territories in his fiction through these objects. Kerrigan demonstrates that these territories are not pure spaces, but that the affluent world of the Irish bourgeoisie influences the desires and orientations of the exploited working class who, within the world of the text, aspire to their wealth and often view the wealthy as prey. The upper classes in turn are depicted as being dependent on the labor of the working classes, particularly in the acquisition and distribution of narcotics. The character of Synnott in *The Midnight Choir* (2006), the most subversive figure in Kerrigan's novels, will be examined in relation to a postcolonial distrust of authority that resists the narrative closure of the traditional crime narrative. Finally, the essay will consider

3. Winston and Mellerski, *Public Eye*, 51.

4. Beyer, "Third Ireland," 77.

areas unrepresented in Kerrigan's fiction, the points in the narrative where the phenomena in question—the byzantine network of influence beneath Irish society, the global financial system, the European continent—are too complex to register through a singular crime narrative.

Kerrigan's Dublin tetralogy comprises *Little Criminals* (2005), *The Midnight Choir* (2007), *Dark Times in the City* (2009), and *The Rage* (2011). They can broadly be described as crime thrillers, but contain elements of police procedurals and social realism. While the four novels are loosely connected, with recurring characters such as the Garda detective Bob Tidey and the criminal Jo-Jo Mackendrick, Kerrigan makes no attempt to construct a serial narrative across the series. Like the classical detective stories, each of Kerrigan's novels is organized around a particular crime: a kidnapping in *Little Criminals*, police corruption in *The Midnight Choir*, the attempted murder of a police informant in *Dark Times in the City*, and a security van heist in *The Rage*. Rather than a narrative arc, the constant across the tetralogy is the Dublin setting.

Fredric Jameson notes that Raymond Chandler's crime fiction depicts a moment already happened, embodying a nostalgia for the recent past.[5] Kerrigan has acknowledged the influence of Chandler on his work, but his novels draw from the immediate present of the author, so that across the four novels a developing situation is traced in which a financial boom becomes a credit crunch, and finally a recession. Kerrigan's novels eschew nostalgia for any particular time period. The time between *Little Criminals* and *The Rage* is, for example, marked by Rose Cheney's preoccupation with burgeoning property prices in *The Midnight Choir*,[6] which in turn becomes an obsession with how far prices have fallen in *The Rage*.[7]

The tetralogy recounts this rupture, but also registers the continuity in conditions between the prosperous economy and what Beyer, drawing from Jane Casey's short story "Inheritance" (2011), calls "the third Ireland," where citizens adjust to the reality of austerity.[8] In *Little Criminals*, Ireland

5. Jameson, *Raymond Chandler*, 14–16.

6. Kerrigan, *Midnight Choir*, 22.

7. Kerrigan, *Rage*, 111, 118.

8. Beyer, "Third Ireland," 73.

is experiencing an economic boom, but its benefits are not shared equally. In the midst of so-called financial prosperity, Kerrigan depicts the criminal Frankie Crowe collecting his daughter from her crumbling school, its prefab classrooms financed through sponsored walks and donations. For the most part Crowe is an unsympathetic character, but the novel demonstrates that even the sociopathic Crowe has an awareness that the failure of the state is embodied by his daughter being educated in a "shanty schoolroom" with "no ceiling, just steel girders beneath a corrugated roof."[9]

Kerrigan's interest in the quotidian also extends to what Jameson calls "the purchasable environment," the clusters of objects around which desire circulates in the narratives.[10] Kerrigan shows the reader objects both as a critique of the commodity fetishism of the economic boom, and as a demonstration of how reification activates particular objects—like the swanky bar in *Little Criminals* where "everything seemed to have a hard shiny surface, including the barmen"—that pull us in certain directions as individuals and as societies.[11] In the post-crash novel *The Rage*, detectives Rose Cheney and Bob Tidey visit the house of a corrupt banker whose murder they are investigating. Cheney notes that the décor displays a "twelve-year-old's notion of taste" and tells Tidey about the craze among wealthy businessmen for "monster chess sets," declaring "if the new Irish aristocracy had an emblem, that's it—a swanky, overpriced version of a game they can't play."[12] This is an extension of Kerrigan's polemical writing. In his column in *The Sunday Independent*, Kerrigan has excoriated the wealthy's conspicuous consumption during the boom and post-boom periods, regularly recounting the price of items in Dublin's exclusive Brown Thomas store by way of demonstration.[13]

In *Little Criminals*, objects become a means of signifying status and defining in-groups from out-groups. The businessman Justin Kennedy views the furnishings in his house as a "congealed mass that speaks of quality,"

9. Kerrigan, *Little Criminals*, 43.

10. Jameson, *Raymond Chandler*, 17.

11. Kerrigan, *Little Criminals*, 21.

12. Kerrigan, *Rage*, 110.

13. See Kerrigan, "Relax"; and Kerrigan, "We Pay."

Kerrigan writing that "the furniture solid, the walls expensively embellished, there was an unmistakable balance to the room."[14] The particulars of the interior of the Kennedy house are left to his wife and the decorator she hired, referred to by Kennedy simply as "that fruit."[15] Here those deemed surplus to requirements in a masculine world of "handsome strivers" are employed to merely stack the signifiers of distinction in an acceptable order.[16] Jameson suggests that modernity is an era of "stable products" in which "there is no longer any feeling of the creative energy embodied in a product: the latter are simply there, in a permanent industrial background which has come to resemble that of nature itself."[17] In *Little Criminals*, Kennedy dwells in this mass of products assembled by others, securing his identity as a successful businessman in Celtic Tiger Ireland. Later, while reflecting on his career, Kennedy claims ownership of aspects of the built environment around him, noting three buildings "commemorating deals in which he had been involved, and from which he could remember the billing totals to the cent."[18] Here, the objects that make up the interior and exterior environment become a means of securing Kennedy's identity, the labor that created them demeaned or effaced.

Kerrigan depicts a stratified class society through the contrasting relationships to objects in the narrative spaces that working-class characters inhabit. A shopping center on a working-class estate is described as "an embassy installed by outside forces, built with an undisguised hostility towards an alien environment," while in more affluent areas such buildings "might pose as cathedrals of consumerism."[19] In this working-class inverse to wealthy Dublin society, the congealed mass of products with which Kerrigan provides the background contains objects such as a burned-out car

14. Kerrigan, *Little Criminals*, 13.
15. Kerrigan, *Little Criminals*, 13.
16. Kerrigan, *Little Criminals*, 14.
17. Jameson, *Raymond Chandler*, 18–19.
18. Kerrigan, *Little Criminals*, 41.
19. Kerrigan, *Rage*, 114.

that sits on a council estate for days,[20] cans of alcohol consumed by teenagers on housing estates,[21] and Christmas lights on the exteriors of houses that spark competition between neighbors.[22]

Kerrigan's narratives also trace connections between the inhabitants of these separate spaces, subjects often only partially represented in each other's cognitive maps. It is no coincidence that the Irish media report gang violence as taking place in an almost mythical realm called "Gangland," but this act of distancing disguises the firm connections between the lives lived by the working class and the middle class in Ireland. As Nicky Bonner notes in *Little Criminals*, the sudden prosperity of Ireland in the Celtic Tiger era fed the use of cocaine among the newly wealthy, a product provided by the gangs that emerged from the working-class estates to meet that demand.[23] The wealthy lawyer Alex takes cocaine from a tasteful wooden box before she has sex with Danny Callaghan, a driver about to face the consequences of thwarting an assassination attempt by a gang involved in dealing cocaine.[24] The interior of Alex's apartment on the Liffey, overlooking Dublin's financial district, is described as "an upmarket version of Danny Callaghan's own place" situated on an estate dubbed "the Hive," where teenagers drink cider in the communal spaces in a parody of public spirit.[25]

The continuity between these spaces extends to the characterization of those who dwell in them. The criminals in the novels are as entrepreneurial as the businessmen, image-conscious gangsters who read Sun Tzu's *The Art of War* and play golf like corporate CEOs.[26] Gang leader Jo-Jo Mackendrick is described as avoiding armed robbery in preference to "the steady income from what he thought of as the wholesale and service sectors," as well as his legitimate companies for laundering money.[27] Frankie Crowe,

20. Kerrigan, *Rage*, 52.

21. Kerrigan, *Dark Times*, 24.

22. Kerrigan, *Dark Times*, 136.

23. Kerrigan, *Little Criminals*, 85.

24. Kerrigan, *Dark Times*, 122.

25. Kerrigan, *Dark Times*, 49, 112–13.

26. Kerrigan, *Dark Times*, 169, 208.

27. Kerrigan, *Little Criminals*, 66.

the ambitious small-time criminal, mimics business-speak when planning to kidnap Justin Kennedy, reflecting that "it's there to be taken . . . all we need is the balls . . . there's moochers and there's doers . . . moochers take shit. Moochers don't know they're alive."[28] When Crowe meditates on the "Waters and Cox thing" going "pear-shaped," he could well be talking about a merger gone bad, rather than the dissolution of a budding criminal enterprise hatched in Mountjoy Prison with "two hard men from Rialto."[29]

When Mackendrick refuses to clear his kidnapping of the banker Justin Kennedy, Crowe's business instincts flare up into violence, as he executes first Mackendrick, then Mackendrick's bodyguard and mother. Crowe's summation of the killings mirrors his belief that he is merely a businessman extending his ambition. Crowe reflects that "it's the difference between being a loser and being someone who matters. Being ready to fuck anyone who gets in the way."[30] Although there are consistencies across the worlds of business and criminal enterprise, there is still room for misunderstanding between the two. Crowe selects his kidnapping victim by consulting a "rich list" in a Sunday newspaper. When he reads that Kennedy has "landed a private bank," he assumes that Kennedy owns the bank, rather than merely having secured the contract to facilitate the deal.[31] The novel is organized around the resulting kidnapping, Crowe's misunderstanding of the difference between ownership and service provision turning what he assumes will be a simple job into a protracted and steadily more violent event.

This connection between the worlds of business and crime is best summed up by Kerrigan's most unsympathetic character, Detective Inspector Synnott. In *The Midnight Choir*, the corrupt police officer Synnott meets the Minister for Justice, who asks him about the motivations of gangsters. Synnott keeps his observations to himself, but later reflects that the motivations of the criminals are the same as the minister's and his "horsey friends. They want position and wealth with the least amount of sweat possible. They do whatever it takes. . . . If they had the connections to get in on a

28. Kerrigan, *Little Criminals*, 17.

29. Kerrigan, *Little Criminals*, 63–64.

30. Kerrigan, *Little Criminals*, 75.

31. Kerrigan, *Little Criminals*, 25.

stock option or to front a sure-thing property deal, that's what they'd do. Instead, they know how to import coke, organize bank raids, bully a string of prostitutes and wallop the shit out of anyone who looks crooked at them. They're the brightest and most enterprising people in their community."[32] In ways both implicit and explicit, then, Kerrigan maps connections between cognitively disparate worlds, linking the apartments of the wealthy to the flats of the working class. His depictions of criminals suggest that, if the entrepreneurial spirit exists in Ireland, it does so in the criminal gangs that service the cocaine industry as much as in the boardrooms of Celtic Tiger Ireland.

While Synnott is Kerrigan's least sympathetic character, he is also the tetralogy's most formally subversive actant, used by Kerrigan to critique police corruption. *The Midnight Choir* uses the form of the police procedural, with its "multiple focus of characters and crimes," and of all Kerrigan's novels comes closest to Per Wahlöö's notion of using the crime novel as "a scalpel cutting open the belly of an ideologically pauperized and morally debatable so-called welfare state of the bourgeois type."[33] By picking apart Synnott's character over the course of the narrative and refusing the closure often expected of the crime genre, the novel critiques how criminal convictions are obtained, problematizing questions of how the law is enforced.

Initially, *The Midnight Choir* primes the reader to view Synnott in the context of what Winston and Mellerski describe as "a police bureaucracy composed of 'ordinary' citizens intent only on ensuring the preservation of social harmony."[34] This utopian vision disseminated by the police procedural emphasizes the satisfaction of police officers when cracking cases so that "cooperation between the police and society . . . becomes the source of reader satisfaction."[35] In this vein, Synnott begins *The Midnight Choir* as the moral conscience of the police force, breaking the rule that "the team

32. Kerrigan, *Little Criminals*, 235.

33. Knight, *Crime Fiction 1800–2000*, 155; cited in Winston and Mellerski, *Public Eye*, 16.

34. Knight, *Crime Fiction*, 2.

35. Knight, *Crime Fiction*, 7.

always come first" by informing on his colleagues.[36] A pariah in the force for attempting to prevent the beating of Crotty, an IRA member suspected of murdering a female garda in a bank raid, Synnott has been moved from Galway to Dublin to avoid the bullying that recent scandals have revealed any whistle-blower faces in the organization.[37]

But though Synnott testifies in court that Crotty was assaulted while in custody, he perjures himself by fabricating a conversation between himself and Crotty in which the IRA man told him, "My orders were to do the bank. She got in the way. It was nothing personal."[38] Here, Kerrigan begins to cast doubt on the character of Synnott, utilizing what Leroy L. Panek reads as the police procedural's subversive potential to thwart reader satisfaction by casting doubt on the mechanics of crime solving and the application of the law.[39] Unravelling the notion of a police officer as a rational actor pursuing evidence, the novel paints Synnott as operating on passion and hunches, casually adding statements to his notebook to fit his prejudices. In Synnott's hands, detection becomes less a quest for truth than a weaving of convincing stories about events to be passed on to the Director for Public Prosecutions or the media. The police notebook becomes a wish-list of outcomes too convenient for the detective to pass up.[40] Panek discusses the effect of bureaucracy in the police novel, with officers creatively utilizing the form of the report to give an impression of strict adherence to procedure.[41] Synnott's concern in this process is shown to be order rather than law, announced in his aphorism, "When the law

36. Dove, *Police Procedurals*, 68.

37. Kerrigan, *Midnight Choir*, 85–86; for more on the recent Garda whistleblower scandal, see Michael Clifford, *Maurice McCabe: A Force For Justice* (Dublin: Hachette Ireland, 2017).

38. Kerrigan, *Midnight Choir*, 90–92.

39. Panek, "Post-War American Crime Fiction," 167.

40. Kerrigan, *Midnight Choir*, 68, 298–99.

41. Panek, "Post-War American Crime Fiction," 160. Panek cites a passage from William Cauntitz's novel *Black Sand* in which a police officer fills out a report, making sure the "fairy tale complied with department policy and procedures." The officer complains that he has "become a goddam fiction editor."

is a bouncing ball on a spinning wheel, all that a righteous man can aim for is order."[42]

Synnott's narrative trajectory sees the detective travel from principled whistle-blower to casual perjurer to accessory to murder, the last when Synnott fails to intervene as Mackendrick enters the apartment of police informant Dixie, despite knowing that Mackendrick will kill her for cooperating with the police.[43] In exchange for cash, Dixie had provided a false statement to help Synnott charge the jewel thief Joshua Boyce. But Synnott's credibility as "the man who told the truth" is shredded when a serial killer confesses to a murder Synnott had pinned on the victim's husband, and he decides that he cannot continue with the Boyce case under the scrutiny that will result. In the interest of Synnott's notion of order, it becomes easier to let Dixie be killed.[44]

Apart from Synnott's reflection that he will "probably get shifted sideways to some backwater," there is little sense at the narrative's close that the detective will answer for his actions.[45] Kerrigan has shown the force beyond Synnott to be corrupt in the extrajudicial beating of Crotty, so it becomes unclear what power could justifiably call Synnott to account. Matzke and Mühlensen point to the "re-establishment of wholeness and order" at the close of classical detective stories, noting that in postcolonial narratives there is a distrust of this order.[46] *The Midnight Choir* reflects this distrust by resisting a narrative closure that would restore wholeness and order, as well as questioning the law that underpins order in conventional crime novels, suggesting that such order is often in conflict with justice. While Kerrigan professes to writing conservative novels, *The Midnight Choir* demonstrates a radical refusal of closure.

If there is anything missing from Kerrigan's cognitive map in the Dublin tetralogy it is a fully rounded picture of the "cozy cartels" of the Irish elite that Rose Cheney tells Bob Tidey are "as much a part of this country as

42. Kerrigan, *Midnight Choir*, 207.

43. Kerrigan, *Midnight Choir*, 350–51.

44. Kerrigan, *Midnight Choir*, 316–18.

45. Kerrigan, *Midnight Choir*, 323.

46. Matzke and Mühlensen, "*Postcolonial Postmortems*," 11.

the mountains and the bogs."[47] Unlike the extrajudicial beatings, perjury, and falsification of evidence in *The Midnight Choir*, these mechanisms are merely alluded to and remain outside the frame of the narrative. *The Rage* sees Tidey become convinced of the solicitor Connie Wintour's guilt for the murder of the dead banker Sweetman, who was about to confess the details of a corrupt property deal. However, having congratulated Tidey's team for the evidence they have pulled together, Superintendent Malachy Hogg declares they are to be removed from the case.[48] Hogg informs Tidey that "this case has been a matter of concern at all levels—so it was natural that the conclusion of the case would be overseen at a higher echelon."[49] Hogg is inclined to blame Sweetman's murder on Justin Kennedy, who has recently committed suicide, and not to pursue the Wintour connection at all. Later, when Tidey persists with his theory about Wintour, Commissioner O'Keefe warns him that he is "throwing around allegations about the very people who have an important role in getting this country off its knees."[50]

In instances like this, the narrative can only suggest a conspiracy, a nexus of vested interests involving the police, top businessmen, and solicitors. It cannot follow the clues to place the conspiracy on the cognitive map of the text. Although Tidey can exclaim that "blame it on the dead guy" is "a sacred Irish institution," it is an institution that remains relatively untouched and, therefore, unchallenged.[51] These networks of corruption are unrepresentable within Kerrigan's crime narratives, which focus on the quotidian lives of criminals and police.

For Jameson, the conspiracy text signifies an attempt to apprehend the enormity of the global system, valuable in the fact that it expresses a utopian desire to map totality.[52] Kerrigan's crime fiction never shades into the realm of the conspiracy text proper, a large-scale and globalized form that attempts, albeit as Jameson suggests insufficiently, to depict the

47. Kerrigan, *Rage*, 239.
48. Kerrigan, *Rage*, 219.
49. Kerrigan, *Rage*, 221.
50. Kerrigan, *Rage*, 256.
51. Kerrigan, *Rage*, 255.
52. Jameson, *Geopolitical Aesthetic*, 2.

global distribution of power. To do so, Kerrigan would need to depart from the vernacular Dublin crime fiction that defines his work, with its commitment to depicting Ireland through colloquial tics and intensely localized intimacies. In this instance, we could compare the unrepresentable in Kerrigan's narratives to the philosopher Timothy Morton's notion of hyperobjects—objects such as global warming and the internet that are "massively distributed in time and space" and, therefore, impossible to grasp as whole entities.[53] Morton writes that hyperobjects "are nonlocal; in other words, any 'local manifestation' of a hyperobject is not directly the hyperobject."[54]

Within Kerrigan's crime narratives, both the conspiracies that underpin Irish society and objects such as the implementation of the law and the globalized tax system become unrepresentable hyperobjects, depicted only in their local manifestations. In *The Midnight Choir*, for example, Rose Cheney is involved in the prosecution of a corrupt accountant: "The attempts to find a loophole had precedents in various high-profile trials, and the accountants had the money to employ enough lawyers to trawl the books in search of fresh punctures in the law through which [their client] might wriggle."[55] In *Little Criminals*, the global tax system is embodied in figures like Helen Snoddy, who we are assured "always knew the shortest route between any given deal and the nearest tax sanctuary,"[56] or like Kevin Little, the entrepreneur and tax exile who sees himself as a "guardian angel" for a certain section of Irish society.[57] The crime that begins that novel is the robbery of a tax-avoiding cash-in-hand business that becomes the target of Crowe's gang, but it is retribution for Crowe's crimes that becomes the focus of the narrative.[58]

53. Morton, *Hyperobjects*, 5.

54. Morton, *Hyperobjects*, 5.

55. Kerrigan, *Midnight Choir*, 144.

56. Kerrigan, *Little Criminals*, 42.

57. Kerrigan, *Little Criminals*, 196.

58. Kerrigan, *Little Criminals*, 5. Frankie Crowe's informant Leo Titley tells him about the potential holdup on the night of a concert in the backroom of the pub, telling Crowe, "money at the door. The pubs love it, taxman never sees a cent."

It is telling that in describing the extralegal means through which Kennedy raises the ransom for his wife in *Little Criminals*, Kerrigan breaks the narrative voice with direct exposition to explain the mechanics of the complex financial maneuver, the only way this unrepresentable hyperobject can register on the narrative: "The Liechtenstein account was a tax-evasion scheme set up within Flynn O'Meara Tully in the early 1990s. The account was initially held at a Liechtenstein bank, with an array of cut-outs and buffers that made it as investigation-proof as these things get. Over a number of years, the firm's off-the-books earnings were channeled into the account, through a small private bank in Dublin, quietly building into a solid hoard of cash to be shared among a handful of the most senior executives."[59] In addition, the police are shown to be either complicit or uninterested in this process, asking no questions regarding the origin of the money, despite working closely with Kennedy for the safe return of his wife. This reflects the intricacies of the global financial system and the limits of the Irish police force when tackling white-collar crime.

Part of the reason these and other globalized links cannot be represented fully is that Kerrigan's narratives and their semiotic systems are dependent on their Dublin location, referencing local slang, history, and the changing landmarks of the city. There are outside spaces in the novels: the countryside is for laying low and England offers a chance of escape for a criminal, whereas for Dolly Finn, Europe signifies "a whole continent to get lost in."[60] But if Kerrigan were to, for instance, follow Dolly Finn to England between his disappearance at the end of *Little Criminals* and his reappearance in *Dark Times in the City,* the narrative would break down, and all the signs of Dublin with which Kerrigan builds his fictions would be rendered useless as soon as Finn went through the departure gate.

Although Pepper has argued for the crime novel's subversive ability to interrogate society within the bounds of the nation state, with David Schmid he also diagnoses an inability of the form to deal with globalization. Pepper and Schmid suggest that the recent globalization of the crime

59. Kerrigan, *Little Criminals*, 195.

60. Kerrigan, *Little Criminals*, 260.

novel has led to the spread of localism in the genre, with novels serving almost as tour guides for particular settings.[61] Despite being globally distributed, this proliferation of vernacular crime fiction leaves the crime novel impotent in the face of an interconnected world that it cannot fully apprehend. The form proliferates local settings, but fails to register the connections between nodes in a global network. As a result, such localized crime novels are unable to "properly interrogate the complex and overdetermined terrain of global capitalism and the messy business of contemporary geopolitics where the state may have been relativized as a form of political authority and locus of power."[62]

The organization of Ireland's economy around outside forces, as detailed by the historian Conor McCabe—whether in the export of live cattle to England, dependence on the financial services industry, foreign direct investment, or creative tax arrangements—gives those within the state the sense of a moral ground that is constantly shifting.[63] Although Kerrigan's Dublin tetralogy hints at this reality, the narrative style with which he constructs his fictions is unable to fully represent the terrain of transnational capital.

To return to our starting point, the question of whether Kerrigan writes radical or conservative novels is dependent on whether the orientation of our politics in any given moment is based on a local or a global critique. Although Kerrigan's work does not centrally engage with the larger realities of a connected world, on the level of the nation his novels take a scalpel to the conventions and pretensions of the Irish bourgeoisie. Within the reduced scope of the vernacular crime novel, Kerrigan critiques trickle-down economics, class stratification, commodity fetishism, and police corruption. Kerrigan's crime fiction is as polemical and radical as his newspaper columns or nonfiction works, deftly utilizing the crime novel to critique the Irish state in its manifestation as the poster child for both global capitalism and austerity.

61. Pepper and Schmid, "Introduction," 2.

62. Pepper and Schmid, "Introduction," 9.

63. McCabe, *Sins of the Father.*

Bibliography

Beyer, Charlotte. "'The Third Ireland': Inheritance and Postcolonialism in Irish Crime Writing," *Journal of Commonwealth and Postcolonial Studies* 4, no. 1 (2016): 61–81.

Burke, Declan. "A Great Meeting of Criminal Minds at Books '08." *Irish Independent*, 21 September 2008.

Dove, George. *The Police Procedurals*. Bowling Green: Bowling Green Univ. Popular Press, 1982.

Jameson, Fredric. *The Geopolitical Aesthetic*. Bloomington: Indiana Univ. Press, 1992.

———. *Raymond Chandler: The Detections of Totality*. London: Verso, 2016.

Kerrigan, Gene. *Dark Times in the City*. London: Vintage, 2010.

———. *Little Criminals*. London: Vintage, 2005.

———. *The Midnight Choir*. New York: Europa, 2007.

———. *The Rage*. London: Vintage, 2012.

———. "Relax, We're out of the Woods—Again." *Sunday Independent*, 21 August 2011.

———. "We Pay, While the Rich Are Recession-Proofed." *Sunday Independent*, 13 November 2011.

Knight, Stephen. *Crime Fiction 1800–2000: Detection, Death, Diversity*. Basingstoke: Palgrave Macmillan, 2004.

Matzke, Christine, and Susanne Mühlensen. *Postcolonial Postmortems: Crime Fiction from a Transcultural Perspective*. Leiden: Rodopi, 2006.

McCabe, Conor. *Sins of the Father*. Dublin: History Press, 2011.

Morton, Timothy. *Hyperobjects*. Minneapolis: Univ. of Minnesota Press, 2013.

Panek, Leroy L. "Post-War American Crime Fiction." In *The Cambridge Companion to Crime Fiction*, edited by Martin Priestman, 155–71. Cambridge: Cambridge Univ. Press, 2003.

Pepper, Andrew, and David Schmid. "Introduction." In *Globalization and the State in Contemporary Crime Fiction*, edited by Andrew Pepper and David Schmid, 1–19. London: Palgrave Macmillan, 2016.

Priestman, Martin. "Post-War British Crime Fiction." In *The Cambridge Companion to Crime Fiction*, edited by Martin Priestman, 173–89. Cambridge: Cambridge Univ. Press, 2003.

Winston, Robert P., and Nancy C. Mellerski. *The Public Eye: Ideology and the Police Procedural*. London: Palgrave Macmillan, 1992.

PART FIVE

Domestic Noir

14

Serial Domestic Noir

Louise Phillips's Kate Pearson Series

ROSEMARY ERICKSON JOHNSEN

Crime fiction's emergence as a popular genre in twenty-first-century Irish writing is producing critically and commercially successful work of many types, including the political thriller, police procedural, and private eye subgenres. Irish women writers have contributed considerably to the genre's success both within Ireland and on the export markets. Tana French receives a lot of well-deserved attention, but other Irish women are writing novels blending traditional crime fiction subgenres into a popular fusion that is beginning to be called "domestic noir." In a fall 2016 *TLS* review applauding the work of Tana French alongside several British and American writers, Ian Sansom formulates the suspenseful duality of this kind of fiction as "a violent return to life with women as both victims *and* perpetrators."[1] Such a perspective illuminates Louise Phillips's Kate Pearson series, which portrays female characters who are variously victims, perpetrators, and investigators (both official and unofficial). The professional investigations of Phillips's criminal psychologist Dr. Kate Pearson overlap with her personal life and intersect with female characters such as Clodagh McKay in *The Doll's House* (2013) and the titular "Game Changer" of her fourth series novel (2015). My essay's examination of Phillips's series demonstrates how her work offers insight into contemporary Irish society,

1. Sansom, "Only Death," 14.

with particular reference to women's lives and feminist issues, and helps to define the parameters of domestic noir in the face of sometimes-competing demands of series fiction.

Crime fiction is more popular than ever, as evidenced by sales figures, reviews, and the number of first-time authors in the genre. Besides its current popularity, there are good reasons to look to the genre for cultural insight and social commentary. In the context of Nordic crime fiction, one highly visible set of exports, Katrín Jakobsdóttir cites it as "one of the few literary genres which holds the sign of realism aloft and takes up community problems as a subject for debate and examination. But it may be precisely these traits that captivate readers from all around the world."[2] Her description of crime fiction from 2011 takes on even greater impact when we realize that this is the same woman who became the prime minister of Iceland in November 2017; she can speak with rare authority about the pertinence of the genre for examining "community problems" in ways that resonate at home and abroad.[3] Similar beliefs are expressed by Michael Reynolds, the editor in chief of Europa Editions, a press that makes a lot of international crime fiction in translation available to readers in the United States. Reynolds notes that "world noir confronts broad, global themes through an investigation of international crime in its local manifestations. It does so without ignoring real lives—the individual, the human."[4] In Ireland, it has been nearly a decade since Fintan O'Toole pointed to emerging "Irish-set crime writing" as "arguably the nearest thing we have to realist literature adequate to capturing the nature of contemporary society."[5]

Notably, women writers enjoy a growing preeminence in the still-young field of Irish crime fiction. Declan Burke, author, editor, and influential

2. Jakobsdóttir, "Meaningless Icelanders," 48.

3. Jakobsdóttir earned an MA from the University of Iceland in 2004 and has taught classes there and at the University of Reykjavík. Her thesis was on Icelandic crime fiction, and she has published articles on Icelandic crime fiction and children's literature. She was first elected to Parliament in 2007. At the time her essay was published in Nestingen and Arvas's *Scandinavian Crime Fiction*, she was a crime-fiction scholar, writer, and politician.

4. Reynolds, "Preface," 10.

5. O'Toole, "From Chandler," 360.

blogger of Irish crime fiction, draws attention to the success of women writers in his introduction to the 2016 New Island Books anthology of short stories by Irish crime writers, *Trouble Is Our Business.* Calling it "one of the most notable trends" of the 2010s, Burke points to women's dominance in "the number of debut Irish crime novels being published" and their critical success, noting that "the past four winners of the crime fiction gong at the Irish Book Awards have all been women."[6] One of these women is Louise Phillips, whose debut novel introducing criminal profiler Kate Pearson, *Red Ribbons* (2012), was nominated for the Best Irish Crime Novel of the Year. The next book in the series, *The Doll's House*, won the award in 2013, and the third, *Last Kiss* (2014), put Phillips on the short list again. Phillips's website categorizes the Pearson books as "psychological crime thrillers," a descriptive label that suggests the mingling of subgenres characteristic of domestic noir. Given the series' emphasis on women and children—children as victims and women often as adult survivors of trauma—the suspense, psychological exploration, and criminal justice contexts illuminate contemporary Irish society in important ways.

In *Cyber Ireland: Text, Image, Culture* (2014), Claire Lynch notes that "chick lit" by Maeve Binchy, Marian Keyes, and Cecelia Ahern put Irish genre literature on international bestseller lists in part by using "Irish settings and speech patterns"[7] to increase their international success. Lynch summarizes their impact by writing that "Keyes' books are rightly celebrated as contributing to the global industry of popular fiction for women in general, as well as manifesting a consciously Irish model of the genre."[8] Those familiar with the growth of Irish crime fiction have not been slow to see the connections between these two popular genres and the way the success of Irish "chick lit" authors prepared the ground for the twenty-first-century wave of Irish crime fiction. John Connolly, an early, important figure in the genre—in 2009 O'Toole unhesitatingly called him "the most successful Irish crime writer"[9]—points to the debt of gratitude Irish

6. Burke, "Editor's Introduction," 6.

7. Lynch, *Cyber Ireland*, 97.

8. Lynch, *Cyber Ireland*, 98.

9. O'Toole, "From Chandler," 359.

crime novelists owe to these women. "Crime authors have cause to thank the writers of women's popular fiction," Connolly writes, "for encouraging publishers to look at Irish writers not just as a source of literary fiction but also of genre fiction that can succeed commercially. Once female authors such as Maeve Binchy and Marian Keyes began to appeal to a readership in Britain and the US, they fundamentally altered the perception of Irish writing among international publishers and paved the way for explorations of other genre forms."[10]

All of these factors merge into the kind of genre blending that domestic noir specializes in and that Phillips deploys to such effect in her Kate Pearson series. Ian Sansom's review mentioned above observes that women's crime novels from the 1940s and 1950s address "the violence inherent not just in marital but in all family relationships . . . and the possibilities of social as well as sexual transgression."[11] Sansom goes on to link these mid-twentieth-century crime novels by women to "much of the most interesting popular fiction of the past couple of decades,"[12] work that might be classified as domestic noir. Scholarly analysis of such novels has been gaining traction. Earlier scholarly engagement with them generated the concept of "suburban gothic," a classification that captures several of the key themes and strategies of domestic noir. Groundbreaking work in this area—such as Bernice M. Murphy's 2009 study, *The Suburban Gothic in American Popular Culture*—was focused primarily on American primary source material, including not only fiction but also film and other media. Charles L. Crow's study *American Gothic*, published that same year in the University of Wales Press series on Gothic Literary Studies, also examines the suburban as a gothic setting. Recent developments reflect the advancement of "domestic noir" as both classification and analytical heuristic. The title of the 2018 essay collection edited by Laura Joyce and Henry Sutton, *Domestic Noir: The New Face of 21st Century Crime Fiction*, is one

10. Connolly, "No Blacks, No Dogs, No Crime Writers: Ireland and the Mystery Genre," 56.

11. Sansom, "Only Death," 14.

12. Sansom, "Only Death," 14.

indication that both the blended subgenre and its place in scholarly criticism have been established.

Considering the specifically Irish angle on both crime fiction and chick lit, it will come as no surprise that Ireland puts its own stamp on domestic noir.[13] Revelations about past mistreatment that was covered up, such as the Magdalene laundries, have demonstrated that twentieth-century Ireland was not the safe, pious society it was often claimed to be. Crime fiction such as the psychologically oriented investigations of Louise Phillips's Dr. Kate Pearson series can show how the roots of contemporary crime lie in past abuse that was either papered over or accepted as normal at the time. One example, from *Last Kiss*, addresses this directly. When Kate has located the childhood teacher of Sandra Connolly Regan and Alice Thompson, he talks about the strangeness of their upbringing by Alice's alcoholic mother and Sandra's harsh grandmother (who is later revealed to have done much worse things than treat her granddaughter coldly). When asked if he reported any of what he witnessed to social services, he answers that "a lot has changed in this country in thirty years. When those two girls were children, an alcoholic mother was tolerated, and an unloving one was far too common. They were fed, dressed and sent to school. They got on with their education. That was enough for folk not to meddle."[14] Apart from the scandals attached to institutions, this articulation of the prevailing ethos suggests there was ample room for violence and trauma *within* the home. As Irish journalist and crime writer Gene Kerrigan notes in the preface to his volume of Irish true crime stories, "We place the family at the centre of our constitution, but for some there is no more dangerous place than the home."[15]

This is territory within which contemporary Irish women crime novelists have excelled. The current success of Irish crime fiction and the important

13. This is a subject I have explored in essays on Tana French, including a 2014 essay in *Clues* on the dangerous mothers of her first four novels and a 2018 essay in *Domestic Noir: The New Face of 21st Century Crime Fiction*, ed. Joyce and Sutton, which analyzes *The Likeness* and *The Trespasser* in the context of Sheridan Le Fanu, Elizabeth Bowen, and the Tuam babies scandal.

14. Phillips, *Last Kiss*, 355.

15. Kerrigan, *Hard Cases*, 5.

forerunners in chick lit work together to forge a powerful Irish presence in domestic noir. Irish women writers, often deploying female investigators, blur genre boundaries and place traumatic experiences of women and children at the center of their work.[16] Shirley Peterson has shown how Tana French's crime novels "move into the category of trauma novels, balancing subject and method through (often unreliable) first-person narrators, confronting temporal discontinuities and fragmented identity while struggling to assimilate the 'unspeakable' into a coherent causal analysis."[17] Part of what Peterson points to in her analysis is the interaction between the investigator-narrator's interior self and the ongoing investigation. It is no accident that the central characters' own psychological backgrounds and contemporary lives are interwoven with the investigation of the crime plots. Claire McGowan, author of another series featuring a female forensic psychologist, explains in a 2014 *Belfast Telegraph* feature that "I wanted to write a character that wasn't a detective as such, I wanted to be a bit more flexible in what she did. . . . She makes a lot of mistakes in her private life. She is driven and will quite often break the rules."[18] McGowan's description alludes to the deliberate inclusion of the investigator's personal life and background in order to create greater flexibility within the genre.

The Kate Pearson series includes a strong emphasis on the investigator's past, which is excavated for its psychological freight but also comes to bear on present-day events. The formative experience for Kate was being abducted at age twelve. It is a point of motivation for her investigations, and a source of empathy with her patients, victims, and survivors. Initially, she remembers little of the experience. Her memories of it become more complete as the series goes on, however, and by book four it is explored

16. This observation raises the question of women readers, too, but that is beyond the scope of my essay here. As the *Belfast Telegraph* feature on Claire McGowan notes, reflecting McGowan's awareness of these issues in "describing her genre as 'almost women's fiction,' Claire said of her fan base: 'I think there are a lot of women readers. I have had some criticism as there is a lot of looking at personal relationships, but I think the people who read the books enjoy that.'"

17. Peterson, "Voicing the Unspeakable," 109.

18. Fleming, "Crime Pays."

extensively. In *The Game Changer* (2015) it becomes directly connected to her memories of her parents and pertinent to Adam O'Connor's police investigation. The basis of the foundational trauma becomes contextualized and attains direct present relevance within the narrative. In what readers learn of Kate's father's behind-closed-doors behavior, we find another example where, as Peterson puts it in the context of Tana French's crime novels, "a detective's personal trauma is linked to the culture's refusal to address its traumatic past."[19] When crime novelists such as French, McGowan, and Phillips emphasize connections across boundaries of class, age, and professional status, readers can see the commonalities among women's experiences and consider the framework of systems that supposedly protect them. Elizabeth Mannion describes this dynamic at work in Jane Casey's Maeve Kerrigan series: "Commentary, provided largely by Maeve, reveals her own susceptibility to harm, unifying her with women citywide, including victims of crimes she investigates. In addition to emphasizing the vulnerability of young women, this calls into question the distinction between revenge and justice, vigilantism and the rule of law."[20] Mannion's point about Kerrigan's shared experience of women's danger in spite of being a police officer has a corollary in series that feature criminal profilers, like McGowan's and Phillips's.

The nature of the profiler's work, delving into psychology and past trauma, allows crime novels featuring profilers to adopt—at least part of the time—a *professional* point of view within the domestic noir. The vision of a trained expert offers an additional level of insight to what might otherwise be merely confusion and pain. Although Kate Pearson is not a member of An Garda Síochána, she works with them in her professional capacity as an independent contractor. She is first introduced as a credentialed, acknowledged expert, and throughout the series readers observe her at work. The first time she is mentioned, in the second chapter of *Red Ribbons*, she is named with her title as "Dr. Kate Pearson." On the occasion of her introduction, she is giving a talk at Maynooth on her experience as

19. Peterson, "Voicing the Unspeakable," 112.

20. Mannion, "Irish by Blood," 121.

a criminal profiler. The idealized depiction of the event underscores Kate's standing: "The conference had been booked to capacity over a month in advance, which meant a packed room of people, all waiting for Kate's talk. . . . The line-up was impressive, featuring some of the best crime writers and criminology academics in the country."[21] The conference organizer's lengthy introduction of Kate references experience, degrees, and the corroboration of authorities in the United Kingdom and Ireland: "Kate holds a first-class honours degree in Psychology from Trinity College, a Master's in Criminology from University College London and a Doctorate in Forensic Psychology from the University of Nottingham. She has vast experience in the area of criminal profiling, having worked with . . . leading psychologists in the UK. Since her return to Ireland, she has also given some help to An Garda Síochána."[22]

In keeping with the emphasis on Kate's expertise, Phillips's novels also incorporate passages explaining important concepts and criminal-psychological research areas. In this way, some of the author's own extensive research is made available to her readers. In addition to extended definitions of concepts such as narcissism and psychopathology, the novels present descriptions of real-world examples of related phenomena, such as (in *The Game Changer*) the Jim Jones cult that resulted in the deaths of nearly a thousand followers in 1978. In *The Doll's House*, readers learn about the sexual assault protocols followed by the Irish police when Kate contacts the officer in charge of a sexual assault investigation she thinks is related to the case on which she is consulting. As a consulting expert, she is given professional respect undiminished by her unfamiliarity with the process the police launch when a victim files a complaint. She can ask that Detective Hennessy "talk [her] through it from the beginning,"[23] an opportunity for readers to learn alongside her.

Kate's talk in the chapter introducing her character concludes with the caution that profilers must "be mindful not to be led in the wrong

21. Phillips, *Red Ribbons*, 9.

22. Phillips, *Red Ribbons*, 11.

23. Phillips, *Doll's House*, 260.

direction,"[24] an observation that integrates the character's professional background with the requirements of the crime-fiction genre. Throughout the series, Phillips shows how the investigative methodologies Kate uses parallel those used by the police. As Kate is the primary investigator of the series, often her work is what readers observe as it is happening; in contrast, much of the police work occurs off-page and is reported to Kate. For crime-fiction readers, familiar with the basics of police procedures, the parallels between Kate's methods and those of the police investigation are evident. She relies not only on her training in psychology but also on the evidence produced by the police: crime scene photos, autopsy results, observations from CCTV footage, and witness statements. She draws everything together using methods similar to those of the police investigation. For example, the extensive "mind maps" she constructs in *The Game Changer* incorporate evidence, observations, questions, and investigative lines. Yet Kate is no armchair detective; in every book she insists on site visits, and she likes to take her own photos. In *Red Ribbons*, Phillips constructs the report that Kate writes for the police.[25] Readers have followed Kate's research process, observing the work that has gone into the report, before being given its full text, marked out from the narrative by its official format and a distinctive font. After that, readers can observe its reception and impact. O'Connor reports that his superiors were dissatisfied with it: "They were hoping for more. What they want to know is what he'll do next."[26] An annoyed Kate explains, "It doesn't work like that." Unlike the investigators, readers are also privy to the interior monologue of the perpetrator, which shows the accuracy of Kate's work. In some cases, what she presents as a hunch lacking sufficient evidence to go into the formal report is corroborated almost immediately for readers. When she presents the report to O'Connor, she says the killer is trying to "create or recreate an image" and that the posed, buried victims "both looked like angels."[27] O'Connor is weary and openly skeptical, but Phillips gives Kate the victory

24. Phillips, *Red Ribbons*, 14.
25. Phillips, *Red Ribbons*, 203–6.
26. Phillips, *Red Ribbons*, 233.
27. Phillips, *Red Ribbons*, 220.

when only six pages later readers encounter the killer reflecting on his primary victim "the way he'd left her: safe and sound, looking like a perfect angel."[28]

Kate's role as distinguished expert is complicated at times by the mingling of personal and professional challenges, and sometimes the boundaries between the personal and the professional are noticeably porous. In *Red Ribbons*, Kate is in a strained marriage with a young son. When she is first brought into the investigation, Detective O'Connor's insistence on including her expertise in the police investigation leads one coworker to inquire, "How's your Ms Pearson getting along? She's a real beauty, nice and sweet," a characterization O'Connor responds to by pointing out that Kate is "a respected criminal psychologist."[29] By the fourth book, her marriage is over, and the affinity she felt with O'Connor has developed into personal partnership: they are living together, and Kate is expecting their child. This personal relationship shows how for women the compartmentalization of the personal and the professional can be difficult to maintain. Some of O'Connor's colleagues resent the profiler's role in the investigation, and Kate's personal relationship with him offers a pretext for resistance. Perhaps more troubling is how O'Connor himself allows his personal relationship with Kate to cast doubt on her professionalism: "A lot depended on how she handled this emotionally and . . . he had his concerns that her normally rational thought processes would win out."[30] Tensions between the professional and personal are further developed through Kate's growing awareness that not only is her current family in jeopardy but also that her birth family was directly involved in both the older criminal enterprise brought to light *and* the current crimes in *The Game Changer.*

Kate not only decodes violence in her role as profiler, throughout the series she is subject to it. Kate is abducted, attacked, terrorized; her life is regularly put at risk. More than once she is an object of obsession to a perpetrator who stalks her and breaks into her home before directly attacking

28. Phillips, *Red Ribbons*, 226.

29. Phillips, *Red Ribbons*, 232.

30. Phillips, *Game Changer*, 169.

her. In *Last Kiss*, she finds herself with a knife at her throat as she is forcibly abducted by the killer. Some of these attacks are shocking, even in the context of the genre. In *Red Ribbons*, for example, her young son is abducted with her. In *The Game Changer*, a pregnant Kate is the victim of a planned hit and run: she is on foot, and one of the perpetrator's accomplices drives into her with a car. While such events are not out of place in domestic noir, they begin to put pressure on the conventions of a crime fiction series with its recurring central character. That Kate would be called in to consult on multiple cases in her professional role is plausible; that multiple cases would provide perpetrators who focus on her personally stretches credulity. When the killer in book four is revealed to be a half sister that she never knew she had, a series reader may wonder what could befall Kate in any subsequent case. Perhaps this is partly why the series seems to have ended, with Phillips turning to a new series character, Heather Baxter in *The Hiding Game* (2019).

Phillips also complements the professional perspective provided by Kate's investigations with the related perspectives of other women characters. That all of these contribute to the investigation—and the reader's suspense—is tribute to Phillips's mastery of her complex narrative structure. In *Red Ribbons*, Ellie Brady's memories appear increasingly relevant to the primary criminal investigation. These memories begin to merge with the investigation by way of Dr. Ebbs, Ellie's new doctor at St. Michael's Psychiatric Hospital, where she has been a long-term patient, and part of the suspense comes from readers having to wait for the doctor to take action. In *The Doll's House*, Phillips weaves together the work of Kate and another female character even more directly, without an intermediary figure such as Dr. Ebbs. Clodagh McKay's consultation with a hypnotist provides a different perspective on the recovery of memories that have been fragmented by trauma (such as Kate's own memories of her childhood abduction). The process that readers see Clodagh experience during these sessions overlaps with Kate's treatment of her patient, Imogen, and her analysis of the criminal in the main investigation. Furthermore, readers see how Clodagh's search for answers can mimic Kate's trained investigation, down to Clodagh's search for physical and documentary evidence, her questioning of potential witnesses, and her strategy of voice-recording memories. As the investigations proceed, Clodagh's investigation and Kate's merge; the multiple points of view Phillips provides throughout the novel come closer and closer together with all, including the killer, converging on the same location: Clodagh's childhood house on the Strand Road, Sandymount. Because the childhood trauma experienced by Clodagh and her brother Dominic lies at the core of the crime, Clodagh has special access to the relevant facts as she explores her memories. At the same time, her close involvement blinds her to possibilities and consequently exposes her to renewed danger. The similarities of their investigations illuminate the profiling process, but their differences emphasize the importance of the trained professional. Kate's expertise, deployed in coordination with that of the Emergency Response Unit's hostage negotiator Anne Holt, brings Clodagh out of danger.

Genre classifications are flexible, and this is particularly true of new genres such as domestic noir. Readers, critics, and scholars identify defining limits when these are approached too closely or even transgressed. Perhaps one sign that the crosscurrents Phillips uses so effectively in her profiler series reach a kind of tipping point in the fourth novel, *The Game Changer*, is the way Kate herself is analyzed, morphing from doctor into patient. The fragmented memories of her childhood abduction become filled in and linked to the criminal investigation, but more important in terms of the series trajectory is Kate's shift to being the subject of psychological analysis and manipulation. It seems that everyone in *The Game Changer* has an angle on Kate's psychological makeup and behavior, including her father's friend Malcolm; her live-in partner detective Adam O'Connor; and even the perpetrator, who indulges in a lengthy "reflection on Kate's progress"[31] as she manipulates Kate from afar. Two-thirds of the way into the book, Kate has pathologized herself: "Staring at the mind maps again, she decided the best approach was to separate herself from them, to treat Kate Pearson as a separate entity, someone who was either at the centre or periphery of an investigation. She pressed the red button on her recorder. 'Kate Pearson is the only child of Valentine and Gabrielle

31. Phillips, *Game Changer*, 164.

Pearson.'"[32] When the eminently well-qualified Dr. Pearson has become so entangled in her past that her present functioning is damaged, it becomes difficult to continue moving the series forward. As a profiler, she works as an independent contractor for specific police investigations; if her authority is diminished, she is likely done consulting for An Garda Síochána. In a one-off domestic noir novel, the female protagonist can wind up completely dysfunctional; in contrast, for a series with a consulting profiler to continue, the profiler must maintain professional credibility. On the other side of the genre divide that the Pearson series bridges, the police procedural, characters can drop in and out of the series, even die or otherwise make permanent exits, without concluding the series; again, this is not practicable for a series with a consulting profiler as principal investigator. In a blended genre like domestic noir, writers will test limits. As more works of domestic noir are published and read, consensus will emerge as to its genre boundaries. The Kate Pearson series helps map the territory as it is currently constituted.

Phillips's series is among those written by Irish women that offer insight into contemporary women's lives by including both challenges and opportunities, and showing their multiple personal and professional roles. These works illustrate David Clark's claim that "of all literary forms, it is crime narrative which has most accurately and most successfully mirrored the profusion of transformations which have taken place in Ireland."[33] So, for example, readers see Kate's failed marriage and subsequent relationship with a man she met while consulting in a professional capacity. This pattern has meaning in a purely personal context, but it is also more than that. Although not emphasized in the novel as representing cultural change, Kate's home life speaks directly to those issues that frame Irish women's lives. Kate's husband Declan working in Birmingham for a time may be nothing new for Irish families, but their separation and divorce reflects twenty-first-century Ireland. Furthermore, the presence of other female

32. Phillips, *Game Changer*, 302.

33. Clark, "Mean Streets," 255.

characters whose life experiences intersect with Kate Pearson's allows Phillips to explore topics such as motherhood and child exploitation across multiple sections of society. Finally, this inclusive approach to representation aligns readily with feminist purposes as the investigator turns her circumstances to advantage. Rather than succeeding in spite of them, she is successful precisely because of these overlaps.

In their 2014 special issue of *Éire-Ireland* on "Irish Crime since 1921," coeditors William Meier and Ian Campbell Ross write that its contents indicate "areas for further research that would insert Ireland into major academic conversations about deviance, theories of crime and punishment, and the relationship between crime and society. The rapid growth of crime fiction, true crime, and television programming suggests an urgent need for more extensive critical inquiry."[34] As Irish crime fiction continues to develop, and the genre of domestic noir consolidates its recent gains, the Kate Pearson series offers us insight into genre, culture, and women's issues. Internationally successful crime fiction by authors like Louise Phillips provides guideposts as the slower workings of scholarship begin to catch up with the flourishing primary literature.

Bibliography

"About Louise." *Louise Phillips: Writer.* louise-phillips.com. Accessed 15 April 2018.

Burke, Declan. "Editor's Introduction." In *Trouble Is Our Business*, edited by Declan Burke, 4–6. Dublin: New Island Books, 2016.

———, ed. *Down These Green Streets: Irish Crime Writing in the 21st Century.* Dublin: Liberties, 2011.

Clark, David. "Mean Streets, New Lives: The Representations of Non-Irish Immigrants in Recent Irish Crime Fiction." In *Literary Visions of Multicultural Ireland*, edited by Pilar Villar-Argáiz, 255–67. Manchester: Manchester Univ. Press, 2013.

Connolly, John. "No Blacks, No Dogs, No Crime Writers: Ireland and the Mystery Genre." In Burke, ed., *Down These Green Streets*, 39–57.

Crow, Charles L. *American Gothic.* Cardiff: Univ. of Wales Press, 2009.

34. Meier and Campbell, "Editors' Introduction," 15.

Fleming, Joanne. "Crime Pays for Thriller Writer Claire McGowan as BBC Snaps Up Rights to Her Novels." 24 April 2014. *Belfast Telegraph*, belfasttelegraph.co.uk. Accessed 25 July 2017.

Jakobsdóttir, Katrín. "Meaningless Icelanders: Icelandic Crime Fiction and Nationality." *Scandinavian Crime Fiction*, edited by Andrew Nestingen and Paula Arvas, 46–61. Cardiff: Univ. of Wales Press, 2011.

Johnsen, Rosemary Erickson. "The House and the Hallucination in Tana French's New Irish Gothic." In Joyce and Sutton, *Domestic Noir*, 221–38.

———. "Twenty-First-Century Mothers in Tana French's Crime Fiction." *Clues* 32, no. 1 (2014): 61–70.

Joyce, Laura, and Henry Sutton, eds. *Domestic Noir: The New Face of 21st Century Crime Fiction*. London: Palgrave Macmillan, 2018.

Kerrigan, Gene. *Hard Cases: True Stories of Irish Crime*. Dublin: Gill & Macmillan, 1996.

Lynch, Claire. *Cyber Ireland: Text, Image, Culture*. Basingstoke: Palgrave Macmillan, 2014.

Mannion, Elizabeth. "'Irish by Blood and English by Accident': Detective Constable Maeve Kerrigan." In *The Contemporary Irish Detective Novel*, edited by Elizabeth Mannion, 121–34. London: Palgrave Macmillan, 2016.

Meier, William, and Ian Campbell Ross. "Editors' Introduction: Irish Crime since 1921." *Éire-Ireland* 49, nos. 1–2 (2014): 7–21.

Murphy, Bernice M. *The Suburban Gothic in American Popular Culture*. Basingstoke: Palgrave Macmillan, 2009.

O'Toole, Fintan. "From Chandler and the 'Playboy' to the Contemporary Crime Wave." Reprinted as "Afterword," in Burke, ed., *Down These Green Streets*, 358–61.

Peterson, Shirley. "Voicing the Unspeakable: Tana French's Dublin Murder Squad." In *The Contemporary Irish Detective Novel*, edited by Elizabeth Mannion, 107–20. London: Palgrave Macmillan, 2016.

Phillips, Louise. *The Doll's House*. Dublin: Hachette, 2013.

———. "Double." In Burke, ed., *Trouble Is Our Business*, 315–27.

———. *The Game Changer*. Dublin: Hachette, 2015.

———. *The Hiding Game*. Dublin: Hachette, 2019.

———. *Last Kiss*. Dublin: Hachette, 2014.

———. *Red Ribbons*. Dublin: Hachette, 2012.

Reynolds, Michael. "Preface." In *Europa World Noir Reader*, 7–10. New York: Europa, 2012.

Sansom, Ian. "Only Death Is Consistent: The Nuanced World of Post-War Female Suspense Fiction." Review of *Women Crime Writers: Eight Suspense Novels of the 1940s and 50s*, edited by Sarah Weinman. *TLS* 11 November 2016 (no. 5928): 14–15.

15

Searching for the Missing, Haunted by the Troubles

Claire McGowan's Dr. Paula Maguire

VIVIAN VALVANO LYNCH

Claire McGowan's Paula Maguire series positions a forensic psychologist at the center of the police procedural. Maguire, long settled in London and working with the city's Metropolitan Police, reluctantly returns to her native Ballyterrin in Northern Ireland as part of a cross-border missing persons unit. The haunted history of the North crucially underpins the series and radiates throughout the life of Maguire, whose mother, Margaret, disappeared when Paula was thirteen. The series painstakingly reveals how Margaret's mysterious disappearance was inextricably connected to the Troubles. But Paula is not the sole member of the Ballyterrin community entrapped by the conflict's missing pieces and unsettled memories, and attempts to fill these gaps from the past serve as catalysts to exact stability in the present. Mindful of the field of trauma fiction, this essay will discuss the series as literature of mystery and detection that depends on personal, local, and historical traumas enacted by the Troubles.

Distilling the plethora of scholarship on trauma and trauma theory,[1] Fionna Barber provides a useful entry into this series: "The term 'trauma'

1. A detailed discussion of trauma theory lies outside the scope of this essay. The reader is advised to investigate work by Cathy Caruth, Shoshana Felman, Dori Laub, Susannah Radstone, and Kathleen Costello-Sullivan. Essays by Graham Dawson, Fionnuala Dillane, and Paula McFetridge in the Spring/Summer 2017 special issue of *Irish University Review, Moving Memory: The Dynamics of the Past in Irish Culture*, are also valuable.

can refer to the effects of either physiological or psychological wounding or threat of danger in origin; both can have effects on processes of memory and the individual's ability to cope with the consequences of an event. Traumatic experiences can be life threatening or involve the proximity of the death of others, or they can also result . . . in the unraveling of an individual's sense of self and identity."[2] Robert Garratt distinguishes between "trauma narratives" and "novels about trauma":

> Most novels about trauma employ conventional narrative strategies, points of view, and linear story lines. A trauma novel, by contrast, employs a narrative strategy in which a reconstruction of events through memories, flashbacks, dreams, and hauntings is as important as the events themselves. In a trauma novel, both subject and method become central: in addition to developing trauma as an element of the story and part of its dramatic action, it depicts the process by which a person encounters and comes to know a traumatic event or moment that has previously proved inaccessible.[3]

The first Maguire book, *The Lost* (2013), concentrates on the procedural narrative while introducing the subject of Troubles trauma through Paula. By the fourth novel, *A Savage Hunger* (2016), the narrative strategy expands as McGowan increasingly probes wider communal trauma. This is not to blithely label any of the novels as trauma narratives and remove them from detective literature. Rather, it is to assert that as she composes novels solidly grounded in crime, mystery, and detection, McGowan's narrative forms accommodate the heightened awareness of her characters' traumas. The impact of the Troubles constitutes the foundation, the very cornerstone, upon which these novels are built. Part of McGowan's achievement lies in her adding substantially to literature about the Troubles. Trauma rooted in the Troubles is obviously no newcomer to Irish fiction or, more broadly, Irish literature. However, McGowan's ingenuity in utilizing narratives of crime and detection to effectively convey such trauma is distinctive.

2. Barber, "At Vision's Edge," 234.

3. Garratt, *Trauma and History*, 5.

At the present moment, when well after the 1998 Good Friday Agreement an abundance of Irish literature continues to reckon with the aftermath of the Troubles, her accomplishment is all the more noteworthy. As Freya McClements plainly states in a recent essay, "If there is a lesson in the literature of the Troubles, it is that its legacy is inescapable."[4]

McGowan's Ballyterrin setting is fictional, and "the name translates roughly as 'Border Town,' though it occupies a similar (but not identical) geographical location to [McGowan's] hometown of Newry."[5] We meet Paula, a conventional first-person narrator, in the "Prologue" as she presents at a conference on missing persons. Reflecting on statistics that claim one percent of the missing did not want to go, she ponders: "*When I think about her—which I try not to do—I hope she wasn't in the one per cent. But sometimes, I must admit, I hope she was—because otherwise, it means she* wanted *to go*."[6] In due course, it is revealed that the "she" is Paula's mother. Paula's presentation prompts her assignment to the newly formed Missing Persons Response Unit (MPRU) based in Ballyterrin, where two young girls have gone missing. Tellingly, even as she notices the familiar countryside's charms, she is well aware that "scenery was one thing, twisted hatred another. And the past was still everywhere, creaking with spectral life."[7]

Her family home is shabby and outdated. Her father, PJ, held the uncomfortable position of a Catholic in the RUC (Royal Ulster Constabulary). With the establishment of the PSNI (Police Service of Northern Ireland) after the Good Friday Agreement, he was forced into retirement in the wake of Margaret's disappearance. Their neighbor Pat O'Hara was widowed when the IRA murdered her husband, editor of the local newspaper, as his seven-year-old son Aidan hid in terror. Pat filled a maternal void for Paula.

4. McClements, "Giving Voice to the Troubles." This article is a concise yet splendid overview of Troubles novels beginning with Eamonn McCann's *War and an Irish Town* (1974) and going all the way through to Anna Burns's *Milkman* and Michael Hughes's *Country* (both 2018).

5. McGowan, *The Lost*, Acknowledgments.

6. McGowan, *The Lost*, Prologue.

7. McGowan, *The Lost*, chap. 2.

This first novel's investigations introduce key characters and patterns. One missing girl's body is quickly found, broadening the scope to murder and introducing two central characters who serve as Paula's allies throughout the series: Detective Chief Inspector Helen Corry, Head of Serious Crime (PSNI), and Dr. Saoirse McLaughlin, the local Medical Examiner and Paula's childhood friend.[8] Paula's intrepid investigations and acute deductions move past their current cases, exposing decades-old secrets concerning unwed mothers, babies sent clandestinely to America for adoption, incest, suicides, and guilt so pervasive that it causes a troubled mother to kill her daughter.

Amidst this turmoil, Paula, who is as personally needy as she is professionally adept, manages to sleep once each with her English boss, Inspector Guy Brooking (London Metropolitan Police), and with her old boyfriend, Aidan, besotted by the former and nostalgic about the latter. At novel's end, she has survived being held at gunpoint but is stunned to discover she is pregnant and does not know whether Guy or Aidan is the baby's father. She learns that Sean Conlon, the man suspected of killing Aidan's father and currently jailed on another charge, may soon be released; Conlon has hinted that he knows something about Margaret's disappearance and hopes to exchange information for protection. *The Lost* thus includes the core from which later information about Margaret's disappearance will spring.

The next two novels, *The Dead Ground* (2014) and *The Silent Dead* (2015), conjoin missing persons and murders in ever more macabre scenarios. Both again tie in to crimes and secrets of the past and show Paula as the most discerning contributor to closing the cases. Additionally, trauma deriving from the Troubles becomes a more visible plot component and yields distinctive stylistic choices.

The main narrative of *The Dead Ground* occurs during the 2010 Christmas season, shortly after the action of *The Lost*. Its crimes include

8. Good models for Paula in building self-esteem are Corry, McLaughlin, and the Dublin journalist Maeve Cooley, a friend of Aidan's who provides assistance to Paula in investigations. The reader can see this, but Paula sometimes cannot.

missing and murdered babies, one of whom is a case of infanticide prompted by postpartum depression.[9] Several crimes are committed against women: the brutal murder of a local doctor who provides abortions; the grisly murder of the doctor's pregnant daughter, whose almost full-term baby is ripped from her womb; and the savage attack on Garda Fiacra's pregnant sister. Paula is herself attacked by the perpetrators of these three heinous crimes; a dramatic rescue saves her, and Paula, who has been vacillating as to whether to abort, decides to take the pregnancy to term.

The assault of the Troubles on the present is as central as the crime solving in *The Dead Ground.* While most of the novel is delivered in the third person, its "Prologue," dated 1993, is a second-person reverie of PJ talking to himself. He and his partner, Bob Hamilton (a Protestant), have gone to inform a pregnant woman of the discovery of the body of her husband, an apparent IRA victim. They find the wife savagely beaten. Wielding a kitchen knife, she had performed a ghastly, unsuccessful Caesarean section. This woman is later exposed as the co-perpetrator, along with her sister, of the monstrous murders and attacks on the women in 2010. Having endured a harsh upbringing, including incest, the sisters methodically sought vengeance against those they feel failed the pregnant woman in 1993: PJ, Bob, the father of Garda Fiacra, and the doctor who failed to save the baby. PJ, although aware of Paula's current assignment, has so buried the information that we know from the "Prologue" that it only rises to his conscious memory late in the novel. His repression of that 1993 case is tied to his own trauma: that day in 1993 was the same day that he returned home to find Paula alone and his wife gone.

The Dead Ground shows Paula desperate to know more about her mother. Pat reveals that a few years before Margaret's disappearance, she was at a checkpoint when a British paratrooper was shot. Margaret "tried to help . . . but there was so much blood, and the wee lad screaming and

9. The postpartum depression tragedy exemplifies McGowan's skill in depicting complicated police investigations. The team loses valuable time before concluding that this crime is unrelated to the other abductions and murders. McGowan makes a point of thwarting her investigators, heightening her narrative's authenticity.

dying in her lap. There was nothing she could do."[10] Paula visits her mother's old employer, a solicitor who represented local men accused of IRA activities, where she learns that the police had suspected Margaret shared confidential documents about his cases with the British Special Branch. Later, told that PJ is going to have Margaret declared legally dead so he and Pat can marry, Paula ends the novel overwhelmed by irrepressible grief and paralytic need: "'We're giving up on her. We're saying she's dead. . . . It's just I need her, Daddy. I need her now. You see, I'm pregnant.'"[11]

The Silent Dead delves even deeper into the enigmatic nature of trauma, with more crimes that emanate directly from the Troubles. The missing persons are the notorious Mayday Five, members of Ireland First, a Republican splinter group that refused to recognize the Good Friday Agreement. They are the known perpetrators of a 2006 bombing, who were charged, tried, but not convicted. Their bomb, intended for Orange Order members and a Unionist politician, had detonated too soon and left sixteen dead and scores maimed.[12] Ballyterrin's ex-IRA Mayor Kenny also goes missing, just before he is to take his Parliamentary seat at Westminster. Kenny supported the Good Friday Agreement, while his former comrade Martin Flaherty became the leader of the Mayday Five.

Paula's team vacillates between suspecting an internecine IRA feud and survivors' and victims' families seeking vengeance. Paula correctly concentrates on the latter, but even she will not realize how intricate vendettas can become until late in the novel. The principal strength of *The Silent Dead* is its presentation of the Troubles' bitter, life-altering effects: emotional pain, justice sought, justice denied, quests for retribution, and mental instability.

McGowan multiplies her trauma victims here while experimenting further with narrative delivery. Along with the third-person text concentrated on Paula, she provides a cryptic "Prologue" from a dead woman, several

10. McGowan, *Dead Ground*, 218.

11. McGowan, *Dead Ground*, 268–69.

12. The Mayday Five and Ireland First are fictional. In an Author's Note, McGowan acknowledges parallels between her novel's bombing and the Enniskillen and Omagh bombings.

long extracts from a fictional book by Maeve Cooley titled *The Blood Price: The Mayday Bombing and Its Aftermath*, and numerous sections titled "Kira." Each strand boasts a distinctive tone. *The Blood Price* reads like first-rate investigative journalism; the "Kira" pages are suitably affecting. Kira, a teenager engulfed with grief since she saw her beloved sister, Rose, blown to bits on Mayday becomes the nucleus of the revenge plot, convincing one of the Mayday Five to help her and other victims' families abduct his four cohorts.

McGowan strategically delineates the depths of trauma experienced by Kira and those who join her revenge plans. By the time they are caught, their attitudes have meaningfully evolved. In the stirring denouement, Kira and her group are overcome by remorse before Paula is threatened and three more characters are violently killed. Blood begets blood.

With so many emotionally crippled people in this novel, it may sound as if Paula's personal trauma is ignored, but that is not so. Corry and Guy are concerned for her, even as she fulfills her professional responsibilities admirably. Her dogged inquiries into her mother's case continue as she talks with an elderly neighbor who tells her that she saw two men, "just wee boys playing soldiers,"[13] at her mother's door the day that Margaret went missing; moreover, the neighbor called the police and gave a statement to Bob Hamilton. There is nothing in the police record, and Paula accosts Bob, who is clearly hiding something. Paula is grief-stricken that anyone is a "disappeared," a lost person. She wants them all found, an obvious impossibility. Visiting Conlon in prison, she is convinced that he has solid information about her mother, but he will not speak. Somehow in the course of this breathless novel, McGowan remembers that Paula's baby girl must be delivered, red-haired like her mother and grandmother and named Margaret.

Fearing death as she is prepared for her Caesarean section, Paula exacts Saoirse's promise to see that Guy will pursue the truth about her mother. He learns that Margaret was rumored to be involved with someone in Special

13. McGowan, *Silent Dead*, chap. 14.

Branch. The supposition is that the IRA discovered her passing information from her legal office to Special Branch, and planned to kidnap both her and her contact, but Paula is still left to wonder if her mother is alive.

In *A Savage Hunger*, McGowan composes an even more sophisticated narrative system than in *The Silent Dead*, focusing on one present-day victim but adhering to her familiar themes of deeply traumatized characters and the past impinging on the present. Paula and Aidan have been living together for two years and are about to marry, although paternity of Paula's daughter Maggie is still undetermined. The case concerns Alice, a missing young woman with a history of anorexia; she was last seen at a deconsecrated church (her blood is found at the site) on land owned by Anderson Garrett and his mother. Also missing is a relic, the finger bone of St. Blannad, a fictional fifth-century saint known for fasting and miracles that include feeding the hungry during the Famine. Another young woman, Yvonne O'Neill, earlier disappeared from that same site and was never found. The novel is divided into "Parts" headed by quotations from Lewis Carroll's *Alice Through the Looking Glass*; another mysterious "Prologue," this one from Belfast in July 1981, recounting a scene involving a Hunger Striker and a conflicted gunman; third-person chapters concentrated on Paula's consciousness; masterful segments titled "Alice," in which McGowan allows her missing victim to methodically reveal her background, emotional distress, courage, and keen intellect; and a series of WhatsApp conversations among Alice's three purported school friends (in fact, the two boys raped a drugged Alice and the witnessing girl participated in the cover-up). The effect is staggering.

Alice is brilliant, but severely damaged. She has suffered outrageous abuse and assault, including indecent lack of concern from her parents; mistreatment and forced feeding at an anorexia clinic; cruelty at the hands of school "friends," culminating in the aforementioned rape; and unprofessional, criminal conduct by school administrators who do nothing in response to her reporting of it. Her wounded psyche turns to obsessive religious research and practice, leading to her fixation with St. Blannad. She believes that the saint will assuage her hunger, allowing the old Alice to be replaced by a new, healthy self, capable of starting an independent life. The police work hard, but the crux of the novel is that McGowan's intellectually gifted, emotionally impaired victim ingeniously "solves" her own disappearance. McGowan masterfully discloses Alice's astute hiding and, most importantly, her spying on the friends who violated her and on the police who are investigating her disappearance. Moreover, Alice exposes Garrett, a religious fanatic of a different sort, as the murderer of Yvonne, a religious girl who pitied the Hunger Strikers. Alice graphically explains her motivation for essentially conducting her journey through a looking glass: to indict all those who have hurt her through the years. She succeeds beyond her wildest dreams. All—not just the students—are punished.

If only the other markedly traumatized characters in *A Savage Hunger* could have reached such resolution. Aidan is so distraught at Conlon's release that he attacks him and is arrested for murder on the day that he and Paula are to marry. Bob advises Paula that Conlon was possibly still alive when Aidan left him; perhaps the IRA finished the job to impede discussion of Conlon's past paramilitary activities. This ties in with the novel's elliptical 1981 "Prologue." Paula now knows for certain that her mother was involved with someone from the Special Branch, and she confronts Bob with his suppression of evidence. Bob admits his file tampering, but assures her that he searched incessantly. Paula questions whether she should take Maggie to London, where (still-married) Guy has offered her a position.

The police procedural in *Blood Tide* (2017), in which most of the action takes place on the fictional Bone Island, is formulaic, but the novel is vital for enhancing Margaret's story, especially by giving Margaret and Bob segments of narration. It also illuminates aspects of trauma experienced by Bob, Paula, and Aidan. The astounding "Prologue" is Margaret's, dating from 1993. As she waits for "Edward," her British contact, to take her to safety, she tries to write a note to Paula explaining that she must leave for her family's security and that she will return when possible. She is interrupted by the sound of a car and "Footsteps, coming to her door. They were here. It was too late."[14]

The most powerful sections belong to Bob, who emerges as one of the most remarkable figures in the series, a man who never stopped trying to

14. McGowan, *Blood Tide*, Prologue.

help Margaret. Bob had approached Conlon several times, courageously using information gleaned from his RUC days as threats to elicit information about Margaret. When Margaret was taken to RUC Headquarters after the paratrooper's death at the checkpoint, she had asked for Bob, who recalls this moment as Margaret's transformation. She passionately cried to him, "They . . . shot him. Only a wee lad, nineteen if he's a day. . . . He died in my arms. In my *arms.* Asking for his mummy back in Birmingham or wherever. How is this right? . . . They killed John, and they kill wee lads in the street, and [Aidan], he'll never be the same, and my Paula's crying every night. . . . It has to stop."[15] Through Bob, we discern Margaret's activism and motives. Bob now secretly assists the private investigator Paula hired for both her mother's case and Aidan's. Poignantly, Margaret spoke to Bob with complete trust before her disappearance. She told him about her years of informing, emphasizing that she was leaving town with the contact to protect Paula and PJ more than herself. For all the years thereafter, Bob put himself and his family in grave danger by his searching for her, and he has suffered greatly.

In addition to learning important facts from Bob and her private detective, Paula experiences resurfaced memory. Crucially, she finds it arduous to work the case on Bone Island, which was the setting of the last Maguire family vacation. Haunted by recollections of that holiday, she envisions her mother standing on the windy beach, looking lovely. As she visualizes her mother's body in profile, she suddenly recognizes that Margaret was pregnant. Notwithstanding her unsettled personal life (Aidan, broken by his time in prison, urges Paula to take Guy's offer of a London job, but she walks away when she sees Guy's wife is pregnant), Paula ends *Blood Tide* with far more information about her mother's disappearance than before.

The Killing House (2018), primarily Margaret Maguire's book, ends the series. Its strongest portions are the numerous dated segments titled "Margaret," which narrate, in the third person within Margaret's consciousness, her story from 1993 to 2014. The development of her character and revelation of her ordeal during those years constitute homage to a

15. McGowan, *Blood Tide*, chap. 17.

heroic woman. As her mystery unfolds, we are privy to her fortitude and courage as well as to her love for her family and fear for their safety. In heartrending detail, Margaret emerges as the series' final victim of trauma.

The investigation in *The Killing House* is relentlessly rooted in the Troubles. The dead bodies of a man and a young girl are discovered buried on a known IRA family's farm. Paula, living in London with Maggie and working with Guy (who has not been told that he is, indeed, Maggie's father), returns to Ballyterrin for a wedding and consults on the case at Corry's request. The local team are stymied by the presence of members of the Independent Commission for the Location of Victims' Remains (ICLVR),[16] and apart from Corry, they are relegated to secondary status. Paula, who has no official role, is most effective in solving the multiplying complications that grow from the initial investigation. Concurrently, she quietly continues delving into her mother's fate.

The novel's prime criminal is Paddy "The Ghost" Wallace, an IRA man who has been on the run for ten years. Notorious as the volatile head of a murder and punishment squad, Paddy has been picking off members of his old team because he believed one was an informer. He intensifies the book's 2014 action by anonymously informing the authorities that Margaret Maguire is buried on the Wallace land. Although this is not true, it leads to the exposure of that farm as the place where Margaret was held after being captured by the IRA. We eventually learn that Paddy murdered Conlon in *A Savage Hunger*, having identified him as the traitor.

More important than a detailed chronology of these discoveries is the knowledge gleaned from the novel's cynosure: the account of Margaret's onerous journey. She was interrogated for several days at the farm with the vicious Paddy at the helm. Margaret was terrified, but she never broke. She feared punishment, feared her own death as well as possible death for Paula

16. Established by an intergovernmental agreement between Ireland and Britain, the ICLVR's purpose is "to obtain information, in Confidentiality, which may lead to the location of the remains of victims of paramilitary violence ('The Disappeared') who were murdered and buried in secret arising from the conflict in Northern Ireland" (Independent Commission for the Location of Victims' Remains/An Coimisiún Neamhspleách Um Aimsiú Taisí Íospartach).

and PJ, was beset with anxiety over whether Edward would come for her, and questioned whether her well-intentioned actions were worth it. But she gave Paddy nothing on Edward.

Apparently, there is something about Margaret, perhaps some elemental charisma, which impels a spark of understanding in certain persons. We already know of Bob Hamilton's devotion, and *The Killing House* discloses two more extraordinary examples. Paddy's younger sister Aisling was uncomfortable living under her brother's sway but never dared to disobey him. After helping Margaret and after a few brief conversations about Margaret's beloved daughter, Aisling set her free, telling her to run or become another of Paddy's punishment killings. Margaret ran but was foiled by Conlon. He treated her roughly and condemned her as a traitor, but he too wavers after she tells him, "It's not worth it, this idea of a united Ireland. Do you not see? Nothing is worth killing people for. It's nearly over, for God's sake. Just let it be over. Let me go."[17] Faced by her appeal to some sense of humanity within him, Conlon lets her go. Conlon is surely one of the most complex figures in the series: an IRA gunman, but a conflicted one; a known liar, but an informer. Without him, Margaret would have been killed. Margaret got to a phone and called Edward, who had in fact been searching for her, and who engineered an impressive operation during which the two of them were spirited away to the ferry, and to England, never again to return to Ireland.

Of all the heartbreaking features of the Maguire series, none is more so than Margaret's time in London. It entailed years of moving from one small, nondescript flat to another, always goaded on by sudden fear that someone has discovered Margaret and Edward's identities and location. Margaret loved the devoted Edward and adored their daughter, but she did not have a moment of true peace and security. Coping with all but unimaginable trauma became the activity of Margaret's daily life. Guilt-ridden by leaving Paula and PJ, she constantly feared for their lives. Raising one daughter while knowing that her other girl was suffering immeasurably was agonizing. When Edward was executed in 2006 by a car bomb (plotted

17. McGowan, *Killing House*, chap. 27.

by Paddy), Margaret, amazingly, carried on, knowing full well that she had escaped once again: only her running back to the flat to make sure she had locked the door prevented her from being killed with Edward. From this point on, moving from place to place, she had to live with a new dimension of terror. If a shadowy squad from the old IRA should find her again, they could kill her and Aisling. She was both haunted and hunted.

Late in *The Killing House*, Paddy holds Paula at gunpoint, taunting her by saying that he knows where Margaret lives and can have her killed. Fittingly, Bob Hamilton arrives and tries to save Paula, only to be shot by Paddy. By the time Corry arrives, Bob is dying, his last words to Paula a whispered "Find her."[18] Paddy is duly charged, and Aidan released, but a mind like Paddy's is impossible to decipher. He gives Paula Margaret's latest address. Alone, secretly, Paula goes to her. McGowan sets a quiet, gentle scene as Margaret is called to the door by a puzzled Aisling: "'Oh,' said Margaret. Her hands clenched, rising up despite herself to touch the young woman's face. 'It's you.'"[19] Appropriately, McGowan allows us no further entry into the scene.

Three months later, Paula and Maggie are back living in London. All seems calm, but rosy endings are not for a series such as this. Trauma, even somewhat alleviated, lies deep, and psychological injuries leave irreparable scars. Aidan has been so adversely affected by his imprisonment that Paula wonders what unknown perils the future may bring: "the darkness in him had been fed."[20] As the novel ends, Paula is taking Aidan and Maggie to meet Margaret, but the subterfuge involved in maintaining a relationship with Margaret becomes achingly clear. Margaret has been reunited with her precious Paula, but they must meet clandestinely. She has Aisling, who cannot yet be told about her past, and Maggie, whose identity must remain concealed. Many old secrets have been uncovered, but new ones have taken their place. Particularly dangerous: PJ doesn't know that Margaret is alive, Paula doesn't know whether she'll ever tell Guy that he is Maggie's father,

18. McGowan, *Killing House*, chap. 40.

19. McGowan, *Killing House*, chap. 42.

20. McGowan, *Killing House*, Epilogue.

and Margaret must always live looking over one shoulder. In true Irish literary form, the ellipses in this final novel cannot be filled in. Those ellipses are McGowan's last and most powerful declaration that no complete resolution is possible for personal experiences of the Troubles. The leitmotif of the Troubles remains to the end.

In *Remembering the Troubles*, Jim Smyth aptly refers to "the almost ending of 'the north's' thirty years' war [and] the trauma still raw in a still deeply divided society."[21] McGowan's detective novels distill this "almost ending," exuding trauma as the relic of the Troubles. Grant the last word to *A Savage Hunger*'s Alice, who felt such endearment for a relic: "I looked it up and it's from Latin. It means 'what is left behind.' These days, I find myself thinking about that. A lot."[22]

Bibliography

Barber, Fionna. "At Vision's Edge: Post-Conflict Memory and Art Practice in Northern Ireland." In *Memory Ireland*, vol. 3, *The Famine and the Troubles*, edited by Oona Frawley, 232–46. Syracuse: Syracuse Univ. Press, 2014.

Garratt, Robert. *Trauma and History in the Irish Novel.* Basingstoke: Palgrave Macmillan, 2011.

Independent Commission for the Location of Victims' Remains (An Coimisiún Neamhspleách Um Aimsiú Taisí Íospartach). www.iclvr.ie. Accessed 18 April 2018.

"Killing House." https://www.eliteukforces.info/special-air-service/sas-training/. Accessed 19 April 2018.

McClements, Freya. "Giving Voice to the Troubles: How Literature Has Told the North's Story." *Irish Times*, 6 October 2018. https://www.irishtimes.com/culture/books/giving-voice-to-the-troubles-how-literature-has-told-the-north-s-story-1.3642490. Accessed 15 April 2019.

McGowan, Claire. *Blood Tide.* E-book. London: Headline, 2017.

———. *The Dead Ground.* London: Headline, 2014.

———. *The Killing House.* E-book. London: Headline, 2018

———. *The Lost.* E-book. London: Headline, 2013.

———. *A Savage Hunger.* E-book. London: Headline, 2016.

21. Smyth, *Remembering the Troubles*, 5.

22. McGowan, *Savage Hunger*, chap. 42.

———. *The Silent Dead*. E-book. London: Headline, 2015.

Smyth, Jim. "Introduction." In *Remembering the Troubles: Contesting the Recent Past in Northern Ireland*, edited by Jim Smyth, 1–8. Notre Dame: Notre Dame Univ. Press, 2017.

16

More Than Domestic

Toward a Theory of Maternal Noir in Sinéad Crowley's DS Claire Boyle Novels

FIONA COLEMAN COFFEY

There has been a recent surge in unapologetically commercial crime and detective fiction that eschews the at times burdensome Irish tradition of high literary writing, while engaging with important sociopolitical changes in Irish society. Female crime writers, in particular, are expanding the genre in significant ways while exploring women's relationship to and status within the Irish state. This can be linked, in part, to the international success of domestic noir, which explores the ways that marriage and the domestic space limit and entrap women. Domestic noir has helped shape recent Irish detective fiction, but there is "a trend," as Declan Burke notes, "that is kind of feeding off the energy of [the genre]. It may not be domestic noir itself. But the idea of the woman as a flawed but remarkably interesting central character is certainly coming to the fore in Irish crime fiction."[1] Recent detective novels feature complex, imperfect, and emboldened women who are awakening to the (domestic and societal) deceptions and limitations in their lives, echoing this popular genre's central themes.

The influence of domestic noir on Irish crime fiction has led to the emergence of a new subgenre—a maternal noir—which specifically focuses on the tension between motherhood and career. If domestic noir explores the

1. Barry, "Irish Crime Writing."

confinement and abuse of women within the boundaries of marriage and domesticity, maternal noir shines a light on the systemic lack of fairness that women face when confronting motherhood and demanding careers. Maternal noir features detectives who are mothers, and these investigators actively dismantle traditional expectations of parenthood, rejecting the notion that prioritizing challenging careers necessitates negligent motherhood. They directly tackle the tension between motherhood and career and ultimately take a feminist stance that the professional challenges mothers face are not intrinsic but societally constructed.

Sinéad Crowley's Detective Claire Boyle series forges new ground in this emerging category, blending the structures of hard-boiled detective fiction and the police procedural to emphasize the double standards faced by professional women, particularly around childcare and domestic responsibility. In highlighting these concerns, the Boyle series challenges conventions while simultaneously forging a new path within domestic noir.

British novelist Julia Crouch coined the term "domestic noir" in 2013 when trying to describe her own writing. The domestic noir novel, she says, "takes place primarily in homes and workplaces, concerns itself largely (but not exclusively) with the female experience, is based around relationships, and takes as its base a broadly feminist view that the domestic sphere is a challenging and sometimes dangerous prospect for its inhabitants."[2] The genre portrays the domestic space as one of danger and is characterized by women being deceived, entrapped, or gaslighted by deceitful husbands. B. A. Paris emphasizes that the tension in a domestic noir novel "has to come from a relationship that is founded on lies, or where there is a degree of abuse, whether physical or psychological."[3] Novelist Laura Joyce expands this, viewing the genre as "a capacious, flexible category that encompasses realist writing about domestic violence, intersectional feminism, religion, mental illness, and women's rights but that can also include fantastic and even supernatural storylines."[4] This flexibility includes diverse feminist

2. East, "On the Dark Side."
3. East, "On the Dark Side."
4. Joyce, "The Origins of Domestic Noir."

perspectives as well as the larger project of examining how heteronormative standards inhibit women. Ultimately, Anna Snoektra contends, this approach is part of a larger trend toward "repositioning women in crime narratives. Focusing on them as subjective in the story of their victimization rather than being the ultimate objectification: a dead body."[5]

In line with these developments, a crop of bold, multifaceted, and challenging female detectives—by Jane Casey, Claire McGowan, Alex Barclay, Tana French, Stuart Neville, and others—are populating Irish crime fiction. The emergence of strong, talented female detectives who are empowered with the intelligence, grit, and legal authority to solve crimes (rather than being the victim of one) is perhaps both an antidote to female victimization and a reflection of more women populating these roles in real life. Indeed, Rosemary Johnsen argues that "central feminist issues, including violence against women and questions of sociocultural value (what would someone kill for?), are built right into the conventions of the crime genre,"[6] and thus make detective fiction especially fruitful for feminist projects.

Agreeing with this premise, Merja Makinen challenges the notion that detective fiction is a masculinist project, arguing that "there are two standard assumptions about detective fiction, that it is a male-based genre because of its ratiocinating puzzle-solving element, and that it is an inherently conservative genre because its resolution involves the reinstatement of a hierarchical status quo."[7] She refutes these tenets by citing a rich history of feminist female detectives and demonstrating that "women's gender-specific view allows for a potentially radical input."[8] In fact, Lee Horsley observes that the hard-boiled tradition "has proven to be the most compelling model" for feminist reappropriation and "for the purposes of self-definition."[9] The outspoken, independent, confident, and worldly-wise hard-boiled detective figure lends itself readily to feminist writers as "it

5. Snoektra, "From Bluebeard to Gone Girl."

6. Johnsen, *Contemporary Feminist Historical Crime Fiction*, 9.

7. Makinen, *Feminist Popular Fiction*, 92.

8. Makinen, *Feminist Popular Fiction*, 94.

9. Horsley, *Twentieth-Century Crime Fiction*, 248.

supplies a structure for critique that can be significantly changed by the reversal of a basic binary (white to black, male to female), resituating the protagonist in relation to the existing system."[10]

Indeed, a sustained wave of sleuths with feminist sensibilities began in the 1980s, during which American novelists Sue Grafton, Marcia Muller, and Sara Paretsky created highly successful series featuring hard-charging female investigators.[11] The 1980s standardized the woman detective who refused to allow gendered expectations to alter her approach to her work. Margaret Kinsman notes, "with very few parents, children or spouses in the picture, the literary creations were answerable first to themselves (perhaps the ultimate feminist act) and then to their clients and their communities of neighbors, friends and relations."[12]

Rejecting the classic loner detective narrative favored even by the progressive women crime writers of the 1980s, maternal noir repositions women as talented investigators as well as mothers, daughters, and sisters who remain accountable to familial ties and responsibilities. Pregnancy and parenthood are central to the subgenre, and problematize the traditional police procedural, which tends to push any domestic responsibilities to the margins of the plot and the detective's identity. Maternal noir thus establishes new tropes that build upon domestic noir and that assert a feminist interrogation of motherhood. While domestic noir exposes the ways in which the traditional patriarchal structures of marriage trap women, maternal noir focuses on how pregnancy and motherhood affect women when they operate within traditionally male-dominated arenas such as policing, crime, and detective work. The female detectives populating recent Irish crime novels are strong-willed and dedicated, but many of them knock up against double standards and the societal expectation that they be fully present mothers while juggling demanding careers that inherently limit their ability to fulfill those very expectations.

10. Horsley, *Twentieth-Century Crime Fiction*, 248.

11. Kinsman, "Feminist Crime Fiction," 153.

12. Kinsman, "Feminist Crime Fiction," 155.

Mothers and pregnant women are often targets in crime fiction,[13] as they represent a particularly vulnerable portion of the population. However, pregnant women have recently emerged as the sleuths instead of merely the victims. Pregnant detectives have appeared in crime fiction such as British novelists Mark Billingham's *In the Dark* (2008) and Susie Steiner's *Persons Unknown* (2017), American novelist Emily Littlejohn's *Inherit the Bones* (2016), and Scottish novelist Denise Mina's *The End of Wasp Season* (2011) as well as her Paddy Meehan series. They have also been prominent in film and television, from Marge Gunderson in *Fargo* (1996) to the BBC crime drama *Collateral* (2018). In Irish novelist Claire McGowan's Paula Maguire series, forensic psychologist Maguire is pregnant over the course of three novels, tracking a murderer of pregnant women in the second before finally giving birth in the third.

Sinéad Crowley's Detective Claire Boyle series—*Can Anybody Help Me?* (2014), *Are You Watching Me?* (2015), and *One Bad Turn* (2017)—follows Detective Boyle as she hunts down killers while juggling pregnancy, motherhood, marriage, and her husband's growing resentment of her career-mindedness. All three novels feature female protagonists and female victims as well as Detective Boyle, and each tackles the challenges of parenthood, career, and relationships set against the backdrop of gritty, murderous crime sprees.

Can Anybody Help Me? tackles the isolation of early motherhood and the dangers of online forums that connect vulnerable women with each other. When several young mothers from the online forum NetMammy go missing, Boyle must race to find the killer who is masquerading as a supportive mom online, luring young mothers to their deaths. This first novel features Yvonne, a homemaker, who feels isolated at home with a baby and disconnected from her husband, Gerry, who is busy at work. She also seems to be experiencing postpartum depression: numb, disinterested, and lethargic, she turns to NetMammy to connect to other moms. However, it

13. Examples include Emily Schultz's *The Blondes* (2012), Tania Carver's *The Surrogate* (2009), Shannon Kirk's *Method 15/33* (2015), and Kimberly McCreight's *Where They Found Her* (2015), among many others.

turns out that Yvonne's charming, handsome husband has been having an affair. He and his lover have been drugging Yvonne and using a fake Net-Mammy profile to spy on her and gain insight into her psychological state so they can eventually stage her suicide in a convincing manner. Yvonne has no idea that her husband is gaslighting her or plotting her death; her new-born baby, her isolation, and her fragile mental state make her particularity vulnerable to deception.

This first novel has classic elements of domestic noir set within the standard police procedural: the appearance of domestic bliss undercut by a husband plotting against his unsuspecting wife, warping her perception of reality. However, *Can Anybody Help Me?* moves firmly into the territory of maternal noir because Boyle is herself heavily pregnant while hunting down the serial killer of young mothers. This juxtaposition of hunting killers while simultaneously generating new life is striking, as is her ambivalence about becoming a mother. Boyle's professional dedication pushes her to an unhealthy brink that threatens her pregnancy. Moreover, she and her husband continuously clash over what is appropriate risk for a pregnant woman, making Boyle's relationship to motherhood even more fraught.

While the inconvenience and physical alienation of pregnancy is explored in the first novel, *Are You Watching Me?* delves into Boyle's disinterest in the banality of motherhood. Driven by the excitement and intellectual vigor of her career, Boyle wants no part in Mommy and Me music classes or pureeing her own organic baby food. Soon after giving birth, Boyle is back at work pursuing a murderous stalker who is targeting Liz Cafferky, the beautiful, young communications executive for a men's homeless shelter in Dublin. Cafferky took this menial-wage job because she feels indebted to her boss for helping her get sober. An old college friend cajoles her into appearing on TV as the public face of the shelter, a role that her naturally shy self abhors. A young man who sees the show becomes obsessed and begins stalking her at the same time that several men from the shelter end up dead. Liz is thus manipulated and threatened by the men around her while Boyle struggles to reconcile traditional expectations of motherhood with the demanding role of an investigator, reflecting both domestic and maternal noir elements within the novel.

One Bad Turn finds Boyle back in full swing, with her husband taking care of most of the domestic work and childcare. The tension in their marriage, which is evident in the first two novels, comes to a head when she stumbles into a hostage situation at her doctor's office. Eileen Delaney had kidnapped the daughter of her childhood friend, Dr. Heather Gilmore. Gilmore's ex-husband, a corrupt Celtic Tiger real estate investor, defrauded Eileen, leaving her and her son homeless. Eileen's son died under suspicious circumstances after accusing Gilmore's husband of dishonest dealings. Men dominating, cheating, and lying to the detriment of the women around them are clearly found in all three of Crowley's novels, reflecting the rise of domestic noir and the growing feeling that women are being gaslighted by the men around them. Here, as throughout the series, Boyle struggles to balance her career with her husband's expectations of her as a mother, situating the novel firmly within the maternal noir category.

Boyle's initial ambivalence toward her pregnancy and its effect on her career is indicative of the uneasy relationship between motherhood and work that is found in maternal noir. Crowley writes of Boyle's unapologetic careerism in a matter-of-fact manner: "Claire loved being a detective. The job was everything she had always dreamed it would be: challenging, busy, never boring."[14] Defiantly disinterested in treating her pregnancy as any sort of impediment, Boyle chafes at her family and colleagues' delicacy surrounding her condition: "They just didn't get it. None of them did. Pregnancy wasn't an illness. She could still do her job. Had to. There was a woman dead, and it was up to her to find the killer."[15]

Boyle's primary relationship with her pregnancy is one of inconvenience and physical discomfort periodically punctuated by moments in which others subsume Boyle's whole self in their own concepts of maternity and pregnancy: "Welcome to pregnancy; leave your individuality and your name at the door of the antenatal ward."[16] Boyle's devotion to her job filters through every aspect of her pregnancy. At a prenatal appointment

14. Crowley, *One Bad Turn*, 13.

15. Crowley, *Can Anybody Help Me?*, 234.

16. Crowley, *Can Anybody Help Me?*, 1.

with her husband, Matt, Boyle is distracted from the ultrasound by her anticipation of a verdict in a serial rape case that she investigated. After the appointment, Claire jumps at the chance to return to work, thinking: "A nice person would have said no; let the others handle it. After all, there was nothing she needed to do. But Claire knew she wasn't always a nice person, and in fairness, Matt had known it too when he married her."[17]

Throughout the series, Boyle focuses on her career to the increasing detriment of her marriage. *Are You Watching Me?* explores the tension between Boyle's professional drive and Matt's expectations that she prioritize motherhood over work. The strain in her marriage escalates as Boyle refuses to acquiesce to her husband's limiting assumptions. Matt is initially understanding and agrees to take on most of the domestic responsibilities, but Boyle still chafes at the confines of marriage and motherhood: "Her husband's hand stroked her shoulder blade and she shifted a couple of inches away. There was too much work stuff, too much baby stuff, too much of everything stuffing up her head."[18] The claustrophobia and absolute exhaustion of domestic responsibility suffocates Boyle: "For a fleeting moment, she wished she was single. No Matt, no Anna. No one to ask her how the day had been. No demands, no questions. No hugs, even. She'd trade them all. Trade them for an empty house with a warm bath and a bottle of red."[19]

Crowley is relentless in illustrating how motherhood can simultaneously elicit love *and* resentment, another hallmark of maternal noir. Boyle's refusal to feel shame is an overt rejection of maternal guilt and of the notion that women should try to "have it all." She does not succumb to the feelings of inadequacy common among mothers when they inevitably fail to juggle competing personal, familial, and professional demands. Instead, she rejects the very notion that she should *have* to juggle at all.

Matt's increasing resentment at having to sacrifice his own career for domestic duties boils over in *One Bad Turn*. His patience and support wear

17. Crowley, *Can Anybody Help Me?*, 6.
18. Crowley, *Are You Watching Me?*, 62.
19. Crowley, *Are You Watching Me?*, 330.

thin: "'And you're the only one who can do it?' The coldness again. And, worse still, the sneer in his voice. Claire had closed her eyes as her husband continued, 'A police station full of cops but Sergeant Claire Boyle is the only woman who can ride to the rescue. D'you know what, Claire? If I'd known I was marrying Superwoman I'd have bought you a cape.'"[20] Boyle brushes off his casual sexism and, as his resentment increases, refuses to be complicit in double standards for women. Boyle "sent Matt an apologetic text promising to be home at the vague hour of 'not too late.' A large part of her felt resentment at having to include the apology at all—what was she apologizing for exactly? Doing her job? Attempting to save a young woman's life?"[21] Crowley thus acknowledges without judgment that this duality of maternal love and resentment extends to marriage as well.

Surrounded by male colleagues, Boyle is acutely aware of the ways that men use their work to get out of domestic duties and how readily this is accepted by their families and the culture around them:

> Her male colleagues thought nothing of pulling extra shifts [when] it suited them, or if being at home with the family *didn't* suit them. How often had she heard the lads standing around, laughing about how they'd "got out" of the mother-in-law's birthday or the cousin's wedding because they "had to work," knowing full well no one would argue with them. And always, always, there'd be a wife at home holding the fort, wrapping the presents, dressing the kids, attending the wedding, making the excuses. . . . This morning wasn't the first time they'd had a row about her job since she'd gone back after maternity leave, or indeed the second or the third. Back when she was pregnant, Matt, who prided himself on being a feminist, had been full of plans about being what he termed the "lead parent in the home" and told all and sundry that he'd be happy to curtail his working hours to suit Claire's more demanding, and, let's face it, better paid job.[22]

20. Crowley, *Are You Watching Me?*, 195.
21. Crowley, *Are You Watching Me?*, 232–33.
22. Crowley, *Are You Watching Me?*, 196–97.

However, when Matt is faced with the reality of taking on the majority of childcare responsibilities, he increasingly finds this role stifling, a double standard that aggravates Boyle. Instead of acknowledging the uneven workload that women are unjustly expected to take on, Matt focuses his resentment on his wife's absenteeism and the possible detriment to his own career.

Crowley has described writing Boyle in the tradition of the male detective, flipping conventional gender representations in detective fiction on its head:

> What I was trying to do was write a traditional male cop and make him a woman. And what I mean by that is, in traditional crime fiction, the male cop devotes everything to his job. . . . It is almost expected that he leaves his family. It's quite normal in male crime fiction to see the cop maybe not going to the birthday party or forgetting his wife's birthday but it's okay because he is solving the crime. And I was thinking, if he were a woman taking on that level of work, would people forgive her? . . . [Boyle's] caught between that: she's a great mother but she's also a great garda, and she wants to do both.[23]

As Crowley describes, the traditional hard-boiled detective is either single and unencumbered or neglects his personal and familial responsibilities in the dogged pursuit of justice. In line with this convention, Boyle gets immersed in her investigations, forgetting to eat or check her phone, missing dinners, and working weekends: "Bollocks. Eleven missed calls, three text messages. All from Matt. The first, a gentle, 'how're things? Ring me.' The second, an hour later, 'just let me know all is okay.' The third, sent at midnight, 'Jesus, ring me, Claire. Am worried.'"[24] When Boyle finally arrives home, she can "feel his anger radiate. . . . There would be no cuddles this evening, so."[25]

23. Crowley, "Interview."
24. Crowley, *Can Anybody Help Me?*, 202.
25. Crowley, *Can Anybody Help Me?*, 202.

Despite her devotion to her job, however, Boyle always returns home to her child and her domestic obligations. In contrast to the traditional male detective who tends to be alienated from his family, Boyle is a good mother *even though* she prioritizes her own individualism and work over that of motherhood. And, significantly, she does so without a major internal crisis or a conflicted identity. At the beginning of *One Bad Turn*, Boyle finds herself locked in the bathroom at her doctor's office with her baby, listening to an escalating hostage situation. Boyle manages the stressful situation while simultaneously inhabiting her roles as garda and mother:

> Quickly, Claire began to run through the day in her mind, her thoughts a grotesque parody of the baby books Matt had once been addicted to. Anna had had breakfast at eight and a bottle at eleven, had fallen asleep just after half past twelve. . . . She'd sleep for another twenty minutes maybe, no more. Would need a nappy change by two. Did that give her mother time to disarm a lunatic. . . . Could she make an arrest and still have her baby at home in time for fruit puree and yogurt at three? Claire felt a hysterical giggle boil in her stomach and forced herself to calm down.[26]

Unlike the hard-boiled detective who finds himself alienated from his children, Boyle is determined to be a positive presence for her daughter by modeling the satisfaction that comes from a meaningful career. In creating a talented, successful detective who is *also* a good mother, Crowley filters the hard-boiled tradition through a gendered lens, both playing with and resisting its precepts.

Crowley was surprised by a lack of empathy for Boyle: "When I wrote her, I felt she was an incredibly sympathetic character, but I'm surprised at the number of readers who haven't warmed to her or feel that she has neglected her family for the job. Precisely the point I was trying to make!"[27] Priscilla Walton explains the discomfort that occurs when gender roles are reversed but genre conventions remain the same: "Feminist detective fiction constitutes a reverse discourse exploring positions of resistance and agency

26. Crowley, *One Bad Turn*, 30.

27. Crowley, email correspondence.

that were offered by previous practices but were inaccessible to women. Reinscribing those discourses refuses stereotypical structures at the same time as it reveals their contradictions."[28] Readers who accept certain conventions for men find it uncomfortable to see women within those same criteria. By flipping the gendered precepts of crime fiction on its head, Crowley emphasizes those double standards: "I was, in fact, reacting against an entire genre. I have read so many books where the man gives up everything for 'The Job.' . . . It was accepted, if not expected, that the man would value his work above all else. I started to wonder what it would be like to have a female detective who was just as dedicated to her job as the men traditionally were, but who was a wife and, crucially, a mother as well."[29] Crowley deliberately allows Boyle to operate professionally, demonstrating Boyle's undiminished talent and professionalism despite the intense domestic expectations and demands she negotiates on a daily basis. Crowley goes on to specify that it is Boyle's "relationship with Matt, rather than motherhood that is the issue. . . . She could be the mother and cop she [wants to be] if she had a traditional 'wife' herself but she doesn't and that's how the tension arises."[30] Thus, Crowley demonstrates that having a demanding career and being a good mother is neither antithetical nor unattainable; rather, it is the lack of equal support that women receive from their partners that prevents them from achieving both.

The onerous expectation that women be the primary caregivers is further examined in *One Bad Turn*. This third novel is framed by Boyle's decision not to have any more children so she can refocus on work. At the beginning, Boyle has seen her doctor to discuss getting her tubes tied, but she has not yet told Matt. The book ends with Matt storming out after she tells him she is done having children. Enraged that she has made such an important decision without his consultation, he sneers, "'So it's about the job. . . . The precious job. It means more to you than anything, doesn't it, Detective? . . . And do you have room for me in all of this? Do you have

28. Walton, *Detective Agency*, 93.

29. Crowley, email correspondence.

30. Crowley, email correspondence.

room for me? With your job, and your child, and your responsibilities?'"[31] Throughout the series, Crowley portrays Matt as extremely patient; however, his latent sexism and his lack of self-awareness regarding his expectations for Boyle as a wife and mother come to a head when her desire for a compelling career overpowers *his* desire for more children. As Crowley explains, "One of the most important feminist issues of our times [is] the issue of childcare, who looks after the children when the parent works and who does society expect to do it? I don't think [Boyle] prioritizes work over children, I think she wants to do both. Men have successfully done both for generations, she just wants the same opportunity and feels let down by her husband and what she feels are broken promises."[32] It is unclear at the end of the novel whether Matt will return. However, the breakdown of Boyle's relationship is not the last image that we see. Instead, she returns to work, interrogating a suspect and tying up loose ends. Thus, the book concludes by emphasizing Boyle's identity as a detective, not as a wife or mother.

As more female detectives populate crime fiction, their roles as wives, partners, mothers, and daughters will naturally lead to further examination of gender dynamics within the police force as well as to increased scrutiny of how heteronormative gender values inhibit women professionally and personally. Addressing the issues of childcare and parenthood within a genre that traditionally shuns these topics destabilizes the accepted principle within crime fiction that the most dedicated detective is the one who sacrifices the most. Instead, maternal noir suggests that what is more extraordinary is a detective who allows for a multifaceted life and identity that includes domestic obligations while still pursuing a career that demands complete devotion. That inherent contradiction is at the heart of maternal noir, which both acknowledges and challenges this precept. Indeed, the most feminist thing about Crowley's series is not having a tough female detective as the lead but the idea that she can be *both* a good mother and a good detective.

31. Crowley, *One Bad Turn*, 330–31.

32. Crowley, *One Bad Turn*, 330–31.

While the feminist arguments outlined in the Boyle series regarding childcare and motherhood are neither novel nor radical, maternal noir is significant in that it reflects a distinct *lack* of progress since the start of second-wave feminism. The frustration and sense of incredulity that these issues are still prevalent is palpable throughout the genre. The Boyle series occasionally feels like a throwback—filled with antiquated, almost clichéd dynamics regarding motherhood and career—and this is what should be alarming: these same issues are still being written about in such a persistent manner. As more women reach the upper echelons of professional advancement, the issues of childcare are arguably becoming even more urgent as evidenced by this emerging genre.

While maternal noir is not specific to Irish crime fiction, it is increasingly prevalent in Irish writing because motherhood is so central to Irish identity. The allegory of Mother Ireland and the Catholic Church's role in both venerating and controlling mothers has had a deep impact on Irish culture. Maternal noir deconstructs these precepts within Irish culture while often still positioning motherhood as a positive and rewarding experience. Detective Boyle joins the ranks of pioneering female investigators who are redefining the detective genre as well as contemporary motherhood for twenty-first-century Ireland.

Bibliography

Barry, Aoife. "Irish Crime Writing Is Having a Killer Moment Right Now." *The Journal*, 2 October 2016. http://www.thejournal.ie/crime-writing-ireland-3004564-Oct2016/. Accessed 21 March 2018.

Crowley, Sinéad. *Are You Watching Me?* London: Quercus, 2015.

———. *Can Anybody Help Me?* London: Quercus, 2014.

———. Email correspondence with Fiona Coleman Coffey, 27 March 2018.

———. "Interview with Sinéad Crowley." *Sunday AM*. 11 June 2017. https://www.youtube.com/watch?v=aNBf9of9KVo. Accessed 21 March 2018.

———. *One Bad Turn*. London: Quercus, 2017.

East, Ben. "On the Dark Side: A Look at the Rise of 'Domestic Noir' Novels." *The National*, 15 August 2016. https://www.thenational.ae/arts-culture/on-the-dark-side-a-look-at-the-rise-of-domestic-noir-novels-1.147670. Accessed 21 March 2018.

Horsley, Lee. *Twentieth-Century Crime Fiction*. Oxford: Oxford Univ. Press, 2005.

Johnsen, Rosemary Erickson. *Contemporary Feminist Historical Crime Fiction*. New York: Palgrave Macmillan, 2006.

Joyce, Laura. "The Origins of Domestic Noir." The Writer's Center Norwich, 13 April 2017. https://www.writerscentrenorwich.org.uk/article/the-origins-of-domestic-noir/. Accessed 21 March 2018.

Kinsman, Margaret. "Feminist Crime Fiction." In *The Cambridge Companion to American Crime Fiction*, edited by Catherine Nickerson, 148–62. Cambridge and New York: Cambridge Univ. Press, 2010.

Makinen, Merja. *Feminist Popular Fiction*. London: Palgrave, 2001.

Snoektra, Anna. "From Bluebeard to Gone Girl: Why I'm Proud to be Part of the Domestic Noir Comeback." *Guardian* (Manchester), 7 September 2016. https://www.theguardian.com/books/australia-books-blog/2016/sep/07/from-bluebeard-to-gone-girl-why-im-proud-to-be-part-of-the-domestic-noir-comeback. Accessed 21 March 2018.

Walton, Priscilla L. "Does She or Doesn't She?: The Problematics of Feminist Detection." In *Detective Agency: Women Rewriting the Hard-Boiled Tradition*, edited by Priscilla L. Walton and Manina Jones, 86–117. Berkeley: Univ. of California Press, 1999.

17

Between the Lines

Liz Nugent's Malignant Protagonists

BRIAN CLIFF

Irish crime fiction has clearly established itself as a thriving strand of contemporary Irish literature, no longer a new arrival but increasingly integral. As varied voices develop many of the familiar subgenres of crime and mystery fiction, one significant subgenre has been domestic noir, adapted in Irish fiction by a range of contemporary writers, most recently including Jo Spain and Catherine Ryan Howard among others. Although her work predates the recent coinage of the term, one of domestic noir's forebears is Patricia Highsmith, whose distinctly harrowing narrative tone was scarce in Irish crime fiction until recently.[1] Liz Nugent's three novels to date—*Unravelling Oliver* (2014), *Lying in Wait* (2016), and *Skin Deep* (2018)—have, however, done much to bring Highsmith's particular strengths into Irish crime fiction.

Despite their tonal and stylistic distinctiveness, Nugent's novels share recurring themes with other Irish crime fiction such as Tana French's *Broken Harbour* (2012), Claire McGowan's entire Paula Maguire series (2013–18), Sinéad Crowley's Claire Boyle series (2014–), Benjamin Black's *Christine Falls* (2006), Brian McGilloway's *The Nameless Dead* (2012), and Arlene Hunt's *Missing Presumed Dead* (2007). These themes include

1. For an extended discussion of the term's origins, see Joyce and Sutton, *Domestic Noir.*

the regulation and repression of female sexuality through the Magdalene laundries and the mother and baby homes, as well as maternal violence, particularly central to French's *Broken Harbour.* Structurally, Nugent's novels also have something in common with Gene Kerrigan's intercut, communal narratives, which shift like Nugent's between varied and conflicting perspectives. Despite the thematic, structural, and tonal consistency of Nugent's three novels, however, they are standalones, with no recurring characters and few recurring locations (beyond Dublin and its suburbs in the broadest sense). In this, Nugent's work reflects a general pattern in domestic noir, a subgenre that does not regularly lend itself to the series protagonists that the marketplace often favors. One byproduct of this market pressure may be to mitigate against representing the varieties of experience (particularly women's experiences) that provide much of domestic noir's narratives, as they do in Nugent's own novels.

Nugent has written that she finds "it relatively easy to get into the mindset of sociopathic characters like Oliver in *Unravelling Oliver* and Lydia in *Lying in Wait*,"[2] or her most recent protagonist, Delia, in *Skin Deep.* Indeed, a notable absence of remotely likable main characters has been integral to her novels' critical success, and gives the lie to the idea that crime fiction protagonists—particularly women—need to be relatable or likable. Instead, working within a palette that includes Highsmith's varied shadowy inks as well as those of Irish novels like Patrick McCabe's *The Butcher Boy* (1992) and John Banville's *The Book of Evidence* (1989) (which she has cited as an influence),[3] Nugent's character-driven novels immerse their readers primarily in the disturbing first-person perspectives of highly unreliable, unstable narrators. As much as any of her peers, and more than most, Nugent has made a signature out of characters poised on a razor's edge of empathy and evil. These characters are, as Jane Casey has suggested, "unforgettably monstrous,"[4] and yet Nugent sustains a kind of empathy with their real sufferings, moving deftly between two poles:

2. Nugent, "Not Everyone Murders People in Their Sleep."

3. Nugent, "Not Everyone Murders People in Their Sleep."

4. Jane Casey, back jacket of Nugent, *Lying.*

one that allows a reader to empathize—however uneasily—with broken protagonists who do ill out of trauma, and one that allows a reader to judge those protagonists for the ill they do.

Despite not being a conventional series, Nugent's novels are marked by some defining continuities, including this tension between empathy and evil, as well as narrator-protagonists whose deep dysfunctions hinge on their relationship to their children and to their own parents.[5] This familial emphasis draws on elements of what Margot Backus has described in another context as the Irish family gothic (also a significant presence in French's and Declan Hughes's novels) and on analogous patterns that are clear in Highsmith's work, as well as in Ross Macdonald's decaying California families. Nugent intensifies this gothic-family strand in part by shifting among multiple first-person perspectives within each novel. These perspectives offer no more than a partial sense of events, often juxtaposing contrasting versions of a story, like the yawning gulf between Delia's memory of island life and the experiences of the other islanders in *Skin Deep*.[6] Through this structure, Nugent depicts lives woven out of partial truths, some pointedly secretive and some simply unrecognized by the characters.

Within their families, all of Nugent's main characters suffer grievously from clerical governance of sexual morality (often further refracted through class). Banished as an illegitimate child who embodies the failings that led his father to leave the priesthood,[7] Oliver can see from a boarding school window the family home at which he is never welcome; driven away by familial shame and clerical authority, Delia finds herself married

5. On noir's capacity for confounding gender assumptions, see Abbott, *Street Was Mine*. On maternal guilt in noir crime fiction, see Horsley and Horsley, "*Mères Fatales*," in which the authors argue that "the sympathetic representation of . . . insecure, fragmented female identities, subverts the idealized cultural possibilities of stereotypical femininity" (374). See also Di Ciolla and Pasolini, "Violent Mother."

6. This yawning gulf bespeaks Delia's trauma as much as the islanders' subjectivity: as Horsley and Horsley suggest of "female noir," "the gaps in understanding and memory among guilty mother figures are evidence of the fragmentation of secure, normative identities" ("*Mères Fatales*," 396).

7. Nugent, *Unravelling*, 130, 135.

and pregnant in London, far from the sea that she craves. Nugent's novels convey the distorting weight of these clerical and social forces as they pass down the generations, crushing the characters' lives under the weight of those legacies.

In representing these legacies, Nugent's novels construct a very specific sense of place and time, setting many core events in the 1980s, a decade depicted as a kind of suspended lull between the changes of the late 1960s and the boom that began in the mid-1990s, amidst what now seem perhaps to have been the last gasps of clerical dominance. This dominance is evidenced in *Lying in Wait* and *Skin Deep* by references to a series of contentious 1980s referenda. In *Lying in Wait*, Karen cannot leave her grim marriage to Dessie to be with Laurence explicitly because the 1986 referendum to legalize divorce had just failed (a 1995 referendum paved the way for allowing divorce, albeit under restrictive guidelines, now set to be less so following the May 2019 referendum).[8] Through Delia's conflicting experiences, *Skin Deep* makes more extended references to the 1983 abortion referendum, which resulted in the Eighth Amendment enshrining constitutional barriers against abortion, barriers only undone by another referendum in May 2018.[9] Strikingly, Nugent does little or nothing to translate such details for readers unfamiliar with Irish social contexts, never belaboring the point and displaying little anxiety about holding the reader's (especially the non-Irish reader's) hand. *Lying in Wait*, for example, does not explain why Laurence finds it so hard to acquire condoms in 1984 Dublin,[10] nor does it explain much about the mother and baby home to which Annie was sent.

8. Nugent, *Lying*, 260.

9. Nugent, *Skin*, 125. Delia describes marching in the anti-abortion campaign, and not bothering to vote, "because I never thought it was something that would affect me" (Nugent, *Skin*, 125). It does directly affect her, though, when she is unable to secure an abortion, and when her adoptive parents are prevented only by Delia's hasty marriage from sending her to a mother and baby home. One would be hard-pressed to distill the absence of empathy more sharply than Nugent does here.

10. Nugent, *Lying*, 149.

While the novels narrate these characters' traumas at the hands of authority and of their own families with pronounced empathy, that empathy is also sharply limited by the characters' insistent—even evil—sociopathy. Oliver claims, for example, that his acts were motivated by "poverty and desperation," leading him to commit "an awful and dreadful deed that I would not have even considered if I'd had my father's financial support at the time."[11] The novel offers little evidence, however, that Oliver has ever been much better than this "dreadful deed" would suggest. Instead—from its opening line, "I expected more of a reaction the first time I hit her"[12]—*Unravelling Oliver* builds a picture of his character as consistently calculating, making this statement of "desperation" less a cause for empathy and more a disingenuous papering over of the voids in his soul.

This mix of empathy and evil sustains the three novels, with the narrator-protagonists living through the fractured prism of their own vanity, insecurity, and narcissism, failings that are much more apparent to those around them than they realize. Rationalizing away their sins, and in the process only revealing more about themselves, Nugent's main characters often congratulate themselves on their morality in the same breath as they express a malignant self with no real understanding of others. Oliver's closing line—"I try to be good"—is, for example, surely news to those around him.[13] This acidly distills his self—narcissistic, vicious, rationalizing—even as it models Nugent's concise construction of character and her impressive ability to add a closing sting to a sentence, a chapter, a novel. Delia displays a similarly obtuse morality when she takes pride in her refusal to reply to her abandoned son James's letters: "I was not heartless enough to write and tell him that I didn't want anything to do with him. Instead, I did nothing."[14] When James grows increasingly angry—the novel depicts his gradually curdling view of women, echoing Delia's own father's rages—she manages to take this as further vindication: "I had been right not to get

11. Nugent, *Unravelling*, 179.

12. Nugent, *Unravelling*, 1.

13. Nugent, *Unravelling*, 231.

14. Nugent, *Skin*, 307.

involved with my son. He was obviously a very damaged individual, full of hatred and anger."[15] It is quite an astonishing moment, this profound failure to accept any degree of responsibility for her son's pain. With their focus on such poisoned relationships rather than the crimes themselves (extensive and brutal though those crimes are), Nugent's novels are more about character than about linear plot or its constituent actions, and are all the more disturbing for that.

The secondary characters do much to color both the empathy and the revulsion these narratives foster. In *Unravelling Oliver*, Moya—Oliver's married neighbor, with whom he is having an affair—depicts herself as the injured party when she discovers that Oliver has been seeing yet another woman: "Yes, yes, I was cheating on Con, Oliver was cheating on Alice, but I thought we were cheating *exclusively*."[16] Moya's sins and shortcomings are remarkable, but also mundane in their familiarity, as are those of other characters throughout the novels. Amidst a cast of largely unpleasant characters, such that moments of genuine kindness stand out in sharp relief, the banality of offenses like Moya's intensifies the sense of Oliver's, Lydia's, and Delia's departures from even such debased norms.

Through such patterns, Nugent insistently foregrounds her narrators' malevolence, not least in Lydia's perfect opening line, as evasive as it is blunt: "My husband did not mean to kill Annie Doyle, but the lying tramp deserved it."[17] This sentence encapsulates everything about Lydia's character, with that hinge "but" pivoting from a plea for understanding toward a brutal contempt, the latter all the more acute for the former's brief feint at sympathy. On the very next page, Lydia makes this brutality still more explicit, revealing between the lines that she herself delivered the fatal blow, enraged by Annie having deceived them (at Delia's insistence, Andrew paid Annie to serve as a surrogate, whom he could impregnate and whose child could then be raised by Andrew and Lydia as their own, but Annie apparently faked her pregnancy). Lydia characteristically compounds rather than

15. Nugent, *Skin*, 336.
16. Nugent, *Unravelling*, 121.
17. Nugent, *Lying*, 3.

mitigates the revulsion of this revelation by congratulating herself on her charity: "I like to think I did the girl a kindness, like putting an injured bird out of its misery. She did not deserve such consideration."[18]

As this perverse self-congratulation suggests, throughout the narrative Lydia's performed empathy provides only the thinnest of veneers over her sociopathic narcissism. She cries crocodile tears about having to cut so many corners that her son Laurence has to go to a school where he is desperately unhappy, but she won't sell any of their land, won't surrender her credit accounts at Dublin's swankiest department stores, and certainly won't change her illegal and expensive plan to have Annie act as a surrogate.[19] Despite this performance, in quieter moments she acknowledges this incapacity, as when she notes that she "couldn't feel [Annie's] mother's anguish. I tried, but I couldn't imagine it."[20] Her incapacity stands in stark contrast to other characters, including her son, Laurence, who rather poignantly "knew what it felt like to be ignored, but . . . wasn't sure what it felt like not to be noticed. I imagine they are very different experiences."[21]

This shadow of empathy is regularly paired with a denial of responsibility. When Andrew dies from a heart attack amidst "the stress of it all," Lydia holds "Annie Doyle entirely responsible."[22] Here and elsewhere, Lydia elides her own role so definitively that it seems clear she simply does not recognize her guilt. In one such moment, when she and Laurence falsify letters to make Annie's family think she is alive and in hiding, Lydia—unnervingly and delusionally—revels in the prospect that this counterfeiting "could only bring us closer,"[23] like some demented family craft project. Andrew's family—not without cause—blames her for his early death, pointing to his desperation to keep her in the style to which she'd become accustomed, a desperation that led him to illicit investments that have shattered his own and his mother's finances before the novel even

18. Nugent, *Lying*, 4.
19. Nugent, *Lying*, 9.
20. Nugent, *Lying*, 45.
21. Nugent, *Lying*, 143.
22. Nugent, *Lying*, 89.
23. Nugent, *Lying*, 172.

opens.[24] This returns the novel to that finely honed tension between empathy and evil, as Lydia's role in Andrew's death also reflects her experiences of the power structures operating around gender. By gambling away his mother's savings, for example, Andrew fits into Nugent's strong narrative thread of men victimizing women, of women being—as she comments in an essay that followed the successful 2018 campaign to repeal the Eighth Amendment—"silenced and imprisoned in their bodies and their marriages for too long."[25]

Even with its insistent sense of this contorting context, one that shapes all three of Nugent's novels, *Lying in Wait* gives depth to Andrew's family's rage by tying his death to his acute stress not only over Annie's murder (though, of course, his family knows nothing about that) but also over Lydia's callousness about her death. Even as she recounts these details, however, Lydia continues to evade responsibility. What she leaves out for much of the novel, and then mentions as an aside, is that she refused to eat for a week, until Andrew in desperation consented to her surrogacy plan.[26] That this manipulative quality is central to Lydia's character—rather than solely a desperate, grief-stricken response to the very real agony of her "nine miscarriages"[27]—is made clear by Lydia's passing reference to having used the same hunger strike strategy to get what she wanted as a child.[28] Quietly accruing such details across its ornately grim narrative, *Lying in Wait* makes it hard to argue with the adoption psychiatrists' assessment that Lydia "had not dealt properly with issues in [her] childhood."[29]

Indeed, that childhood, traumatic as it was, is one of the primary complicating factors in Nugent's characterization of Lydia. When Lydia and her sister were young, their mother ran off with her lover, a scandal for which the girls paid dearly, isolated from their peers, whose "parents thought

24. See, for example, Nugent, *Lying* 252, 276.

25. Nugent, "Gothic."

26. Nugent, *Lying*, 88.

27. Nugent, *Lying*, 86.

28. Nugent, *Lying*, 129.

29. Nugent, *Lying*, 87.

that we might be a bad influence."[30] This ostracism is at the back of the entire narrative, all the way through to Lydia's reclusiveness as an adult—"I have never mixed with outsiders"[31]—and her excessive dependence on Laurence. Even amidst this harrowing portrait, however, we learn that Lydia drowned her sister, an act clouded by time and perspective, but one troubling enough that their father banished Lydia to live with a distant aunt for "nearly a year."[32] Through these juxtapositions of misery and malignancy, Nugent establishes both Lydia's capacity for evil and ample grounds on which a reader can empathize with her.

The rest of the novel builds carefully on this, using a subtle narrative structure to develop an increasingly grotesque central character, one marked by callousness, narcissism, moral obtuseness, and calculated manipulation. As the novel proceeds, these varied failings block out more and more light as Lydia entraps Laurence into complicity with hiding Annie's true fate, manipulates him with a fake suicide attempt, and finally frames him for Annie's murder. Through all of this, Lydia drives Laurence to a heart attack, one that—unlike Andrew's—doesn't quite kill him, instead leaving him "mentally a child" and entirely dependent on her.[33] This grim fate is made far more visceral by Nugent's rich investment in character, by Lydia's wounded rage as she turns sharply against him ("You rejected me. . . . You should have obeyed me"), and by her delight in his diminished state: "I got what I wanted. My boy will be home with me for ever. He will never argue and he will do as he is told. . . . I control every single thing about him, and he does not question me."[34] Nugent begins *Lying in Wait* with Lydia in appalling form, and richly develops it to this haunting outcome, creating a character at once fundamentally destructive in her boundless narcissism and shaped by profound grief, without offering any way to reconcile those two assessments.

30. Nugent, *Lying*, 123.
31. Nugent, *Lying*, 135.
32. Nugent, *Lying*, 120.
33. Nugent, *Lying*, 294.
34. Nugent, *Lying*, 293–94.

For all of the oxygen Lydia takes up, she is far from the only contributor to the novel's bleak landscape. Even Laurence—who offers some of Nugent's more acidly funny lines, as when he notes he "was not concentrating on schoolwork at all, preoccupied as I was by the fact that I was living with a liar and a murderer, probably"[35]—lies and stalks Annie's surviving sister Karen. Karen's husband, Dessie, is defined by his fragile masculinity, concerned primarily with what others will think of him if they know about Annie's past or if they see Karen's modeling pictures, while Annie's father is so unaware of what he did to Annie by sending her to a mother and baby home that he thinks she would return voluntarily to one. Even Laurence's gentle but jilted girlfriend, Bridget, distributes humiliating naked photos of Laurence, "revenge porn" before that term existed. As with Moira in *Unravelling Oliver* and multiple enabling characters in *Skin Deep*, however, some of Nugent's sharpest observations are reserved for bystanders who benefit from the perceived failings of the women they themselves judge, like the bartender who kept serving a drunken Annie, or the lecherous detective on Annie's case.

Emphasizing this sense of complicit bystanders and collateral damage, a harrowingly bleak coda reveals that Karen—tricked by Lydia into believing Laurence killed Annie—has abandoned her modeling career and gone back to the abusive Dessie. She ends the novel entirely isolated by Dessie's misogynistic insecurities and Lydia's murderous pathologies, drinking too much and trapped in a loveless marriage, with two children who don't even like her. In these closing pages, *Lying in Wait* turns the focus from the baroque intensity that occupies much of the novel—Annie's murder, Andrew's death, Laurence's incapacitation, Lydia's unbridled malignancy—to something much more mundane in its scope. Karen's end is all the more acutely grim because she is far more sinned against than sinning, and because the external contours of her lonely life are a daily reality behind Lydia's headline-grabbing family gothic. Although Karen's chapters may initially seem secondary, her life unraveling is the mechanism by which much of the novel's contextual material—particularly the varied

35. Nugent, *Lying*, 56.

mistreatments of women, from Dessie's abuse and Annie's trauma to the moralistic feeding frenzy of the press when Annie's past is revealed—is made central to the novel's emotional force, anchored as that force is in character. Sexual moralities and gender norms that are maintained through varieties of shame have undone both Lydia's and Karen's lives. That shame and the control it is used to exert—among mid-century Irish society's original sins, in Nugent's fierce telling—filter down through the generations here, in *Unravelling Oliver*, and again in *Skin Deep*.[36] In depicting this corrosive process, Nugent offers her characters the empathy so very few of them can offer each other. Through such tensions and emphases, Nugent's work at its best blends an almost claustrophobic immersion in a pathological narrator with a wider narrative sense of community and empathy, one largely if not wholly unavailable from that narrator, giving her novels an acutely powerful sense of darkness and light. The consistency of this sense is perhaps these novels' signal strength.

Where *Lying in Wait* immerses the reader in a decaying Dublin mansion, the grim roots of *Skin Deep* are off the west coast of Ireland, on a small island with a dwindling population and a particular shortage of women. Reflecting the islanders' fear that their community will cease to exist if the county council deems island life no longer sustainable, Martin has from early on told his daughter Delia—the main narrator—that she is "the future of this island . . . the one that matters."[37] It is quickly clear, however, that she is valued only as a breeder: her father, she is told, "didn't love you, he loved your potential to be a mother."[38] This value structure

36. In *Skin Deep*, Delia's adoptive father Alan's own father was blamed for an out-of-wedlock pregnancy for which another man, of much higher social and economic standing, was responsible (Nugent, *Skin*, 123). This experience not only distorts Alan's life but also contributes to Delia's suffering: when he prevents her from traveling to England for an abortion, it is, she perceives, "Alan's revenge on the Russells for the loss of his father's good name. A scandal from a previous generation had to be paid for. By me, by Peter, by Harry and by our baby. But everyone paid in the end" (Nugent, *Skin*, 136). Delia may be malignant, but *Skin Deep* does much to confirm her observation here.

37. Nugent, *Skin*, 15.

38. Nugent, *Skin*, 368.

is disturbing enough even before the narrative couples it with her father obsessing about her beauty. Long after the horrifically violent death of her family and her exile from the island at a young age, his obsession continues to shape Delia, not least in her regular dismissal of others' anger as "Jealousy," which allows her even as an adult to believe "I was better than all of them, and more beautiful. Daddy was right all along."[39]

Skin Deep is characteristic of Nugent's work in the way it unfolds through a nonchronological structure, which allows it to build its momentum in varied and surprising ways. Although Delia's narcissism is established in short order, she shows more flashes of empathy than do Oliver or Lydia, but such moments remain fragmentary and fleeting, in the nature of exceptions that prove the rule. Far more fundamental to her character are the signs that "There was always something wrong and twisted about" Delia,[40] as the other islanders see it and as she herself testifies when she describes hurting her infant brothers "to see which of them would cry the loudest,"[41] displaying a revelry in the suffering of others more ominous than conventional sibling envy. Tom, her father's best friend, similarly recalls how, "From an early age, Delia stirred trouble in that family. I saw it with my own eyes. . . . 'Mammy was bold and Daddy smacked her and then she was crying,' she said, only a toddler, but with a sly smile on her beautiful face."[42] When she revisits the island as a young pregnant woman and is promptly forced to leave again—despite their desperation to keep the population stable, they loathe her too much to accept her back—Tom's mother, Biddy, tells Delia they always saw a corruption in her, even as a baby: "There's innocent and there's guilty, and then there's malice. And there was always malice in you. Don't think we don't know it. We watched you from a baby."[43] Although Tom, Biddy, and the other islanders have their own agendas, and—in an echo of Andrew's family holding Lydia responsible—although they blame

39. Nugent, *Skin*, 61, 336.

40. Nugent, *Skin*, 366.

41. Nugent, *Skin*, 29.

42. Nugent, *Skin*, 363.

43. Nugent, *Skin*, 114.

her alone for the wrongs committed by her father, the novel offers no indication that she ever grew out of this "malice."

As if to confirm the islanders' assessment, Delia closes the chapter in which she attempts to return to the island and give birth there with—even allowing for her desperation and fragility—a breathtakingly wrong statement, "He loved me the most," entirely missing the point of the revelation that her father killed her entire family.[44] Slipping such a poisoned barb in at the end of a chapter like this is a central pattern in Nugent's novels' unsettling rhythms.[45] Despite glimmers of understanding—Delia does recognize when her own actions "exposed" her so "everyone could see the warped and ugly truth" about her[46]—Delia in the end feels as little empathy as do Nugent's other protagonists, and is bewildered when she encounters it in others, like a foreign language she cannot speak.[47] In this, Delia is perhaps distinguished by degree more than kind: even fewer of the secondary characters here than in *Lying in Wait* or *Unravelling Oliver* display any sustained empathy, and few see—or care about—the damage they do. Much of that damage is done to Delia, who suffers greatly, often at the hands of genuinely appalling people. While this suffering fosters empathy with her, much of Delia's own behavior—like Lydia's—makes that empathy ultimately unsustainable. To put this another way, as Declan Hughes does, it is "never easy to like" Delia, "and yet Nugent's prodigious storytelling gifts and unsparing eye for malice, cruelty and human weakness make her a compelling and at times even sympathetic character."[48]

This tension—Delia *is* an awful person, *and* much wrong has been done to her—is at the crux of how Nugent's three novels to date succeed. Oliver, Lydia, and Delia all suffer deeply awful childhoods in ways that are central to each novel, but that is never quite enough for the novels to excuse them. Nugent creates such rich fiction by investing even viciously off-putting characters with a degree of humanity, grounding them in enough

44. Nugent, *Skin*, 119.

45. See also Nugent, *Skin*, 198.

46. Nugent, *Skin*, 228.

47. See, for example, Nugent, *Skin*, 39 and 124.

48. Hughes, "*Skin Deep* review."

complexity to allow a spark of empathy before they snuff it out. This pattern is perhaps the most foundational strength of these three novels, and one of the clearer ways in which the legacy of Highsmith—who "seduces the reader into feelings of empathy with her murdering heroes"[49]—might be most clearly seen.

Nugent walks this uneasy line so very well, creating malignant characters while maintaining a quietly insistent attention to the things from which these characters suffer, with no soothing reconciliation of that tension. In ways recognizable to varied readers—of Patricia Highsmith and Ross Macdonald, of contemporary domestic noir, and of modern Irish fiction more generally—Liz Nugent's works are thus partly historical novels, rooted in the characters' parents' pasts, in previous generations of malignancy, and in the shame and suffering that spread their stain down the generations, ruining a succession of lives. Indeed, these novels focus less on whodunit—largely revealed in Nugent's opening sentences—than on the creeping, crawling, cancerous families behind the crimes, on the complex pathologies and sociopathies of her characters. Although Nugent's work derives much narrative pleasure from its depiction of evil, its ability to surprise stems not from that evil but from the thorny sophistication with which she unravels her characters' lives.

Bibliography

Abbott, Megan E. *The Street Was Mine: White Masculinity and Urban Space in Hardboiled Fiction and Film Noir.* Basingstoke: Palgrave Macmillan, 2002.

Backus, Margot. *The Gothic Family Romance: Heterosexuality, Child Sacrifice, and the Anglo-Irish Colonial Order.* Durham: Duke Univ. Press, 1999.

Di Ciolla, Nicoletta, and Anna Pasolini. "The Violent Mother in Fact and Fiction." In Joyce and Sutton, *Domestic Noir*, 137–58.

Horsley, Katharine, and Lee Horsley. "*Mères Fatales*: Maternal Guilt in the Noir Crime Novel." *Modern Fiction Studies* 45, no. 2 (1999): 369–402.

Hughes, Declan. "*Skin Deep* Review: Dark Monster of a Book about Beauty and Identity." *Irish Times,* 7 April 2018. https://www.irishtimes.com/culture/books

49. Peters, "Literary Antecedents," 16. Peters also quotes Gillian Flynn making much the same point about Highsmith's capacity to unnerve the reader ("Literary Antecedents," 13).

/skin-deep-review-dark-monster-of-a-book-about-beauty-and-identity-1.3448060. Accessed 10 May 2018.

Joyce, Laura, and Henry Sutton, eds. *Domestic Noir: The New Face of 21st Century Crime Fiction.* London: Palgrave, 2018.

Nugent, Liz. "The Gothic Horrors of 1980s Ireland." *Crime Reads*, 13 June 2018. https://crimereads.com/the-gothic-horrors-of-1980s-ireland/. Accessed 20 June 2018.

———. *Lying in Wait.* Dublin: Penguin Ireland, 2016.

———. "Not Everyone Murders People in their Sleep." *Irish Times*, 24 June 2017. https://www.irishtimes.com/culture/books/not-everyone-murders-people-in-their-sleep-1.3120959. Accessed 15 June 2018.

———. *Skin Deep.* Dublin: Penguin Ireland, 2018.

———. *Unravelling Oliver.* Dublin: Penguin Ireland, 2014.

Peters, Fiona. "The Literary Antecedents of Domestic Noir." In Joyce and Sutton, *Domestic Noir*, 11–25.

Contributors

. . .

Index

Contributors

Anjili Babbar completed her PhD at the University of Rochester and two MA degrees at the University of Rochester and McGill University. Her research on Irish crime fiction is the logical confluence of childhood obsessions with *Columbo* and *Inspector Morse* and her work in Irish Studies (representations of Irish folklore in popular culture) and criminality (literary forgery and deception). Her first book, *Finders: Justice, Faith, and Identity in Irish Crime Fiction*, is forthcoming from Syracuse University Press.

Gerard Brennan coedited *Requiems for the Departed* (2010), a collection of crime fiction based on Irish myths. His novels include *Wee Rockets* (2012), *Fireproof* (2012), and *Undercover* (2014). Brennan holds an MA in Creative Writing from Queen's University Belfast, where he also earned his PhD in English with the thesis *Disorder* (a novel) and "Behaviourism and Hammett's Hardboiled Crime Fiction Legacy" (a critical component). *Disorder* was published by No Alibis Press in 2018.

Declan Burke is the author of *Eight Ball Boogie* (2003), *The Big O* (2007), *Absolute Zero Cool* (2011), *Slaughter's Hound* (2012), *Crime Always Pays* (2014), *The Lost and the Blind* (2014), and *The Lammisters* (2019). *Absolute Zero Cool* won the Goldsboro Award for Best Humorous Crime Novel in 2012. Declan also edited *Down These Green Streets: Irish Crime Writing in the 21st Century* (2011), *Trouble Is Our Business* (2016), and (with John Connolly) *Books to Die For* (2013). *Books to Die For* won the Anthony Award for Best Non-Fiction Crime. Declan is a former UNESCO/Dublin City Council writer-in-residence.

Brandi Byrd has recently completed her PhD at University College Dublin, studying memory and narrative in contemporary Irish fiction. She has presented research on Irish crime novels by Tana French, Brian McGilloway, David Park, and Glenn Patterson. Her recent essay, "'To Know This, and in Shame to Turn Away':

Institutional Abuse and the Ethics of Witnessing in Paul Murray's *Skippy Dies*," was awarded the 2017 ISAANZ Irish Studies Postgraduate Essay Prize.

Nancy Marck Cantwell (PhD, University of Illinois) is professor and chair of the English Department at Daemen College in Amherst, New York. Her scholarly work investigates texts produced by nineteenth-century novelists from England, Scotland, and Ireland. Recent publications include essays in *Nineteenth-Century Gender Studies*, *Études Irlandaises*, and *Supernatural Studies* as well as book chapters in *Jane Austen and Philosophy*, *Biographical Misrepresentations of British Women Writers of the Long Nineteenth Century*, and *The Contemporary Irish Detective Novel.*

Brian Cliff is a visiting research fellow in the School of English at Trinity College Dublin, where he was a lecturer and assistant professor from 2007 to 2019. His recent publications include *Irish Crime Fiction* (2018); *Synge and Edwardian Ireland* (2012), coedited with Nicholas Grene; and a reprint of Emma Donoghue's *Hood* (2011), coedited with Emilie Pine. He co-organized "Irish Crime Fiction: A Festival" in November 2013, and is currently working on a monograph about community and contemporary Irish writing.

Fiona Coleman Coffey holds an M.Phil from Trinity College, Dublin and a PhD from Tufts University. She is associate director for the Center for the Arts at Wesleyan University. Her research focuses on women in Irish drama, theatrical responses to the Troubles, and Northern Irish crime fiction. She is the author of *Political Acts: Women in Northern Irish Theatre, 1921–2012* (2016) and has contributed to *The Contemporary Irish Detective Novel*, *Radical Contemporary Theatre Practices by Women in Ireland*, and *The Theatre of Marie Jones.*

Bridget English holds a PhD in English from Maynooth University. Her research interests lie in theories of the novel, modernism, and the medical humanities. Her monograph, *Laying Out the Bones: Death and Dying in the Modern Irish Novel* (2017), examines the ways that Irish wake and funeral rituals shape novelistic discourse, arguing that the treatment of death in Irish novels offers a way of making sense of mortality and provides insight into Ireland's cultural and historical experience of death.

Richard Howard is an early career researcher who earned his PhD from Trinity College Dublin in 2016, and was funded by the Irish Research Council. His research interests include Irish science fiction, weird fiction, genre fiction, and critical theory. His research has appeared in *Medical Humanities*, *Irish Studies Review*, and *Irish University Review*. He also writes fiction and has had work published in *Weird Tales*, *Electric Velocipede*, and most recently in Jeff and Ann VanderMeer's anthology *The Bestiary*.

Rosemary Erickson Johnsen is associate provost and associate vice president of academic affairs at Governors State University, near Chicago. A professor of English, she has published a book, *Contemporary Feminist Historical Crime Fiction* (2006), and essays on crime fiction, Irish literature, and public scholarship. Johnsen is a two-time National Endowment for the Humanities grant recipient (2017 and 2018), and she is on the editorial advisory board of the *Journal of Popular Culture*.

Joe Long earned his MA in Irish Studies from New York University with the thesis "Family and Community on the Waterfront: Irish Life in Chelsea and Greenwich Village." His study of Irish immigration to Lower Manhattan is archived in the Oral History of Irish America Project at New York University's Glucksman Ireland House. In addition to his research on the history of Irish longshoremen, Joe has been instrumental in promoting Irish crime fiction on both sides of the Atlantic.

Vivian Valvano Lynch is Professor Emerita of English, St. John's University, New York. The author of *Portraits of Artists: Warriors in the Novels of William Kennedy* (1999), her research areas include James Joyce and contemporary Irish and Irish American fiction and drama. Lynch has published numerous essays on the works of Joyce, Kennedy, Seamus Deane, Jennifer C. Cornell, Sebastian Barry, Patrick O'Keeffe, Rona Munro, and Claire Keegan. She is a coeditor of the *Irish Literary Supplement*, for which she frequently reviews.

Elizabeth Mannion is a teacher and researcher with a focus on drama and an interdisciplinary range of Irish studies. She is the editor of *The Contemporary Irish Detective Novel* (2016) and the author of *The Urban Plays of the Early Abbey Theatre* (2014). Her research has appeared in numerous journals and anthologies, most recently *A History of Irish Working-Class Writing*. She teaches at Baruch College in New York.

Shane Mawe is an assistant librarian at Trinity College Dublin, and has worked on various library exhibitions, including one featured in Trinity's 2013 Irish Crime Fiction festival. Longtime interests in crime fiction and music saw him draw parallels with the lives of Rory Gallagher and Dashiell Hammett in *Stagestruck: The Official Rory Gallagher Fanzine.* He also contributed to *Down These Green Streets: Irish Crime Writing in the 21st Century.*

Caitlín Nic Íomhair lectures in Irish-language literature at Maynooth University. She is a scholar of Trinity College Dublin, where she completed her BA and PhD. Her thesis on the work of Biddy Jenkinson won the Ferguson Memorial Prize. Her current research interests include post-Christianity and ecology in contemporary Irish poetry, the work of Máirtín Ó Cadhain, and retracing the vocabulary of sex and sexuality in modern Irish-language fiction.

Eunan O'Halpin is Bank of Ireland Professor of Contemporary Irish History at Trinity College Dublin and director of the Trinity Centre for Contemporary Irish History. His most recent monograph is *Spying on Ireland: British Intelligence and Irish Neutrality during the Second World War* (2008). His research interests include Afghanistan and the belligerents during World War II and fatalities during the Irish revolution (1916–21).

Maureen T. Reddy, professor of English at Rhode Island College in Providence, Rhode Island, has been teaching and writing about crime fiction for thirty years. Her publications on crime fiction include two books, *Sisters in Crime: Feminism and the Crime Novel* (1988) and *Traces, Codes, and Clues: Reading Race in Crime Fiction* (2003), and many articles. In 2013, Reddy won the Popular Culture Association's Dove Award for contributions to the serious study of crime fiction.

Index